V&R

Research in Peace and Reconciliation

edited by
Martin Leiner

in co-operation with

Benoît Bourgine (Louvain-la-Neuve),
François Dermange (Genf), Dennis Doyle (Dayton/Ohio),
Matthias Gockel (Jena), Makoto Mizutani (Kyoto),
Arie Nadler (Tel Aviv), and David Tombs (Belfast/Dublin)

Volume 1

Vandenhoeck & Ruprecht

Latin America between Conflict and Reconciliation

Edited by
Martin Leiner and Susan Flämig

Vandenhoeck & Ruprecht

With 4 Figures and 10 Tables

Cover: El Salvador, © Susan Flämig

Bibliographic information published by the Deutsche Nationalbibliothek
The Deutsche Nationalbibliothek lists this publication in the Deutsche Nationalbibliografie;
detailed bibliographic data available online: http://dnb.d-nb.de.

ISBN 978-3-525-56011-2
ISBN 978-3-647-56011-3 (E-Book)

Printed and bound in Germany by Hubert & Co, Göttingen

Printed on non-aging paper.

Content

Susan Flämig/Martin Leiner

Reconciliation in the Middle of Dispute

Introduction to the Series

In the last two decades, studies in Conflict, Peace and Reconciliation have undergone an important quantitative as well as qualitative evolution. In 2010, there were more than 100 different B.A., M.A., or other institutional programs that included these subjects worldwide.[1] The UNESCO database on Peace Institutes counts some 600 institutions in almost 90 countries. Without a doubt, these subjects draw increasing interest, especially among younger scholars, and due to the political transformation in many countries since the end of the Cold War, a lot of data has become accessible. The increasing interest can be attributed to the expanding field of research not only through system changes in Eastern Europe, the end of the military dictatorships in Latin America, the peaceful political transformation in post-Apartheid South Africa, but also the atrocities against human dignity in Bosnia-Herzegovina, Rwanda and many other places, the civil wars in "failing" states like Somalia or Congo, the UN-missions and the wars in the aftermath of 9/11. Very often, these scholars not only describe and explain their case or phenomenon of interest, but also put forth possibilities to overcome violence and avoid the mistakes of the past.

What about the scientific quality of this research? In December 2003, Gerald Steinberg from Bar Ilan University, Ramat-Gan, presented a critical paper at the UNESCO conference on "Educating towards a Culture of Peace"[2]. He offers a critical summary of his evaluation of Peace Studies Programs around the world:

"Peace education, like many other topics in the social sciences, is susceptible to the tensions between the academic objective of value-free analysis, on the one hand, and particularist as well as highly subjective advocacy, on the other. In many cases, social sciences have difficulty in coping with this tension, and this is particularly true for peace education."[3]

1 This is an important figure, compared to the fact that the first Peace Studies Program was established in 1948 at Manchester College in Indiana (USA), an institution of the Church of the Brethren, and that for 20 years almost no other program existed in this field. Only in the late 1960s a broader academic interest in these studies can be observed.

2 "The Thin Line between Peace Education and Political Advocacy: Towards a Code of Conduct." A revised version of this paper is available at: http://faculty.biu.ac.il/~steing/conflict/Papers/UNESCOPeaceStudies.pdf (accessed on Oct 1, 2010). We quote from this version.

3 Op.cit., p. 1.

In particular, Steinberg deplores the elimination of the 'realist' Hobbesian position from reading lists in Peace Studies Programs, the ideological influence of postmodernism and the tendency to incriminate unilateral countries like the U.S. and Israel.[4]

Besides these basic methodological and ideological problems, Steinberg also speaks about "the failure of peace studies to provide empirically useful analysis and prescription for resolving or managing ethno-national conflicts".[5] He attributes this to the complexity of the subject, the tendency of many scholars to emphasize a particular approach and the "relative lack of systematic investigations and empirical evaluation of the relevant theories and models".[6] "Most theories and models appear to be tautological in nature, without independent and externally measurable variables with which to determine the link between cause and effect or to measure success or failure."[7] "Evaluative and comparative methodologies [...] based on empirically observable variables that are derived from the theories and models in the peace studies literature, are necessary to remedy this weakness in the field."[8]

This critical evaluation from an Israeli 'realist' and empirical point of view certainly does not do full justice to the issue. Nevertheless, when it is situated within the history of peace research and confronted with the actual complexity of the field, it can be helpful to determine where we stand and what the future tasks of peace studies are. It also helps to determine the specific location of the new series we start with this book.

In general, we can distinguish three approaches in the field of peace research: firstly, research marked by innovative individuals, secondly, research in specific academic disciplines and thirdly, interdisciplinary research. The *first phase* started in the 1960s and 1970s. By this time peace studies was no more limited to the specific approach of the "peace churches" like the Mennonites or the Church of the Brethren and their seminaries. Peace Studies was chosen by scholars with clearly other religious and philosophical backgrounds and became a topic of wider interest at the same time. In this phase the discussions were nourished by innovative ideas of individuals like Johan Galtung, Dieter Senghaas and Alva Myrdal. Characteristically, these individuals were trained in several disciplines, like sociology, political science, history, economics, mathematics, philosophy or psychology. They engaged in practical peace work as well as academic research, and they also had the courage to develop new ideas in emerging fields of research, including those

4 It is an evident weakness of Steinberg's article that he does not demonstrate the neutrality he requires of other scholars, especially when he talks about Israel and the U.S. Nevertheless, this weakness does not diminish the overall value of his critical observations, even if these are extreme views.

5 Op.cit., p. 5.

6 Op.cit., p. 7.

7 Op.cit., p. 8.

8 Op.cit., p. 7.

that did not directly belong to their own field of expertise.[9] These fathers and mothers of modern peace research used a transdisciplinary approach, which we will discuss below. They also took part in the founding of important academic institutions of peace research, like the Stockholm International Peace Research Institute (SIPRI, 1966) in Myrdal's case or the Peace Research Institute in Oslo (PRIO, 1959) in Galtung's case. Galtung also founded the first academic journal devoted to the topic of this book, the *Journal of Peace Research* (1964). Senghaas directed a research group at the Peace Research Institute, Frankfurt (PRIF).

It was only more than three decades later that scholars like Galtung and Senghaas presented their definitive global theory of peace.[10] But it is very likely that these theories have been the horizon their work aimed at for a longer period. Transdisciplinary complexity and the embedding into a certain world view are two of the characteristics of these works.

The "civilizing hexagon" of Dieter Senghaas illustrates the transdisciplinary complexity of these and other contemporary theories in the field of peace research. Senghaas distinguishes six factors capable of strengthening or weakening opposing parties in a conflict situation:

The Civilizing Hexagon

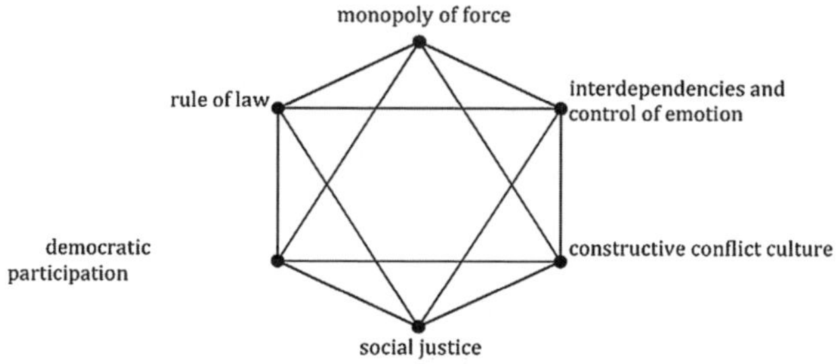

Terms like "social justice" and "constructive culture of conflict" show that Senghaas, unlike Steinberg, integrates normative aspects in his work.

9 Cf. the development of a news values theory by Galtung and Mari Holmboe Ruge: "The Structure of Foreign News. The Presentation of the Congo, Cuba and Cyprus Crisis in Four Norwegian Newspapers", in: *Journal of Peace Research* 2 (1965), p. 64–91. Senghaas has worked on economic aspects of underdevelopment and even on the relation of music and peace. Myrdal was interested in questions of growth of population and the transformation of the family.

10 Cf. Dieter Senghaas (2004), Zum irdischen Frieden. Erkenntnisse und Vermutungen. Frankfurt/M.: Suhrkamp; Johan Galtung (1996), Peace by Peaceful Means: Peace and Conflict, Development and Civilization. Oslo: PRIO and London/Thousand Oaks/New Dehli: Sage Publications.

Johan Galtung elaborates the religious and philosophical ideas that underlie his work. Many of his ideas come from Buddhism[11] and Daoism[12], but more importantly he argues for a transcendence of all religious beliefs in order to find a more peaceful common approach to peace where all the religions can contribute valuable concepts.[13]

The *second phase* of peace research is characterized by studies that more clearly belong to one single academic discipline. Specialists of different disciplines managed to establish relevant topics and projects within the scientific community of their own disciplines. In political science, for example, concepts of peace-building were developed from the field of international relations. Social psychologists described the "psychology of reconciliation"[14] and legal scholars worked on concepts like justice, human rights and constitutional theory in order to contribute to peaceful development in different regions of the world. Institutes like the U.S. Institute of Peace (USIP, founded in 1984) employ more than 70 specialists from different disciplines to engage in research on current as well as fundamental issues. In general, one can say that in the second phase the center of gravity of peace research shifted from Scandinavia to the U.S. In addition, there were many examples of empirical and historical research of good, sometimes even better, methodological calibre. Nevertheless the complexity of the problems in peace research, the ongoing historical development of many conflicts and the enormous costs to perform solid statistical field studies limited the possibility to establish a great number of empirically valuable studies in peace research. We only need to imagine how difficult it is to transform Senghaas's hexagon into empirically observable variables and to validate them by field research. Thus, we can only agree with Steinberg's observation that there should be more empirical studies.

In the *third phase* of peace research, empirical validation of theories has become less important than interdisciplinary combination of different theoretical approaches. Mediation, as an interdisciplinary methodology combining elements mainly from law and psychology, was an additional driving force behind the new interdisciplinary approach.

In recent years, scholars noticed that factors like culture, religion, collective memory, local traditions[15] and regional particularities play an important role

11 Cf. Ricard L. Gage (ed.) (1995), Choose Peace. A Dialogie between Johan Galtung and Daisaku Ikeda, London/Sterling/Virginia, 79–95.

12 Cf Johan Galtung (1996), Peace by Peaceful Means: Peace and Conflict, Development and Civilization. Oslo: PRIO and London/Thousand Oaks/New Dehli: Sage Publications, 43 ss.

13 Cf. Johan Galtung/Graeme MacQueen (2008), Globalizing God: Religion, Spirituality and Peace, Oslo: Transcend University Press.

14 Cf. now the comprehensive volume: Arie Nadler, Thomas Malloy and Jeffrey D. Fisher (2008), The Social Psychology of Intergroup Reconciliation. Oxford: Oxford University Press.

15 For example, in different villages in Bosnia-Herzegovina conflicts between Serbs, Croats and Muslims evolved in different ways. Cf. Bar Simon Tor (2003).

in the evolution of conflict and peace. The same strategies for peace can succeed in one region and fail in another.[16] One lesson to be learned from this is that peace research should focus on the particular context of a conflict and then describe or explain the available data. In this endeavour, different disciplines should work together. A typical result of such an approach is the book *Herding Cats: Multiparty Mediation in a Complex World*, which was published in 1999 by the U.S. Institute of Peace.[17] Twenty of the 25 contributions in the book are case studies of conflicts, like Northern Ireland, Burundi or Tajikistan.

In general, this is still the main approach today. Whilst the increasing number of institutions for peace in the 1980s had a lot to do with the "Peace Movements" in countries like Germany or the U.S. and the initiative of Christian Churches,[18] the 1990s witnessed a huge increase of research in different religious, secular and philosophical or political contexts. However, a rise in the number of institutes working on peace research does not necessarily lead to an improvement in quality of research. At least, the best academic institutions share the effort to become more scientific in methods and research and reject unilateral points of view or "political correctness" that eliminates important theoretical approaches. We should always seek to improve the historical, conceptual and empirical quality of peace research.

In the series that begins with the present publication we want to contribute to this interdisciplinary region-centered scientific research. We collect studies by experts and innovative young scholars from different countries and different disciplines, in relation to conflicts in different regions of the world. We plan to publish volumes in regard to the following regions: Latin America, Sub-Saharan Africa, East Asia and Australia, the Indian Subcontinent, North Africa and Middle East and Europe, Ancient Sovjet-Union and North America. A volume with theoretical texts will complete the series.

Most of the texts of the present volume have been presented at a workshop or summer school. In July 2009, with the help of the Volkswagen foundation, we could invite 35 scholars from Argentina, Chile, Peru, Guatemala, the US, the UK, South Africa, Hong Kong, Iraq, Japan, Germany, France, Switzerland, Austria, and Italy to discuss the transition processes in Latin America after the period of dictatorship in many countries.

Moreover, the present work represents a first step in an effort to move beyond the current dominating approach. The use of one or all of the following three perspectives could lead in this direction:

16 For example, the Sant'Egidio peace initiative was fairly successful in Mozambique, whilst in Algeria its effect was limited.

17 The editors were Chester A. Crocker, Fen Osler Hampson and Pamela Aall.

18 In Germany, the Roman-Catholic "Institute for Peace and Theology" in Hamburg is an example of how peace research is established institutionally through the church. In a more practical way, and from the theological perspective of the Mennonite tradition, John Paul Lederach, among others, developed methods of intervention to foster sustainable peace.

From a Local to a Comparative and Transcultural Perspective

There are universal aspects in all conflicts and in all peace-building processes. Often, starting from a focus on regional, cultural and particular traditional factors, these universal aspects have to be rediscovered. In contrast to a specifically modern perspective, we contend that the epistemological status of these universal aspects is open to change. Universal commonalities are no invariant factors that can be applied to every conflict in the world; they are rather something to be found after first having compared other conflicts in the world. The comparative perspective is of increased importance in our approach than in previous publications on the same topic. For instance, we want to investigate how people from South Africa, who are convinced by the work of the Truth and Reconciliation Commission (TRC), react to discussions in Chile about the necessary end of impunity. We want to study what people in Poland, who work on the history of German-Polish relations, think about the question of how to deal with the past in the relationship between Japan and Korea. What are the similarities, and differences between the massacres in Srebrenica and Kigali? We hope that comparisons of this kind can help to discover universal aspects and to describe the specificities of the different conflicts and peace processes in a more exact way. These comparisons can provoke new questions, open new trajectories for future research and help to find new practical ideas to improve peace-building.

In addition, we argue for a transcultural perspective. Cultures have never been closed entities. Colonialism, migrations, cultural and economic exchange has created a reality in which different cultures live together, new transcultural identities are formed and have become more common. It is obvious that in this respect the impasses of communitarian approaches must be overcome. Wolfgang Welsch's concept of transculturality[19] and similar approaches, also those preferring hyperculturality to transculturality[20], become increasingly important. Addressing this issue we accepted the article on the Brazilian minority in Japan in the present volume.

19 Cf. Wolfgang WELSCH (1999), "Transculturality – the Puzzling Form of Cultures Today". In: Mike Featherstone and Scott Lash (ed.), Spaces of Culture: City, Nation, World. London: Sage, 194–213.

20 Cf Byung-Chul HAN, Hyperkulturalität. Kultur und Globalisierung. Berlin 2010.

From Interdisciplinary to Transdisciplinary Research

Inspired by the classical texts of peace studies and by a desire to overcome an interdisciplinary approach that functions as a mere addition, we seek to pay tribute to the complexity of conflicts and thus promote transdisciplinary research. As there is no generally accepted definition of the term "transdisciplinary", we have to explain in detail what we mean.[21] We will discuss the three major threads of transdisciplinarity in the German-speaking discourse.

The first question is: how to find unity between the different approaches of the different disciplines as well as the different perceptions of the practical experiences on the ground? The second question is: what to think about the value-oriented perspective and the philosophical and religious elements in the theories of scholars like Galtung or the Christian elements in the peace work of Mennonites like John Lederach?

Our starting point for the first question is the position of the German philosopher Jürgen Mittelstraß. For Mittelstraß, transdisciplinarity is a principle of how to organize science and scientific research. It does not imply a new methodology but a new level of cooperation. Whereas interdisciplinarity designs a concrete cooperation of several disciplines working on a particular topic, transdisciplinarity means a *continuous cooperation* of different disciplines. These disciplines accept changes in the orientation of their scholars and the boundaries of disciplines in the process of cooperation. This requires, more or less, four new orientations for research practices:

1. The unlimited will to learn from other disciplines and the acceptance to change the concepts and theories of one's own discipline
2. The gain of interdisciplinary competence, up to the point where one can productively discuss the work of the other discipline
3. The capacity to reformulate the approaches of one's own discipline in the light of interdisciplinary competence
4. The formulation of a common text in which the unity of transdisciplinary argumentation replaces the simple aggregation of different results from several academic disciplines.[22]

This understanding should be completed by what Mittelstraß calls a more practical transdisciplinarity as well as by attempts of some scholars who want to establish transdisciplinarity as a new method.

Even if it takes substantial effort to realize this kind of transdisciplinarity, the position of Mittelstraß could form a basic consensus for cooperative

21 Cf. Gertrude Hadorn Hirsch et al. (ed.) (2008), Handbook of Transdisciplinary Research. Dordrecht: Springer/NL.

22 Cf. Jürgen Mittelstrass, "Methodische Transdisziplinarität", in: Technikfolgenabschätzung. Theorie und Praxis. 14/2; June 2005, p. 18 – 23.

transdisciplinary research. However, the notion of practical interdisciplinarity and transdisciplinarity as methods should be developed further.

With Matthias Bergmann, the second important author in the German debate, we can distinguish between two processes: a process of problem-solving in the life-world *(Lebenswelt)* and a scientific process aimed at an increase of knowledge. They intersect in various ways, but they should be seen as two different processes.[23] It is obvious that practical processes of peace-building and academic processes of peace research offer various possibilities of mutual interaction, but it is also important to see the autonomy of practice and academic research. "Transdisciplinarity implies that the precise nature of a problem to be addressed and solved is not predetermined and needs to be defined cooperatively by actors from science and the life-world. To enable the refining of a problem definition as well as the joint commitment in solving or mitigating problems, transdisciplinary research connects problem identification and structuring, searching for solutions and bringing results to fruition in a recursive research and negotiation process. Transdisciplinarity thus dismantles the traditional sequence leading from scientific insight to action."[24]

The main problem with Bergmann's conception is, that the life-world is only associated with practical research, but it has to be related to the sciences as well. As Edmund Husserl showed in his book *Die Krisis der europäischen Wissenschaften und die transzendentale Phänomenologie*[25], science can only reduce the complexity of the life-world. It always remains dependent on the life-world.[26] Therefore, transdisciplinary research as a whole has to be aware of being embedded in the life-world. Practical lessons learned from the life-world form the common ground for the evaluation of all theories in transdisciplinary peace theory as well as practical peace work. In the life-world and the – still differently interpretable – experiences we find the unity between the different approaches of the different disciplines as well as the different perceptions of the practical experiences on the ground. All the different sciences are abstractions from the life-world. They can contribute to a common image by discussing the interpretation of the experiences in the life-world.

This perspective allows us to answer the difficult question of values in transdisciplinary research. Scholars like Edmund Husserl and Max Scheler showed that there is always a value-feeling in the life-world. Consequently,

23 Cf. Matthias Bergmann et al. (2005), Qualitätskriterien transdisziplinärer Forschung – Ein Leitfaden für die formative Evaluation von Forschungsprojekten, ISOE Studientext, Frankfurt/M.: Institut für sozial-ökologische Forschung.

24 Urs Wiesmann et al. (2008), "Enhancing Transdisciplinary Research. A Synthesis in Fifteen Propositions". In: Hadorn Hirsch et al. (2008), op.cit., p. 436.

25 3rd ed. Edited by Elisabeth Ströker (1996), Hamburg: Meiner.

26 In a slightly different way, such dependence recently has been emphasized by Julian Nida-Rümelin (2009), Philosophie und Lebensform. Frankfurt/M.: Suhrkamp.

value-free research is an abstract way of thinking and it should be integrated into a more complete vision. This is also the aim of another group of academics, the research group of the Swiss Academies of Arts and Sciences directed by Gertrude Hirsch-Hadorn. This group tries to integrate social aspects like the common good of society into the concept of transdisciplinarity.[27] However, in our opinion, this idea does not give enough respect to the freedom of research and the individuality of every scholar. Research should not be limited by the definition of common good of a society, but by the researcher's individual understanding of peace, values and by the worldview of the scholar. In the context of discovery this individual value-oriented approach is the only possible approach, even if it does not appear explicitly. However, in the context of justification, the research has to integrate the experiences on the ground, and the results of this approach have to be argued for in different publics such as the scientific community. Only an approach that can translate its values into the values of other religions and cultures can be convincing in the globalized scientific community. At the same time an academic approach that can convince peace workers on the ground can be considered successful.

Transdisciplinary research, if not at the expense of the quality of disciplinary methodological research, can integrate values and worldviews. This encouraged us to integrate philosophers and theologians of different religious backgrounds into our program. A Buddhist understanding of peace seems to us as important as a Mennonite or an atheist one. The inclusion of these views is an important attribute of Christian peace research.

Media- and Symbol-oriented Perspective

Conflicts and peace processes are deeply engaged in highly symbolic communication. National and religious symbols and their history play a crucial role in the understanding of the development of conflicts as well as of peace processes. Even during World War II cities like Leningrad and Stalingrad in the Soviet Union or Königsberg and Freudenstadt in Germany had to suffer more because of their symbolic meaning and not because of their strategic importance.

The media often amplifies this kind of symbolic communication. They inform and create the public and its perception of conflict or peace. Even certain acts of terror, for example, seem to be more important as communicative acts than as destructive acts. At least, this is the thesis of

27 Cf. Wiesman et al. (2008), "Enhancing Transdiciplinary research. A Synthesis in Fifteen Propositions", op.cit., p. 436 – 441.

Andreas Elter's book *Propaganda der Tat* (2008), which examined the actions of the RAF in the 1970s.

This symbol and communication oriented interpretation of conflict and peace processes is another mark of our research that will be explored further in subsequent publications.

The Hölderlin Perspective

Within the field of peace research, in Jena we follow a particular approach called the Hölderlin-perspective. The German poet Friedrich Hölderlin (1770 – 1843) gave his name to this kind of research, when he wrote on the last pages of his novel *Hyperion:* "Versöhnung ist mitten im Streit und alles Getrennte findet sich wieder".[28] Our perspective is the antithesis to a widespread perception in the field of political science, where reconciliation is seen as an event that occurs only after the end of violent conflict, sometimes even many years later, after a successful peace-building process.

The latter view is a challenge to the idea of Christian theology that the fundamental reconciliation, between God and humankind, already has occurred. John Riches, a scholar of New Testament Studies, underlines this point, when he describes the particularity of the announcement of the Kingdom of God by Jesus:

> Kingdom is not established only where other rulers have been overthrown; rather God's power erupts in the midst of oppression, forgiving and healing, and wherever that power is, there is cause for rejoicing. The world is not, that is to say, given to Satan, or to Caesar, until God will restore his rule over it by destroying the alien rulers. On the contrary, God is already present in this 'evil age', overcoming it by mercy.[29]

In Protestant Systematic Theology, it is quite common to adopt this point of view. Our small attempts at reconciliation only try to mirror, in a human way, God's act of reconciliation.[30] The German theologian Jürgen Moltmann closes

28 Friedrich Hölderlin (1998), Sämtliche Werke und Briefe. Michael Knaupp (ed.). Vol. 1. Darmstadt: Wissenschaftliche Buchgesellschaft. p. 760: "Reconciliation is in the middle of dispute and all things separated find each other again."

29 John Riches, Jesus and the Transformation of Judaism. London 1980. 93 f.

30 In particular, Karl Barth's doctrine of reconciliation and his essays on political topics were marked by this perspective, which in principle presupposes the great reconciliation. Cf. Mathias Gockel/Martin Leiner (2008), "Kritik und Versöhnung – Karl Barth und die DDR". In: Martin Leiner/Michael Trowitzsch (ed.), Karl Barths Theologie als europäisches Ereignis. Göttingen: Vandenhoeck&Ruprecht. 79 – 119. Cf. also for a compelte interpretation of the doctrine of reconciliation of Karl Barth: Benoît Bourgine, L'herméneutique théologique de Karl Barth: Exégèse et dogmatique dans le quatrième volume de la Kirchliche Dogmatik. Leuven: Peeters 2004.

his book "Ethik der Hoffnung" (ethics of hope) by a chapter with the title "Und Frieden mitten im Streit" (And peace in the middle of dispute).[31] He explains this concept as follows:

Nach Eph 2 und Kol 1 hat Gott durch die Hingabe Christi 'Frieden' geschaffen zwischen Heiden und Juden, indem er 'die Feindschaft tötete durch sich selbst' (Eph 2.18) und Frieden verkündete denen, die nahe waren, und denen, die ferne waren. Im Kolosserbrief wird zu diesem konkreten Frieden zwischen Juden und Heiden die kosmische Dimension hinzugefügt, dass Gott durch Christus alles mit sich versöhnt hat, es sei auf Erden oder im Himmel, indem er Frieden machte durch sein Blut am Kreuz' (1,20). In der menschlichen wie in dieser kosmischen Dimension ist es wichtig zu erkennen, dass der Friede von Gott schon gemacht ist, es also für Menschen darauf ankommt, zu erkennen und anzuerkennen, was objektiv sub specie eternitatis schon da ist, es sei in menschlichen Konflikten oder im Weltall. Gott war in Christus und versöhnte den Kosmos mit sich selbst' (2 Kor 5,17). Das ist der 'Friede mitten im Streit': In der Tiefe der lähmenden und oft tödlichen Konflikte der Völker herrscht schon dieser Gottesfriede.[32]

In a Christian context, we integrate a Christian self-understanding into our research with a claim that the great reconciliation already has been achieved. This inspires our own practice of reconciliation.

Moreover, in the Hölderlin perspective we pay attention to the elements speaking for and perhaps even leading towards reconciliation in a conflict: internal and external groups and individuals who disagree with the conflict, common laws and customs, moments of economic cooperation, common feelings, correlations of acting and reacting etc. We are particularly interested in exploring how these elements develop in a conflict. What role do people who never wanted the conflict to become violent play in a peace process? Sometimes peace is made between the strong actors in a conflict, and the difficult work of people who were willing to end the conflict is not sufficiently acknowledged. This is true, for example, in the case of the 300,000 moderate Hutus who were killed in the Rwanda genocide and are almost forgotten. Or we can think of the German officers who tried to kill Hitler on July 20th, 1944. Their plans did not fit the goals of the Allied powers. Their conservative and Prussian attitude was criticized even in the works of German historians, and for a long time the Christian motivation of many of them has not been understood adequately.[33] Sometimes people who are not willing to participate

In a similar way, Friedrich SCHLEIERMACHER spoke about the deep peace present in the middle of conflict, for example, in his Sermon for Christmas on Mt 10, 34.

31 Jürgen MOLTMANN (2010), Ethik der Hoffnung. Gütersloh: Gütersloher Verlagshaus. 265.

32 Jürgen MOLTMANN (2010), Ethik der Hoffnung. Gütersloh: Gütersloher Verlagshaus. 265. See also Timothy HARVIE (2009), Jürgen Moltmann's Ethics of Hope: Eschatological Possibilities for Moral Action, Ashgate.

33 Cf. Martin LEINER (2004), "Zu theologischen Motivation des Widerstands gegen das 'Dritte Reich'". In: Martin LEINER/Hildigund NEUBERT/Thomas A. SEIDEL/Ulrich SCHACHT (ed.): Gott

in the escalation of conflicts play an important role in the peace process. Abraham Lincoln's position in the American Civil War is a case in point. This was also the case in South Africa and in some countries of Eastern Europe. Interesting questions in this context would be: Is there a better quality of peace because people not interested in the escalation of conflicts can really foster reconciliation? Or is it just the opposite, because the systemic change is too soft? Furthermore, what is the role of institutions that are not part of the violent conflict in the process of transformation? What are the results when the actors of peace are not the actors of a conflict?

With these four approaches, the comparative and transcultural, the transdisciplinary, media and symbol-oriented interpretations and the Hölderlin-perspective, we hope to contribute to the further evolution of peace research. The awareness of practical experiences and disciplinary quality should engender a better distinction between scientific from the nonscientific approaches in Peace Studies. A global perspective will bring together people researching ways to foster lasting peace and harmony in the 21st century.

References

Bor Siman Tov, Yaacov, ed. (2003). From Conflict Resolution to Reconciliation. Oxford: Oxford University Press.

Bergmann, Matthias et al (2005). Qualitätskriterien transdisziplinärer Forschung: Ein Leitfaden für die formative Evaluation von Forschungsprojekten. Frankfurt/M.: Institut für sozial-ökologische Forschung.

Crocker, Chester A./Fen Osler Hampson/Pamela Aall, ed. (1999). Herding Cats: Multiparty Mediation in a Complex World: USIP.

Elter, Andreas (2008). Propaganda der Tat. Frankfurt: Suhrkamp.

Gage, Richard, ed. (1995). Choose Peace: A Dialogue between Johan Galtung and Daisaku Ikeda. London/Sterling/Virginia: Pluto Press.

Galtung, Johan (1996). Peace, Development and Civilization. London/Thousand Oaks/New Dehli: Sage Publications.

Galtung, Johan/Mari Holmboe Ruge (1965). The Structure of Foreign News: The Presentation of the Congo, Cuba and Cyprus Crisis in Four Norwegian Newspapers. Journal of Peace Research (2):64–91.

Galtung, Johan/Graeme MacQueen (2008). Globalizing God: Religion, Spirituality and Peace. Oslo: Transcend University Press.

Gockel, Matthias/Martin Leiner (2008). Kritik und Versöhnung – Karl Barth und die DDR. In Karl Barths Theologie als europäisches Ereignis, edited by M. Leiner and M. Trowitzsch. Göttingen: Vandenhoeck & Ruprecht.

mehr gehorchen als den Menschen – christliche Wurzeln. Zeitgeschichte und Gegenwart des Widerstands. Vandenhoeck & Ruprecht Göttingen.

Hadorn Hirsch, Getrude et al, ed. (2008). Handbook of Transdisciplinary Research. Dordrecht: Springer Netherlands.

Han, Byung-Chul (2005). Hyperkulturalität: Kultur und Globalisierung. Berlin: Merve Verlag.

Harvie, Timothy (2009). Jürgen Moltmann's Ethics of Hope: Eschatological Possibilities for Moral Action. Surrey/Burlington: Ashgate.

Husserl, Edmund (1996). Die Krisis der europäischen Wissenschaften und die transzendentale Phänomenologie. edited by E. Ströker. Hamburg: Meiner.

Hölderlin, Friedrich (1998). Sämtliche Werke und Briefe. edited by M. Knaupp. Darmstadt: Wissenschaftliche Buchgesellschaft.

Leiner, Martin (2004). Zur theologischen Motivation des Widerstands gegen das 'Dritte Reich'. In Gott mehr gehorchen als den Menschen - christliche Wurzeln: Zeitgeschichte und Gegenwart des Widerstands, edited by M. Leiner, H. Neubert, T. A. Seidel and U. Schacht. Göttingen: Vandenhoeck & Ruprecht.

Mittelstraß, Jürgen (2005). Methodische Transdisziplinarität. Technikfolgenabschätzung. Theorie und Praxis 14 (2):18 – 23.

Moltmann, Jürgen (2010). Ethik der Hoffnung. Gütersloh: Gütersloher Verlagshaus.

Nadler, Arie/Thomas Malloy/Jeffrey D. Fisher (2008). The Social Psychology of Intergroup Reconciliation. Oxford: Oxford University Press.

Nida-Rümelin, Julian (2009). Philosophie und Lebensform. Frankfurt: Suhrkamp.

Schleiermacher, Friedrich. Christ Bringing a Sword: Christmas Sermon. In Selected Sermons of Schleiermacher: translated by Mary F. Wilson. New York: Funk and Wagnalls.

Senghaas, Dieter (2004). Zum irdischen Frieden: Erkenntnisse und Vermutungen. Frankfurt/M.: Suhrkamp.

Steinberg, Gerald (2003). The Thin Line between Peace and Political Advocacy: Towards a Code of Conduct. In UNESCO Conference on Educating towards a Culture of Peace. Bar Ilan University, Ramat-Gan.

Weingardt, Markus (2007). Religion macht Frieden. Stuttgart: Kohlhammer.

Welsch, Wolfgang (1999). Transculturality: The Puzzling Form of Cultures Today. In Spaces of Culture: City, Nation, World, edited by M. Featherstone and S. Lash. London: Sage.

Wiesmann, Urs (2008). Enhancing Transdisciplinary Research: A Synthesis in Fifteen Propositions. In Handbook of Transdisciplinary Research, edited by G. Hadorn Hirsch et al. Dordrecht: Springer/NL.

Susan Flämig/Martin Leiner

Introduction to the Present Volume

The title of the book, Latin America *between* conflict and reconciliation, allows for two interpretations: One reading reflects the view that the region's past is not only shaped by fierce conflicts but also by attempts of fostering reconciliation in the middle of conflict, as some of our contributions show. The second understanding points to the reconciliation that is yet to happen and this is linked to the broader issue of justice. Most of Latin America has left their pasts of dictatorial regimes behind and the national elites like to see their continent as a zone of peace, compared to other parts of the world.[1] The transition of the political systems from dictatorial to democratic is predominantly considered as completed. Dealing with Latin America's past means dealing with the human rights violations of the dictatorships of the 1960s–1980s. Truth Commissions were an essential instrument of uncovering past crimes. However, in many cases the truth came without justice; and perpetrators were not held accountable. There were no far-reaching vetting processes and the reparations policy was rather restrictive. The impunity that prolonged and delayed regime changes has been harshly criticised within the human rights discourse. In the last 5 – 10 years, there have been serious efforts to bring perpetrators to trial, the Pinochet case being one of the most prominent examples. Prosecutions now also play an important role in the transitional justice processes in Argentina, Peru and Uruguay.

However, justice is not only a matter of judicial processes, but is closely related to the precarious social realities that many Latin Americans still experience. In El Salvador, for example, historic injustices were the root cause for the civil war of the 1980s. The establishment of a democratic system, however, did not diminish the vast social divisions in the country. Instead, many people still experience deep socioeconomic insecurity, in addition to a general feeling of insecurity caused by excessive violence that is symptomatic of many places on the continent.

The increase instead of a diminution of violence in democratic systems gave rise to more research. Whereas empirical findings prove the rise of violent and criminal incidents like assaults, homicide, kidnapping, rape, drug trafficking and human trafficking, theoretical explanations and classifications of the

1 Herz, Monica (2010), Concepts of Security in South America. In: International Peacekeeping 17/5, 598 – 612.

phenomena vary. Some scholars have described a shift of violence from the political sphere to the social sphere. The violent dichotomy of dictatorial regimes and the regime opposition no longer exists. Instead, it seems like violence became ubiquitous in many societies. This perspective carries the risk that politicians blame societal circumstances for the violence and assume no responsibility. It does not take into account that violence, despite its changed appearance, is a product of political (in-) action. It also goes along with the widespread assumption that conflicts in Latin America (except Colombia) belong to the past. This, in turn, has made the continent significantly less attractive to Peace Studies. With the present volume we want to contribute to raising new awareness for the continuing conflicts in the region. At the same time, options to condemn and overcome new and old conflicts are analysed, and examples of encouraging work for reconciliation are presented.

The volume comprises two sections: The first part is a collection of studies of Latin American cases that approach the topics of reconciliation and conflict resolution within and in the aftermath of dictatorships and civil wars from different perspectives and academic disciplines. The second, less comprehensive part is dedicated to experiences with reconciliation, conflict resolution and migration from a global and comparative perspective. The book includes several contributions that reflect on the Hölderlin perspective of reconciliation in the middle of dispute (Freudenberg, Rojas, and Tombs). Some contributions aim to deepen our theoretical understanding of reconciliation. They explore the diversity of interpretations of the term (Lira and Loveman) and elaborate the specific benefit of reconciliatory approaches for sustainable peace (Flämig, Hasenclever and Sändig, Thesnaar). Other articles concentrate on particular conflicts (Chacón and Mucha, Nanteuil).

At the end of the civil war in 1992 El Salvador underwent major security reforms which are central in Susan Flämig's contribution. Particularly police reforms were designed to generate a new democratic and service-oriented security force that reunites former combatants from opposing parties in one institution. The failure of the reforms in the long term is, among other reasons, due to the disregard of individual and collective values and beliefs of the police, she argues. According to Flämig, the renunciation of violence among security forces will not be achieved through a mere technocratic reform process, but requires a deeper transformation and rehumanization of the police forces.

The life and writing of Bishop Oscar Romero is still a source of inspiration for many people inside and outside El Salvador. His work in the middle of violent dictatorship and within a church that was traditionally loyal to the regime is portrayed by David Tombs. He shows how parts of the Catholic Church adopted a more confrontational approach to the authoritarian state and thus challenged the church to reorientate itself to social justice concerns during the 1970s and 1980s. Although Romero did not explicitly speak about reconciliation, his desire to build a church that unites a socially divided society indicates not only his commitment to liberation, but also to justice-based reconciliation.

Matthieu de Nanteuil's article is by far the longest in the book. Nanteuil develops his politological and sociological analysis of the situation in Colombia in great detail and offers valuable insights from the French-speaking perspective on questions of conflict and peace. Scholars like Michael Foucault, Emile Durkheim (division of work) and Georges Bataille play a significant role in his argumentation, as well as Zygmunt Bauman. Its central thesis is that the Colombian conflict cannot be fully understood without recognising the country's aspiration to belong to the Western liberal tradition. At the same time, the main political players in Colombia rely on the continuous existence of armed conflicts, including the various forms of violence that are part of it, so that it is very difficult to develop an "ethic of social ties."

Beyond outlining the most salient characteristics of Colombian society, Nanteuil analyses the internal "divisions of labour", which create a paradoxical relationship between Colombian society and modernity. He concludes with some perspectives for an alternative vision of Colombian society.

Mariana Chacón and Witold Mucha analyse the role of indigenous movements within the transitional process to democracy in Bolivia and Peru. Chacón and Mucha show how in past conflicts as well as in contemporary politics leaders claimed and claim to speak for "the indigenous population", although in reality it is about a diverse range of groups with different interests. A louder "indigenous voice" opens a path for better participation in the political process, as the case of Bolivia shows. In Peru, in contrast, the majority of the indigenous groups have not benefited from any political measures concerning their rights. The authors point to the persisting risk of political instrumentalisation of the indigenous identities.

Against the background of political reconciliation proposals discussed in Latin America, and particularly in Chile, in the 1990s, Elizabeth Lira and Brian Loveman illustrate the different meanings of reconciliation derived from various cultural, religious, social and historical traditions. They trace the trajectory of the concept from its origins in Judeo-Christianity to a totalistic and perverted use under the Spanish inquisition to a more justice-oriented understanding of reconciliation within a theology of liberation. According to the authors, the overlapping and sometimes contradictory notions of the concept are still apparent in the post-dictatorship discourse. Therefore, the term continues to be susceptible to political instrumentalisation.

The Chilean Labour Union advocated human rights within a legal system that was continuously restricted by the military government, as Hugo Rojas points out in his contribution. He also shows how the complaints presented to the International Labor Organization during the dictatorship not only served as a legal strategy, but also represented an important historical record. It proves the detention, torture and murder of thousands of Chilean workers, whose cases were acknowledged by the National Commission on Torture and Political Imprisonment in 2004 on the basis of these documents.

Katharina Freudenberg explores the human rights work in the Evangelical Church of the Río de la Plata (IERP) during the dictatorship in Argentina. She shows how in the middle of violent crimes and human rights violations the church provided victims with pastoral, social and judicial support. This church was part of the Ecumenical Human Rights Movement (MEHD) that seeked to raise awareness on the practice of "disappearances" and was based on a theology of liberation. Its work included active help for affected family members as well as a documentation of the cases which was invaluable after the end of the dictatorship.

Kanan Kitani's article deals with a rather exceptional transcultural topic: the migration of Brazilians to Japan and their religious life. In a country with less than 1 % of the population being Christian, the mainly Catholic migrants represent a crucial Christian group in Japan. Kitani examines the churches at which the Brazilians gather, with a particular focus on their general low visibility in Japanese society, their influence on the Japanese religious sphere, and their important social role for migrants.

In contrast to many countries in Latin America, in South Africa, not justice but reconciliation was at the heart of the post-Apartheid public discourse. The work of the Truth and Reconciliation Commission and the debates that evolved around it gave impetus to more research about the topic. Christo Thesnaar looks at reconciliation from a pastoral perspective. He considers both reconciliation and healing as deeply theological issues and proposes a shift within Christian pastoral theology from resolution-oriented approaches towards a hermeneutic, understanding-seeking approach to healing. The article also illustrates that healing is not necessarily limited to an individual and spiritual dimension as often assumed in European and North American theology. Healing is also a collective process of restoring harmony and thus ensuring the functioning of a community.

The book concludes with Andreas Hasenclever and Jan Sändig's contribution. They give an overview of the emergence of the peacebuilding concept in the international arena and place reconciliation within this context. The authors contrast liberal, institution-centred approaches to peacebuilding with communitarian, community-centred models. Communitarian approaches bring the importance of reconciling divided societies to the centre stage. The liberal peacebuilding agenda, thus, needs to be complemented by a pro-active promotion of reconciliation. Such an approach, labelled as hybrid peacebuilding framework, unites liberal institutions and local social realities.

As editors of the volume, we would like to thank expressly our co-workers: David Gippner, Matthias Gockel, Monika Merrbach, Sven Ojeda-Febles, Peggy Stöckner, Benita Sumita, and Markus Voss-Göschel, who invested a lot of their precious time into the publication and amelioration of this book.

We also thank the Volkswagen foundation, who gave an important grant for a Summer School on Latin America, where most of the texts have been presented and discussed. The Evangelische Kirche in Mitteldeutschland and the Ernst-Abbe-Stiftung also helped us to finance the publication.

References

Herz, Monica (2010). Concepts of Security in South America. In: International Peacekeeping 17/5, 598–612.

I. Case Studies

Susan Flämig

The Ethical Dimension of Security Sector Reform

Police Reforms in Post-War El Salvador

Introduction

Security sector reform (SSR) is conceptually a framework for transforming state security systems that accommodates all relevant state and non-state actors; it is based on democratic norms and principles of good governance (OECD/DAC 2001). Many of these principles and norms were included in the reform process that took place in El Salvador after the end of the civil war in 1992. Especially the creation of a new civilian police was received with a lot of optimism. The success of the transition, however, was limited, as security actors were not able to manage the violence and crime which extend from the post-war years to the present day. One reason for the poor performance of the police, I argue, can be found in the disregard of individual and collective values and norms of security actors and of the broader society that influence state institutions. A consideration of those aspects would add an ethical dimension to the concept of SSR. The following article aims to explore this idea by reflecting on the literature from the field of reconciliation and connecting it to the case of the Salvadoran police. It starts with a critical review of the concept of SSR, showing that such a technocratic approach lacks the ethical dimension of a transition process, a dimension that is more often addressed in research about reconciliation. Thereafter, a brief overview of El Salvador's peace process is given. In the fourth part I examine the intentions and shortcomings of the police reforms, asking why the value of nonviolence is still not sufficiently recognised in practical police work, despite the introduction of new education programmes, frameworks, and mechanisms. I conclude with the suggestion that a rehumanized approach is necessary to overcome a security paradigm that evolved during military dictatorship and civil war.

Ethical Dimensions of Security Sector Reform

SSR is a concept that aims at creating a functioning security system with democratic and accountable actors (Brzoska 2000, OECD/DAC 2001, Wulf 2004). Thereby it should minimise the risk of conflict and open a space for development. It is a state-centred concept that focuses on a wide range of actors and often comprises measures of institutional restructuring, for example introducing civil control of the military, separating external defence from public security or initiating professionalization programmes for the police.

The concept emerged in the 1990s and gained particular attention in development policy-oriented circles. It is often donor-driven and has been criticised for a lack of contextual understanding of the environment of the countries in which it ought to be implemented (Egnell/Halden 2009).

SSR tends to place the formal transformation at the centre of a reform process: authoritarian and non-transparent structures, for example, should be changed by removing personnel and by territorial separation of the military and police; human rights violations by security forces ought to be prevented or minimised by introducing new doctrines, establishing oversight bodies and changing the curriculum.

The concept does not include a focus on the persons working in these institutions and their personal histories that shape their attitudes and impact on their performance. Equally a state's security policy is based on norms and values and an understanding of what security means that is based on local history and traditions. These aspects are still often neglected in the state-building debate.[1] In El Salvador, we can observe a security approach that was for a long time based on repression and coercion; it was notably protecting the interests of a small elite and left out the majority of the population (Browning 1971, Holden 2004). This approach developed during the military dictatorship since 1931, it lasted during the civil war, and the politics of the last 20 years suggest a continuation of this pattern in new forms. One example is the so called "politics of the iron fist", introduced by former President Antonio Saca in 2003 (FESPAD 2003). It identifies youth gangs, the so-called 'maras', as the main source of crime and violence and declares that they are to be fought with rigid and also violent means, including the deployment of military forces. The state's security threat is continuously perceived as coming from inside the country, from its own citizens; whereas the image of the enemy was projected onto the guerrilla previously, it is now associated with the 'maras'.

If a state security approach that is built on repression and an authoritarian culture is to be changed through SSR, the concept needs to be deepened regarding underlying norms and values. In recent years, an intense debate evolved around the transferability or non-transferability of Western norms that shape peace-building and state-building attempts in non-Western countries.[2] In this context the limits of a concept like SSR become apparent. Gaining a better understanding of the ethical side of SSR will not remove the limitations, but it opens a different perspective that may explain one reason for

1 The critique of SSR, based on state formation theory by Egnell and Halden 2009, is an exception.

2 See, for example, the recent publication by Newman, Richmond and Paris 2009.

those limitations. As Lidén (2007:6) put it, "ethics does not produce moral certainty, but it raises the awareness of our already present morality." This can be done by focusing on the culture of state institutions and eventually the employed persons, their attitudes about work, guidelines, politics etc. as well as their relationships with the society, within a hierarchical order or with other state and non-state actors.

Some of these aspects are covered in the debates evolving around policing and ethics (see, for example, Neyroud 2008, Chan 1997). Issues such as the modernization of police forces, the shift in its role from order maintenance to crime fighting, or the relationship with citizens are regarded from an ethical standpoint. This literature, however, concentrates on Europe, the USA, and Australia. Normative policing in the context of peace-keeping and peace-building missions, especially with regard to countries outside the Western Hemisphere has not been sufficiently reflected in research.

Another body of literature that could give important input comes from the field of reconciliation. Reconciliation is a term that is not clearly defined and is filled with various meanings. It appears more often in disciplines like psychology, theology and sociology rather than politics and security studies. In the fields of conflict resolution and peace-building it is often regarded as the ultimate goal of all endeavours to create peace (Ramsbotham et al 2005:231). In this context, some themes stand out in research, all of them linked with each other: First, there is the broad field of uncovering the truth about what happened during war or dictatorship, followed by the question of how to deal with the difficult past (Lederach 1997). These questions are often dealt with in truth commissions that for themselves became a popular object of research (Hayner 2001). Another, closely related field is the problem of how to approach justice in transitional societies. It ranges from questions of reparations for past suffering to socio-economic inequality to justice sector reforms (Mani 2002, Rigby 2001). Thirdly, in a long-term perspective, forgiveness is a topic that does not only appear on an interpersonal level, but is also debated in a bigger societal and political context (Auerbach 2004).

It is striking that within this whole body of literature, security forces are predominantly seen in their role as perpetrators. They have often been deeply involved in atrocity and abuse, in many cases they were the essential instrument of state terror. In the field of SSR, in contrast, security forces represent those actors who are carrying out the plans of creating peace, stability, and security that is based on respect for human rights. SSR designs them to be members of a democratic institution and eventually also members of the society.

These two roles are almost diametrically opposed. Moving from the former violent position towards an accountable and democratic police or military force demands a huge personal and cultural change which can be described as rehumanization. Ramsbotham et al (2005, p. 244) describe rehumanization as the challenge to overcome the polarization between conflicting parties: "The deeper process of reconciliation cannot be reached while dehumanized images of the enemy are still current (…).” Overcoming polarization means to reach a stage where a mutual acknowledgement of suffering and loss becomes possible. If one of the parties is represented to a large extend by state security forces, and on the other side large parts of the population are suffering because of state terror, a rehumanization of security forces poses the serious challenge for victims and the larger society of deconstructing the image of security forces as perpetrators and enemies. It also requires the security forces themselves to gain a new understanding of their role and to face up to the questions of whose security, for whom and by what means. These questions need to be asked on a macro level among political decision-makers and opinion-formers. On a micro level it stretches the importance of basic requirements in a process of reconciliation: firstly, (re-)establishing relationships between opposing parties or between state and citizens, and secondly, creating space to manage and solve conflicts without violence (Kriesberg 2001, Bar-Tal and Bennink 2004, Bloomfield 2006) which also applies to security forces and related reforms. Institutional rearrangements can help to bridge differences and overcome polarization, but only if the importance of the restoration of relationships and the renunciation of violence are taken into consideration as well. Before looking at the institutional restructuring in El Salvador's security landscape and its shortcoming in addressing the problems of the post-war years, some key points about the peace process are depicted.

El Salvador at the Threshold of Peace

It was hoped that the peace agreement of 1992 would end twelve years of civil war in the small Central American country and signal the starting point for an effective transition to peace. Almost 50 years of a brutal military dictatorship preceded the war that claimed 75,000 lives and that highlighted the deep social inequalities. The insurgent group Farabundo Martí National Liberation Front (FMLN) arose in the 1970s as part of a resistance movement against the dominance of a small oligarchy that owned most of the agro-economically important land as well as the economic capital since independence. These dominant elite's interests were protected by an extremely violent state security apparatus, notably its military and paramilitary forces. Against the global background of the Cold War, the military was financially and logistically supported by the United States and the Reagan Administration (Torres-Rivas 1997:222). A stalemate prevented a victory by either the state security agents or FMLN, and the peace endeavours of regional governments and alliances like the Organisation of American States (OAS) as well as the Catholic Church could not end the conflict. It was only after the international situation changed in 1989/90 that the FMLN and the right-wing government formed by Alianza

Republicana Nacionalista (ARENA) came together for official peace negotiations under the auspices of the United Nations (UN). After two years at the negotiating table an agreement was signed that embodied the hope of ending open hostilities and the inequalities whilst also opening a path towards more security and justice.[3]

The peace-building process was supported by the United Nations Observer Mission in El Salvador (ONUSAL) from 1990 to 1995. The agreement included far-reaching security reforms designed to transform the police into a democratic and accountable actor, diminish the power of the military, and dissolve all paramilitary forces (Acuerdo de Paz 1992). Given that a relapse into war has been staved off, El Salvador is still regarded as a success story within the UN. However, social and economic questions were only marginally negotiated, even though they were a decisive source of conflict. They remain unresolved, as many scholars have found (de Soto/del Castillo 1994, Studemeister 2001, UNDP 2009).[4] Although the economic system has changed through the introduction of market liberalisation measures in the 1990s, it is nonetheless still oriented towards the interests of a small oligarchy.[5] Another crucial obstacle to more equality is the level of crime which has increased dramatically since the peace accords and the continuation of violence.[6] Besides the fundamental changes that the security system underwent, many Salvadorans perceive violence and insecurity at the same levels as during the civil war or, at times, even worse (IUDOP 2002). This gap between the intention of the reforms and the reality will be explored in greater detail by looking at the case of the police.

A New Security System and its Shortcomings

Security reforms were unequivocally at the heart of the peace agreement, and the final accord comprised far-reaching decisions and measures designed to transform the security forces that were involved in much of the violence

3 For details about the negotiations see Doyle et al (1997), Hampson (1996), de Soto (1999).

4 The Human Development Report (2009) found that the Gini index for measuring inequality in El Salvador lies at an average of 49.7 between 1992 and 2007, which is among the highest in the world.

5 The new economic system is characterised firstly by an elite that underwent a modernization from agro-economic exports to the financial sector and secondly by *maquilas* which can be described as factory enclaves of international companies that make use of local labour, but the capital stays outside the national economy. Thirdly remittances from emigrated family members represent almost 20 per cent of the GDI (Human Development Report 2009, Zinecker 2007).

6 A study by Fajnzylber, Lederman and Loayza (2001) showed that there is a link between inequality and crime by analysing the correlation between the Gini index and homicide and robbery.

during the dictatorship and the civil war.[7] The reforms aimed to produce a democratic, citizen-oriented security sector which respects human rights. This was clear enough from the different measures taken at the time: (1) The restructuring of the military and police forces was based on the principle of separation of powers; based on this, the police was to become a civilian and accountable actor, the power of the military was to be diminished, and all paramilitary forces were to be dissolved (Acuerdo de Paz 1992). (2) Human rights violations committed during the civil war were investigated by a truth commission and an ad-hoc commission.[8] (3) Further institutions like the Ombudswoman for the Defence of Human Rights (PDDH) and the National Council for Public Security (CNSP) were launched to increase the democratic orientation of the sector.

At the time, the window of opportunity seemed large enough to bring a profound change in the security system and to transform a violent and repressive state. Although challenged by various practical and political problems, the reforms moved beyond the documentation stage and were in fact implemented in the first two to four years after the war. A lot of optimism accompanied particularly the police reforms. The inclusion of former combatants from both conflict parties as well as civilians into the new Policia Nacional Civil (PNC) was regarded as an important step towards the attainment of a reconciled and peaceful society (Hampson 1996:166). Bringing former enemies together in one institution was at the time unprecedented, and it served to establish some trust between the two parties as well as between the police and the population (Spence et al 1994, Neild 2002).

However, the optimism did not last long. Violence after the peace accords has been escalating rather than diminishing. Crime rates increased dramatically after the peace agreement and are still at a high level (Call 2003, FESPAD 2003, World Bank 2011).[9] Studies have found that El Salvador has one of the highest homicide rates in the world (UNODC 2011). Police forces themselves have been involved in cases of human rights violations and criminal activities, such as cases of torture, arbitrary arrests, and excessive use of violence against prisoners as well as discrimination against women, homosexuals, disabled persons, and persons of indigenous origin (FESPAD 2006). They are also accused of being involved in organised crime and drug trafficking. In 2003 the UN Human Rights Committee positively noticed that the PNC had set up a division for human rights; at the same time the academy continuously admitted trainees suspected of having committed human rights violations

7 The report of the truth commission found the state security forces responsible for 85 % of the human rights violations committed during the civil war, and 5 % to be the responsibility of the FMLN (Commission on the Truth for El Salvador 1993).

8 Although an amnesty law impeded persecution (Popkin 2000).

9 Statistics vary significantly, depending on the sources. Most of the data used in different studies comes from the PNC, the Public Attorney's Office, the Institute for Forensic Medicine (IML) and the Directorate of Statistics and Census (DIGESTYC).

(UN Human Rights Committee 2003). It furthermore criticised other malpractices, for example the cases of female police officers who become victims of violence, and the lack of transparency about investigating such incidents. Thus, there is a major discrepancy between the intention of the reforms and the development of the institution in reality.

There are several reasons for the on-going violence on one side and the weak performance of the police on the other side. Causes, forms, and diffusion of violence are highly debated in the newer literature about El Salvador. Whereas some scholars see a shift from political violence to criminal and ubiquitous violence (Torres-Rivas 1999), others argue that violence has been part of day to day life since El Salvador became an independent state and that violence still has a political dimension (Hume 2009, Moodie 2010). The situation, of course, has changed: new security actors emerged, most notably private companies who provide security on commercial terms only whilst being insufficiently covered by legislation (Melara Minero 2001). Youth gangs and, in recent years, criminal networks are at the centre of the public security discourse. They represent an immense problem, although it is not clear how much of the violence can be attributed to which group (UNDP 2005, Peetz 2004). However, along with those scholars that question the separation of violence between being political or criminal, it can be asked whether violence became apolitical at all. In fact, El Salvador is depicted as a non-conflict, "normal" country that has to deal with criminal violence just as other countries have to. It makes the problem of violence a societal problem and disconnects it from political (non)action. It allowed the ARENA government to ignore the importance of developing an inclusive and comprehensive security policy. Violence is deeply related to the lack of economic and social opportunities for a large part of the population that did not profit from the liberalization of markets; it is also a result of a deficient reintegration of combatants, easy access to arms, and a deficient justice sector.

It is evidently a difficult societal, political, and economic environment in which the newly established PNC must try to provide security. Its weak performance is due to very practical shortcomings like underpayment, short education periods without follow-up training or supervision, and a lack of functioning oversight mechanisms (Neild 2002, Zinecker 2007, Beltrán 2009). In addition, transformation did not reach to the deeper levels of attitudes, norms, and values that impact on the design and performance of the sector. In a study for the Washington Office on Latin America about the police's performance, Beltrán (2009) notes that respect for human rights as well as the introduction of new policing concepts like community policing clearly have made their way into the educational system. However, theoretical knowledge often is still not applied in practice, as one police commissioner states in the report: "The recruits can understand a bit about what community policing means, but they don't implement it in practice. And there's the difficulty, trying to internalize the concept instead of just memorizing the concept and saying what it is." (p. 11) A member of an observing human rights NGO notes that "We have an academy where humanistic and human rights topics have acquired a merely formal character (...) We have a police force (...) that is quite weak with respect to the doctrine and legal framework of human rights (...) and the prevention and investigation of crime." Beltrán summarises the situation as lacking an institutionalisation of a new culture and philosophy (p. 11). The value of nonviolence exists in the doctrines and legal frameworks, but it has not been acknowledged in practice.

Within and outside the police a culture of violence has continued: Violence is still regarded as a legitimate mean to enforce what is understood as public security or, more generally, to solve conflicts. If the minimum requirement of a principal renunciation of violence is not given, the chances for rehumanization and relationship-building between former enemies and between security forces and the society are limited. The inclusion of combatants from both sides plus civilians in the PNC was a positive first step towards overcoming enemy images and establishing a conciliatory spirit, but it seems like the peace effort did not reach any further level of rehumanization. During the transformational period there were difficulties in finding enough FMLN ex-combatants willing to join the new police. At the same time, out of a lack of alternatives, many members of the former National Police sought transfers into the new force. Against the agreement and the caveats of the UN two entire paramilitary units were also transferred. It can be assumed that these acts made it more difficult to establish a culture of nonviolence. But there is still a gap of knowledge about how the three different groups that constituted the new PNC perceived each other and worked together.[10] Was it a relationship of victims and perpetrators or between state and non-state armed actors? Was there a change over time, when a new generation of police officers entered the PNC? Answers to these questions would provide an important insight into the (non-) transformation of attitudes and norms. They would highlight the extent to which the inclusion of combatants and civilians in one institution could be seen as a chance to discover and develop common values between opposing and very differing groups (Schaefer 2010).

Conclusion

Even though at the time of the peace agreement security sector reforms (SSR) as a concept had not been developed yet, several steps towards a far-reaching transformation of the Salvadoran security system were undertaken. The

10 Some interviews with members of the PNC have been carried out by Zinecker (2007); she is relating post-war violence mainly to economic deficiencies, but also mentions the shortcomings of the security sector.

measures mentioned above ensured that some essential organisational preconditions for change were met. Institutional change was achieved on a formal level, as Call (2003:828 – 29) noted. However, the new police force faced immense problems in the country and within the institution itself. A deeper transformation in terms of a renunciation of violence and the introduction of a new, democratic, and service-oriented philosophy did not happen. With the idea of SSR, a more comprehensive option of approaching security reforms in the context of peace- and state-building emerged. The concept has been criticised, clarified, and further developed, but it still represents a technocratic concept. The importance of norms and values like nonviolence, respect of human rights, and human dignity is recognised by supporting new legal frameworks, oversight bodies or a different academic curriculum. There is no doubt about the relevance of such measures. In El Salvador, Codes of Conduct for public service officers, based on international regulations, have been introduced as part of the police reforms.[11] They represent a guideline for the development of responsible, accountable, and service-oriented security forces. However, these measures do not automatically change the persons and their attitudes that are at the heart of security institutions. A greater focus on the culture and personal histories of police officers would open a path of understanding reforms as a chance for reconciliation, because it allows seeing the manifold facets of security forces as perpetrators and workers for stability and security. Only if those different roles become clear, a change towards a rehumanized security approach becomes possible. This also requires elaborating and discussing the ethical underpinning of the overall state's security policy and whether it promotes the development of a police that not only acquires theoretical knowledge, but also understands and practices human rights.

References

Acuerdo de Paz (1992). *Carta de El Salvador de fecha 27 de enero de 1992 dirigida al Secretario General por la que se transmite en su totalidad el texto del Acuerdo de Paz entre el Gobierno de El Salvador y el FMLN*, UN Doc. A/46/864–S/23501 (Jan. 30, 1992).

Auerbach, Yehudith (2004). The role of forgiveness in reconciliation. In: Bar-Simon-Tov, Yaacov ed. *From conflict resolution to reconciliation.* Oxford: OUP. 11 – 38.

Bar-Tal, Daniel/Bennink, Gemma (2004). The nature of reconciliation as an outcome and a process. In: Bar-Simon-Tov, Yaacov ed.: *From conflict resolution to reconciliation.* Oxford: OUP. 11 – 38.

11 See, for example, the UN's 1979 Code of Conduct for Law Enforcement Officials and the 2001 European Code of Police Ethics.

Beltrán, Adriana (2009). *Protect and serve? The status of police reform in Central America.* Washington: WOLA.

Bloomfield, David (2006). *On good terms: claryfing reconciliation.* Berghof Report No. 14. Berlin: Berghof Research Centre.

Buchanan, C. and Chávez, J. (2008). *Negotiating disarmament: guns and violence in the El Salvador peace negotiations.* Country Study, No. 3. Mar. 2008. Geneva: Centre for Humanitarian Dialogue.

Browning, David (1971). *El Salvador: landscape and society.* Oxford: OUP.

Brzoska, Michael (2000). The concept of security sector reform. In: Wulf, Herbert ed.: *Security sector reform.* Brief 15. Bonn: BICC. 6 – 13.

Call, Charles T. (2003). Democratisation, war and state-building: constructing the rule of law in El Salvador. In: *Journal of Latin American Studies* 35. Cambridge: CUP. 827 – 862.

Chan, Janet (1997). *Changing police culture: policing in a multicultural society.* Cambridge: CUP.

Commission on the Truth for El Salvador (1993). *From madness to hope: the 12-year war in El Salvador.* Report of the Commission on the Truth for El Salvador.

Doyle, Michael W./Johnstone, Ian/Orr, Robert C. ed. (1997). *Keeping the Peace: multidimensional UN operations in Cambodia and El Salvador.* Cambridge: CUP.

Egnell, Robert/Halden, Peter (2009). Laudable, ahistorical and overambitious: security sector reform meets state formation theory. In: *Conflict, Security and Development,* Vol. 9, No. 1.

Fajnzylber, Pablo/Lederman, Daniel/Loayza, Norman (2001). Inequality and violent crime. In: *Journal of Law and Economics* XLV. 1 – 40.

FESPAD (2006). *Estado de la seguridad publica y la justicia penal en El Salvador 2005.* San Salvador: FESPAD.

FESPAD (2003). *Estado de la seguridad publica y la justicia penal en El Salvador 2003.* San Salvador: FESPAD.

Hampson, Fen O. (1996). *Nurturing peace: why peace settlements succeed or fail.* Washington: USIP.

Hänggi, Heiner (2004). Conceptualising Security Sector Reform and Reconstruction. In: Hänggi, Heiner/Bryden, Alan ed.: *Reform and Reconstruction of the Security Sector.* Münster: Lit Verlag. 1 – 11.

Hayner, Priscilla (2001). *Unspeakable truths: confronting state terror and atrocity.* NY, London: Routledge.

Holden, Robert H. (2004). *Armies without nations: public violence and state formation in Central America 1821 – 1960.* Oxford: OUP.

Hume, Mo (2009). *The politics of violence: gender, conflict, and community in El Salvador.* The Bulletin of Latin American Research book series. Chichester, Malden: Wiley-Blackwell for SLAS.

IUDOP (2002). Los salvadoreños opinan sobre los Acuerdos de Paz y la democracia en El Salvador. Año XVII, No. 1. San Salvador. URL: http://www.uca.edu.sv/publica/iudop/Web/2002/bolet102.pdf [accessed on Jan. 29, 2007].

Kriesberg, Louis (2001). Changing forms of coexistence. In: Abu-Nimer, Mohammed ed.: *Reconciliation, justice and coexistence: theory and practice.* Lanham: Lexington Books. 47–64.

LEDERACH, John P. (1997). *Building peace: sustainable reconciliation in divided societies.* Washington: USIP.

LIDÉN, Kristoffer (2007). *What is the ethics of peacebuilding?* Lecture prepared for the kick-off meeting of the liberal peace and the ethics of peacebuilding project. Jan. 18, 2007. Oslo: PRIO. URL: http://www.prio.no [accessed on July 5,2010].

MANI, Rama (2002). *Beyond retribution: seeking justice in the shadows of war.* Cambridge/Oxford/Malden: Polity Press.

MELARA MINERO, Lidice M. (2001). Los Servicios de Seguridad Privada en El Salvador. In: *ECA* 636. 907–932.

MOODIE, Ellen (2010). *El Salvador in the aftermath of peace: crime, uncertainty, and the transition to democracy.* Philadelphia: University of Pennsylvania Press.

NEILD, Rachel (2002). Sustaining reform: democratic policing in Central America. In: WOLA ed.: *Citizen security monitor.* Washington: WOLA.

NEWMAN, Edward/RICHMOND, Oliver/PARIS, Roland ed. (2009). *New perspectives on liberal peacebuilding.* Tokyo: UNU Press.

NEYROUD, Peter (2008). Policing and ethics. In: NEWBURN, Tim ed.: *Handbook of Policing.* 2nd ed. Cullompton, Portland: Willan Publishing. 666–692.

OECD/DAC (2001). Security issues and development co-operation: a conceptual framework for enhancing policy coherence. In: *The DAC Journal,* Vol. 2, No. 3.

PEETZ, Peter (2004). Zentralamerikas Jugendbanden: 'Maras' in Honduras, El Salvador und Guatemala *(Central America's youth gangs: 'Maras' in Honduras, El Salvador and Guatemala).* In: *Brennpunkt Lateinamerika, No. 5.* June . 49–63.

PNUD (UNDP) (2005). *¿Cuanto le cuesta la violencia a El Salvador?* San Salvador: PNUD.

POPKIN, Margaret (2000). *Peace without justice: obstacles to building the rule of law in El Salvador.* University Park: Pennsylvania State UP.

RAMSBOTHAM, Oliver/WOODHOUSE, Tom/MIALL, Hugh (2005). *Contemporary conflict resolution: the prevention, management and transformation of deadly conflicts.* 2nd ed. Cambridge: Polity Press.

RIGBY, Andrew (2001). *Justice and reconciliation: after the violence.* Boulder: Lynn Rienner.

SOTO, Álvaro de, Castillo, raciana del (1994). Obstacles to Peacebuilding. In: *Foreign Policy* 94/1994. 69–83.

SPENCE, Jack and VICKERS, George (1994). *A negotiated revolution? A two year progress report on the Salvadoran peace accords.* Cambridge, Mass.: Hemisphere Initiatives.

STUDEMEISTER, Margarita (2001). *El Salvador. Implementation of the peace accords.* Peaceworks 38. Washington: USIP.

TORRES-RIVAS, Edelberto (1997). Insurrection and Civil War in El Salvador. In: Doyle, Michael W./Johnstone, Ian/Orr, Robert C. ed.: *Keeping the Peace: Multidimensional UN Operations in Cambodia and El Salvador,* Cambridge: CUP. 209–226.

Torres-Rivas, Edelberto (1999). Epilogue: notes on terror, violence, fear and democracy. In: Kooning, K., Kruijt, D. ed.: *Societies of fear: the legacy of civil war, violence and terror in Latin America.* London: Zed Books. 285–300.

UN Human Rights Committee (2003). *Concluding observations of the Human Rights Committee.* UN Doc. CCPR/CO/78/SLV, (July 22, 2003).

UNDP (2009). *Overcoming barriers: human mobility and development.* Human Development Report 2009.

UNODC (2011). *Global study on homicide: trends, contexts and data.* Vienna.

WORLD BANK (2011). *Crime and violence: a development challenge.* World Bank.

Wulf, Herbert (2004). Security Sector Reform in Developing and Transitional Countries. In: Fischer, Martina/McCartney, Clem/Wils, Oliver ed.: *Security Sector Reform: Potentials and Challenges for Conflict Transformation.* Berlin: Berghof Conflict Research.

Zinecker, Heidrun (2007). *From Exodus to Exitus – in the causes of post war violence in El Salvador.* PRIF-Report No. 80, Frankfurt: Hessische Stiftung Friedens- und Konfliktforschung.

David Tombs

Archbishop Romero and Reconciliation in El Salvador

1. Introduction

The Catholic Church has an extraordinary institutional presence in Latin America. It stretches throughout the vast continent, all the way from the southernmost tip of Tierra del Fuego, right up through South America, Central America and Mexico. Its multinational spread across countries is matched by a remarkable demographic reach within countries. The church's influence extends from the centres of power inhabited by the social elites across to all sectors of society. No other institution does this, not even the state. In some rural areas you might have minimal contact with the state, but the church is present in at least some form and you might have regular contact with it.

As a result, parties involved in a political or social conflict in Latin America are likely to care much more deeply about what the church thinks and says than would be the case in Western Europe. When the church takes a position on a social issue or a political conflict it can be resisted but not easily ignored, the symbolic weight and institutional presence of the church are too great.[1]

Part of the church's sense of itself as a public authority rests on its sense of its history in Latin America. As an institution the church pre-dates the emergence of national territories and national governments in the aftermath of nineteenth century independence. In colonial society the church was one of the three central pillars supporting the ruling system, closely allied to the wealthy landowners and the military. After independence, the church took time to accommodate itself to the new realities but slowly repositioned itself to protect its political position by creating new partnerships with the ruling

1 Only Mexico has a significant anti-clerical streak. In other countries, the political elite may at times have a difficult relationship with the church but they cannot just ignore it. The strength of the Catholic Church's institutional influence rests on a number of factors, these include: a national reach in each country from the capital city to the most remote areas; a transnational reach linking the Catholic Church to other countries in Latin America and around the world; institutionalised presence in social provision, for example, the education system, hospitals, military chaplains; a cultural assumption shared by both governments and the wider public that when the Catholic Church speaks it should be listened to; a respected status making it a relatively 'safe space' which all sectors of society should be able to access. I am particularly grateful for conversations with my colleague Dr. Cath Collins on the social and political aspects of the Catholic Church in Latin America and her insightful suggestions when I was preparing this paper.

elites. These new partnerships allowed it to take a step back from direct political involvement, whilst continuing to maintain a privileged position of power in shaping social policy. When political leaders were sympathetic to the church, as was most usually the case, the church also enjoyed institutional benefits in exchange for its support. When political leaders were less sympathetic to the church, the church could focus on preserving rather than extending its institutional position. During such periods it concentrated its efforts on defending itself against what it saw as unwarranted interference, whilst pressing the government to pursue social policies in keeping with traditional Catholic values. In either case, the guiding principle was invariably institutional interest during the nineteenth and for most of the twentieth century.

One consequence of this long history is that the church typically sees itself – and is seen by others – as having a longer claim to allegiance of citizens than any transient political institution. Whilst political parties, political movements and political leaders have come and gone over the last two centuries, the church has seen itself as an unchanging bedrock on which society can find a sure foundation. Regrettably, however, the church has failed to exercise this powerful influence on behalf of those most in need. On the whole it has been highly conservative and supportive of the ruling civil powers.

During the twentieth century the Catholic Church faced mounting challenges from two different directions, with the spread of secularization on one hand and a vibrant Pentecostal Protestantism on the other. In addition, a third and equally significant challenge to the traditional church emerged from inside the Catholic Church itself. In the 1970s and 1980s – the so-called "era of the military dictatorships" – a significant wing within the church adopted a much more confrontational approach to the authoritarian regimes that had come to power. This progressive wing within the church was an attempt to re-orientate the church to social justice concerns and relocate the church from a position of privilege to a position with the poor.

Oscar Romero, the well-known Archbishop of El Salvador, is a prime example of such a shift. His three year period as Archbishop in the capital San Salvador between 1977 and his assassination in 1980 are a fascinating case-study of the changes that many who were "converted to the poor" underwent. It is well-known that Romero's experiences in defending the powerless and the clergy who served them prompted an initially cautious and conservative Romero to develop a prophetic liberationist challenge to the military government. However, to more fully understand Romero's journey as Archbishop, it is necessary to see his sense of the church's mission in terms of reconciliation and not just liberation.

The political forces of polarisation that Romero faced, and the ecclesial vision on which he based his mission, may offer insight into the positions taken by other courageous church leaders of the time, such as Cardinal Raúl Silva in Chile. It will be suggested that they too may have been guided by an often unstated but crucially important sense of unity and reconciliation in the work of the church in Latin America. To develop this argument it is first necessary to understand the situation of political polarisation which Romero and others in the Salvadoran church faced in the 1970s.

2. Political Polarisation and the "Stretching of the Church" in the 1970s

The political regimes of Latin America in the nineteenth and twentieth centuries typically served the interests of powerful social elites rather than safeguard the basic needs of the poor majorities.[2] In most cases, the ruling parties did not present themselves at the far right of the political spectrum, but were more likely to claim to stand in the "middle ground". The more progressive constitutional legacies from nineteenth century independence, along with a political pragmatism seeking to reach out from a narrow base, and a desire to be seen as a modern Western society, encouraged political parties to claim the central ground wherever possible. However, the deeply rooted structural inequalities in most countries meant that the rhetoric of representative democratic government and the political centre could be highly misleading. In most cases, the "political norm" was centre-right, and in times of crisis it tended to move further to the right.

The church in Latin America typically took its lead from the ruling political regime, and its institutional centre of gravity was similarly "centre-right". For much of its life it was primarily concerned to preserve a mutually beneficial partnership with those in power. Centre-right was therefore its 'natural' social location. Nonetheless, within the church, as in any institution, there would have been tendencies spanning a wider range of the political spectrum from political reformist to political conservative. Individual clergy might find themselves drawn more to one side than the other. Although the gravitational centre of the church balanced out at centre-right, some reformist clergy might find themselves a little left of centre. Such individuals were most likely balanced by counterparts who were equally outside the dominant body to the political right.

Alongside this, as noted above, the church had an historical sense of its spiritual and social mission to the whole of society. This aspect of its historical identity gave it a sense of rightful leadership and social relevance to an even broader constituency along the social spectrum. Whilst it wished to maintain a distance from political extremes to either side (and especially from the far-

2 Such a sweeping claim runs a serious risk of over-simplifying the political history of a continent, but El Salvador, which in the nineteenth century had 'the fourteen families' who controlled coffee production and the export economy, is one of the clearest examples of this.

left), it saw itself as representing and speaking for a relatively wide group. The position of the typical church in Latin American countries is represented in Fig. 1.

In this context, the social divisions that accompanied the political polarisations of the 1970s had far reaching consequences for the church. As hard-line authoritarian military regimes moved political power to the hard right the church was forced to address its relationship with a new political reality.

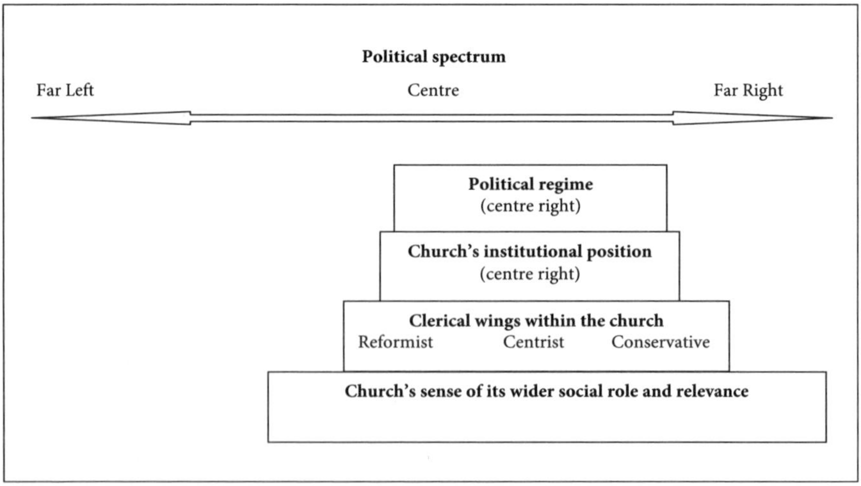

Fig. 1. *The Typical Political Location of the Catholic Church in Latin America*

Instead of making pretence to serve the whole society, the new regimes were more likely to characterise the threat from left-wing revolutionary groups as a de facto situation of war. In this polarised situation the wider population was forced to make difficult choices. Anyone actively opposed to these regimes ran an enormous risk, and anyone not clearly aligned with the regime was under suspicion. Human rights violations against civilians escalated, deaths, disappearance and torture became common place.

Whilst the church's reaction differed from country to country, two prominent patterns can be identified – "shifting" and "stretching". This is to say that in most cases the institutional church found itself shifted into a more oppositional relationship to the regime. Second, political divisions within the church were exacerbated, leading to what might be described as a 'stretching' of the church.

It is important to appreciate that the shifted relationship with governments was not a consequence of church movement along the political spectrum, but rather the opposite. It was a consequence of the church as a conservative institution resisting political pressures to shift and take up a more extreme position. The consequence of this was that the church as a centre-right institution was now located to the left of the regime. As a result, the church had a new relationship of tension with right-wing governments forced upon it.

This is not to ignore the fact that some on the conservative wing of the church moved to the right to preserve their close alliance with political power. However, in most countries this was balanced by a relatively small but significant number of clergy, influenced by liberation theology, being drawn much further towards the left. These constituted a new 'liberationist wing' within the church, positioned much further to the left than the reformist wing had been before them. The overall effect was to dramatically "stretch" the wings of the church in both directions, as represented in Fig 2.

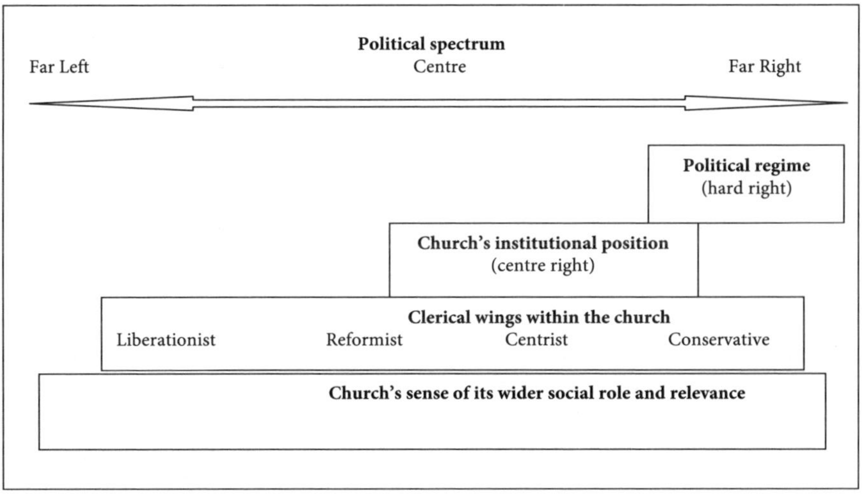

Fig. 2. *Political polarization in the 1970s and its impact on the Catholic Church.*

This "stretching" of the wings of the church was itself bedded into the church's sense of its unity and mission, which fashioned the church's self-understanding as encompassing everyone, even though in practice it had very often fallen far short of this vision during its time in Latin America. Whilst the hard-right might declare war on leftist groups, and had few qualms in seeking to simply exterminate them, the centrist tendencies in the church instinctively sought an alternative.

When faced with a political crisis, the general instinct in the Catholic Church is to be cautious. There is often a temptation to deny that the political crisis exists and dismiss suggestions to the contrary as partisan politics. However, because the church in Latin America was so deeply embedded into the wider fabric of society this flight from reality became difficult to sustain during the period of dictatorships. The church could not isolate itself from events to the extent needed to maintain the pretence that all was normal. The church's social obligations forced it to engage with the consequences of the repression. For example, the dead need to be buried and the church was expected to do this. This brought the church into repeated intimate contact with the painful realities of the situation. It also raised the unavoidable question of how it should respond.

Given the intensity and extent of the repression the suggestion that nothing was really wrong increasingly discredited the church and undermined its status in society. An alternative and more proactive response had to be made. Invariably the church's next instincts were towards moderation, expressed cautiously through calls for a *via media* or a return to how things were previously. The church's conservative bias made it much more comfortable with reforms rather than radical actions.

However, in situations of acute polarisation the church's conservative tendencies and its orientation to inclusion and catholicity can have radical consequences. In such cases, the church typically seeks a position which will not cut it off from either end of the spectrum. If possible it will try to bring the polarised parties together, or at least to narrow the division between them. During the era of dictatorships, this moderating stance often put the church in a difficult position vis-à-vis the two ends of spectrum in many countries. Both the political-left and the political-right were critical of the church for a perceived lack of support.

To add to the church's problems, the social stresses and strains that the church experiences in its external relations are likely to be mirrored by greater internal institutional stress within the church. Existing divisions within the church opened up and became more bitter, as the wider stakes were raised on where the church would position itself politically.

On top of this, both the external tension between the church and the polarised wings of society, and the internal tension within the church itself, contribute to a dramatic heightening of personal stress and tension felt by individuals within the church. This is especially the case for church leaders who are committed to the church's social role as a mediating force, and even more so if they value unity within the church. During the dictatorships, church leaders faced increasing criticism from all sides, from both outside and inside the church. In many countries this included physical attacks on church property and personnel, and even imprisonments, tortures and assassinations.

Notwithstanding the many institutional advantages that the Catholic Church enjoys, the impact of these attacks and the institutional and personal stresses that they create can be unbearable. Against the backdrop of this common pattern, it is illuminating to look at the challenges faced by one of the best known leaders of a national church during this period, Archbishop Oscar Romero of San Salvador.

3. Archbishop Romero, Liberation and Reconciliation

Shortly after Bishop Oscar Romero had been chosen to succeed Archbishop Chávez he gave an interview to the Salvadoran daily newspaper *Prensa Gráfica* (cf. Feb. 10, 1977), in which he made reference to his vision of the church's social ministry. As he put it: "We must keep to the centre, watchfully, in the traditional way, but seeking justice"(Romero 1977, cited by Brockman 1989: 4). His words expressed a caution and conservatism over the role of the church that many progressive priests feared would mark his time as Archbishop. Romero's previous conflicts with the Jesuits and his personal contacts with Opus Dei gave weight to these fears. In a society that was so deeply polarised, with wealth and power concentrated in the hands of so few, a call to keep to 'the centre' sounded like a commitment to the *status quo.* During his time as Archbishop (Feb. 22, 1977–Mar. 24, 1980), Romero learned that keeping to the centre of Salvadoran politics whilst being watchful and seeking justice was an impossible task. He was forced instead to make difficult decisions on which values were most important to him; and as is well known, as Romero grew into his appointment, he consistently chose justice ahead of holding to the centre.

As the political situation in El Salvador deteriorated from 1977 onwards, Romero increasingly adopted "the preferential option for the poor" advocated by liberation theologians and progressive church leaders of the day.[3] This provided him with the ethical and theological basis to confront the injustices of El Salvador's rich and powerful rather than seek an illusory neutral or apolitical centre ground. Romero came to see that the church could not just ignore the divisions in Salvadoran society and pretend they did not exist. On the contrary it was often necessary to expose these divisions for what they were. Holding to the centre did not and could not address the fundamental division in society.

In the aftermath of the murder of his friend Rutilio Grande (Mar. 12, 1977), Romero informed the newly elected President that he would not participate at official government events until a thorough investigation had been conducted into the killing (cf. Romero 1977, cited by Brockman 1989: 11). This was a promise that he kept throughout his period as Archbishop, and which served as a constant reminder of the divisions between church and government.

In this context, the language of liberation that was being developed by prophetic theologians, church leaders, priests, nuns, and lay communities offered a powerful language for Romero to express the political dimension of faith. He set out this vision most systematically in his four pastoral letters, "The Easter Church" (Apr. 10, 1977), "The Church, the Body of Christ in History" (Aug. 6, 1977), "The Church and Popular Political Organizations"

3 The term was formally endorsed by the Latin American bishops at CELAM III in 1979.

(Aug. 6, 1978), and "The Church's Mission amid the National Crisis" (Aug. 6, 1979).[4]

More than thirty years after Romero's death these letters (some written with the help of the Jesuits at the University of Central America) remain models of pastoral and political theology.[5] However, interpretations of Romero that draw heavily on these sources to point to his liberationist outlook may fail to adequately reflect an equally important dimension of his life and work that is highlighted in his personal diary: his commitment to unity. In particular, some accounts of Romero's personal journey present it as a relatively simple albeit highly dramatic change (or even "conversion") from a conservative to a liberationist outlook in 1977. This interpretation can obscure the underlying continuity in his concerns between when he was Archbishop and before, which may be gleaned from his diary.[6] This continuity is to be found in Romero's commitment to unity. It involved overcoming divisions in the church and in society, and also overcoming divisions between the church and society. Appreciating Romero's concern for unity and therefore his Christian sense of reconciliation is at least as important for an understanding of his theology, ministry and life journey as understanding his Christian sense of liberation.

Romero's Commitment to Unity and Reconciliation

Romero held the sanctity, authority and unity of the church in the highest regard. It is unlikely that Romero would have made such a bold option for the poor without these three ecclesial concerns. For example, Rubén Zamora suggests that it was Romero's sense of the sanctity of the church that compelled him to take his determined stance after the death of Grande.[7]

4 Cf. Oscar Romero. Voice of the Voiceless: The Four Pastoral Letters and Other Statements. trans. M. Walsh (1985). Maryknoll NY: Orbis Books. Abridged from Spanish orig. La voz de los sin voz: la palabra viva de Monseñor Oscar Arnulfo Romero. Cardenal, R., Martín-Baro, I., and & J. Sobrino J. ed. (1980). San Salvador: UCA Editores.

5 On help received from César Jerez, Jon Sobrino and Ignacio Ellacuría for the third and fourth letters, see Romero's own diary; Oscar Romero. *A Shepherd's Diary.* trans. Irene B. Hodgson (1993). London: Catholic Fund for Overseas Development and Catholic Institute for International Relations, esp. 51 (Apr. 28, 1978), 184 (Apr. 6, 1979), 241 (May 28, 1979).

6 There are a number of risks in using a personal diary for research of this kind. These include the danger of 'proof-texting' by citing short passages out of context, and also the possibility of uncritically replicating a subjective viewpoint as the authoritative truth on a course of events. The latter concern is especially important because as a public figure Romero may have opted for discretion in his diaries; see, for example, the contrast between his account of his trip to Rome in 1979 described in the diary with the recollections of César Jerez in López Vigil, María (2000) *Oscar Romero: Memories in Mosaic.* trans. Kathy Ogle. London: Catholic Fund for Overseas Development. Nonetheless, the diaries are a crucial resource for understanding how Romero saw what he was doing and wished it to be seen by others. They supplement the outstanding biography by James R. Brockman (1989). *Romero: A Life.* Maryknoll, NY: Orbis Books.

7 Rubén Zamora interviewed for BBC Radio 4 "Requiem for Romero" (Mar. 5, 2005).

Likewise it was the authority of the Medellín texts from CELAM II (1968) and social teachings like Paul VI's *Evangelii Nuntiandi* (1975) that convinced him to stick to his course in the face of fierce opposition.[8]

Above all, however, it was Romero's commitment to unity that explains so much of what he did. Romero's personal motto "Sentir con la Iglesia" ("To feel with the Church") reflects his life-long concern for unity with the church and unity of the church. Despite the conflict with his fellow bishops, and the opposition of the *nuncio* (Emanuele Gerarda) and the mistrust in Rome, Romero always believed that what he did was in accordance with church teaching and a means to build greater unity in the church (cf. Romero 1978 and 1979: 23, 43).[9] Prior to his time as Archbishop much of his concern with progressive priests was that they were dividing the church. As Archbishop, Romero had to endure this criticism himself, from the rich, from articles in the press, from the *nuncio* and especially from fellow bishops during their often rancorous meetings.

Many of Romero's most prophetic acts were influenced by the importance that he placed on church unity and bringing people together. Romero liked to speak to the whole Archdiocese through radio YSAX, using the radio to "gather" his whole flock around him for his services in the Cathedral, even though people might be physically distant from him in remote villages (cf. Romero 1978 and 1979: 186–188, 199–201 and 494).[10] Likewise, in the aftermath of Grande's death, there was the symbolic unity of the famous single Mass for the whole Archdiocese (1977) to bring everyone together.[11]

Romero's pain and distress at divisions within the church are clear in many of his diary entries. Underlying his concern for unity was a theological and ecclesial understanding of the church as the body of Christ expressed in his Second Pastoral Letter "The Church, the Body of Christ in History" (Romero 1980: 63–84).[12] This was based on verses in the Pauline Epistles that speak of

8 Brockman suggests that Romero had given the Medellín documents little attention before becoming Archbishop. They may have become so important for Romero as Archbishop because they provided ecclesial authority that he might have found difficult at a personal level.

9 On the Salvadoran Bishops conference Bishops Revelo (auxiliary of San Salvador), Bishop Aparicio (San Vicente), Bishop Barrera (Santa Ana) and Bishop Alvarez (San Miguel and military vicar) were often in conflict with Romero and his other auxiliary Rivera y Damas; see, for example, Romero's account (Apr. 3, 1978) of the controversy over a critical letter that approximately 200 priests had sent to the papal nuncio and their study of the preparatory document for CELAM III (Apr. 17, 1978).

10 His 8am Sunday morning services were broadcast by radio YSAX and his diary reflects his annoyance when the radio station broadcast was intentionally blocked by his opponents as in April 1979 and then the radio station bombed in Feb. 1980.

11 An act repeated after the death of Fr. Rafael Palacios (June 30, 1979); Romero 274. cf. n. 5. It seems that initially Romero was in two minds over the single Mass for Grande, since his instinct for unity seemed to clash with his concern over church tradition and procedure. It was only when César Jerez supported the Mass with an appeal to the church father Ireneas that Romero felt sufficiently confident to make a final commitment to it.

12 Jon Sobrino is commonly acknowledged as writing the first draft for this; see Brockman p. 60.

believers as constituting the body of Christ (for example, 1 Corinthians 12. 27, Rom 12.5, Eph. 1. 22–23) and also the new emphasis in post-Conciliar theology on the church as the people of God. When speaking at Aguilares (June 19, 1977), to reconsecrate the church after a month-long military takeover, Romero used the understanding of the unity of the body in Gal. 3.26–29 to distinguish Christ's liberation from false liberations. For Romero, liberation and reconciliation went together. In Romero's words:

> Baptism made us one body with Christ, and in Christ we are one with him and cannot betray all that flows from that: the new human being. It is a new being with a heart cleansed of all sin, a new person who does not speak with animosity in the heart, who never furthers violence, hatred, or rancor… Let his eucharist, which is a call to reconciliation with God and our brothers and sisters, leave in all hearts the satisfaction that we are Christians (Romero 1977, cited by Brockman 1989: 63).

For Romero this theological and ecclesial vision applied to the unity of society, as much as to the unity of the church. As he indicated in one of his cathedral homilies (Apr. 23, 1978), 1 Peter 2.9 called people together as more than a spiritual community but also as a political and social community and 'a holy nation'(Romero 1978 and 1979: 49). If the people of El Salvador (which literally means 'the Saviour') were divided it was the role of the church, and Romero's responsibility as Archbishop to bring them together, no matter how much personal suffering this might involve.

Furthermore, Romero's dedication to church and social unity was matched with a *personal instinct* for bringing people together that he never lost. His first action in his visit to Rome in June 1978 was to pray for unity at the tomb of St Peter (cf. Romero 1978 and 1979: 67). Romero also refers with approval to the public audience with the Pope that he attended a few days later (June 21, 1978), in which Paul VI described the great mission of the church as sowing unity, peace and joy in Christ in the midst of humanity (cf. Romero 1978 and 1979: 68). Even in the final sentence of his fatally interrupted address at the anniversary mass for Sara Meardi de Pinto on the day he was murdered, Romero was saying: "Let us join together, then, intimately in faith and hope at this moment of prayer for Doña Sarita and ourselves"(Romero 1980, cited by Brockman 1989: 192).

It was this personal instinct for bringing people together that prompted him to try mediation in many of the difficult situations that he faced as Archbishop, offering his services when asked to help resolve tensions in particular parishes, or intervene in workers' strikes, kidnappings, hostage takings, and building sieges.[13]

Romero's diary cannot confirm this (since it begins Mar. 31, 1978) but there is good reason to believe it.

13 See, for example, his account of dissension within the parish at Ciudad Arce between the parish

Romero's commitment to unity never changed; it is more his realisation that this could not be done by holding to a spurious centre ground that marks his transformation as Archbishop. He saw the preferential option for the poor as a means to achieve unity rather than an alternative to unity. For Romero, it was the way whereby everyone could find their proper place together in a just and harmonious society.

Romero and the Theology of Reconciliation

Despite Romero's concern for unity he never developed an explicit theology of reconciliation that might have held together the political and theological challenges that such work involves in a social conflict characterised by injustice. In fact, the word reconciliation is almost wholly absent from Romero's speeches and writings as Archbishop.[14] Nor does the theme of reconciliation feature significantly in his sermons. The word he uses for Christ's work of salvation on the cross is most usually *redemption* rather than *reconciliation.*

In one intriguing entry in his diary (July 15, 1979) he comments:

> And in the evening I was visited by the vice president of the Movement of International Reconciliation, which has its headquarters in Vienna. She came to offer us their cooperation to promote in El Salvador an activity related to non-violence or, more positively, to justice and peace. I liked her idea very much, but I felt I could not accept it on my own and, because of this I asked if we could meet again tomorrow evening, along with some of my advisers (Romero 1978 and 1979: 53).

Sadly there is no mention of any such meeting in the diary entry for the next day nor is there any explanation for this omission, or any account of how Romero's advisers reacted to the suggestion. However, there are at least four reasons why Archbishop Romero and his advisers may have been wary of 'reconciliation' to describe the work of the church and the political dimension to faith, and therefore why he did not develop his theology of reconciliation in more explicit terms.[15]

priest and the sister who promoted base communities. Romero wrote in his diary: 'I was interested in bringing a message of unity to the entire Christian community'.

14 Here the contrast with liberation is especially telling. For example, there is no index entry for reconciliation in *Voice of the Voiceless: The Four Pastoral Letters and Other Statements*, whereas the references to liberation are plentiful.

15 For a good summary of Romero's interpretation of liberation as expressing the political dimension to faith, see 'The Political Dimensions of the Faith from the Perspective of the Option for the Poor' Address by Archbishop Romero on the Occasion of the Conferral of a Doctorate, Honoris Causa, by the University of Louvain, Belgium, Feb. 2, 1980; reprinted in Romero 177–187. cf. n. 4. The closest Romero came to a sustained presentation on reconciliation was in his homily of 16 March 1980.

First, the predominant sense that reconciliation had (and still has) in Catholic theology was not political reconciliation but sacramental reconciliation. Unlike liberation, which linked the political and the theological together in a very direct way, the tendency was to see reconciliation in theological terms that ignored the political dimension and focussed exclusively on the sacramental and spiritual overcoming of division between God and people.

Second, even in its political terms, "reconciliation" and "liberation" seemed to point in opposite directions and define different political commitments. As José Comblin points out, in his important piece "The Theme of Reconciliation and Theology in Latin America" (*Revista Eclesiástica Brasileira* 1986: 272–314):

> In the context of social conflicts, the theme of reconciliation forms part of the ideology of the dominant classes, of those classes which occupy privileged positions. The appeal to social reconciliation obscures the desire and the project of maintaining the established situation. In this then, reconciliation consists in the exploiters and the exploited renouncing their claims and accepting the existing situation. The discourse of social peace is the natural discourse of the dominant classes. Frequently, bourgeoisie Catholics appeal to the necessity for peace and for social reconciliation in order to struggle against the popular movements (cf. MacLean 2006: 135–170).

The danger of the language of reconciliation being appropriated for conservative politics was especially true in El Salvador, where the PCN – the *Partido de Conciliación Nacional* (National Conciliation Party) – was the political party name of the ruling military government. In such a context, neither Romero nor any other figure sympathetic to liberation theology would be likely to find the term reconciliation helpful for expressing a vision of peace built upon justice.

Third, despite his respect for scholarship, Archbishop Romero's interests were always practically and pastorally inclined. During his time as archbishop he faced almost weekly crises and he had little time to spend on systematic and academic reflection. Thus despite his concern for Christian liberation, his development of liberation as a theological theme is less systematic than in the works of Ellacuría or Sobrino, both of whom worked at the University of Central America and wrote for a more academic audience. Furthermore, the fruitful dialogue between Romero and the Jesuits aimed at deepening their understanding of liberation had no parallel around reconciliation. Neither Ellacuría nor Sobrino prioritised the theme of reconciliation, probably for the reasons already given, and their writings would not have given Romero particular encouragement to think about reconciliation in a more systematic way.

Finally, Romero himself may in any case have viewed his commitment to reconciliation primarily as a foundational value, which needed little further explication beyond practical work for unity. For him ecclesial and social unity guided everything that he did as an outworking of faith and did not need to be justified by further argument or scrutinised in further reflection on reconciliation, even if there had been time to undertake this.

Whatever the precise balance between these factors may have been, and whatever additional factors might also have been involved, the result was that Romero did not speak or write about reconciliation in the way he spoke and wrote of liberation. As a result, his emphasis on unity can be missed and his attitude to liberation can be misinterpreted as *putting the poor in opposition to the rich* in ways that created social divisions. He certainly had critics at the time who made this mistaken complaint. In contrast, it is much more accurate to see Romero as *recognising that Salvadoran society divided the poor from the rich.* He saw the church as called to overcome these divisions and build a true social unity rather than pretend that the divisions did not exist.

A Cross of Unbearable Stress

According to Ricardo Urioste, Romero's personal aide, "Archbishop Romero was the most loved person and the most hated person in this country" (cited by Miglierini 2010). On Mar. 24, 1980, Mar. 24 Romero was cut down by an assassin's bullet whilst celebrating Mass at the hospital chapel. The murder was the final culmination of hostility and attacks from three different directions.[16] First, from the right-wing press, who made scandalous and entirely unfounded allegations against Romero. For example, *La Opinión* published a front page photo of Romero with an enlarged headline 'Monsignor Romero Directs Terrorist Group' and a smaller headline proclaiming that Romero was 'a great ally of subversives'.[17] Second, there were also attacks from the government and social elites who had initially welcomed his appointment as Archbishop, and who felt 'betrayed' by the stance he took.[18] Third, he faced

16 The United Nations truth commission formally ascribed responsibility to a group led by Roberto d'Aubuisson. D'Aubuisson was a former army major who was widely credited with the creation and organisation of death-squads responsible for the disappearances and deaths of political activists, union leaders and others who might challenge the ruling regime; United Nations (1993). Truth Commission for El Salvador. *From Madness to Hope: The 12-Year War in El Salvador.* New York. 127. D'Aubuisson died in 1992, but the right-wing ARENA party, which he founded, was in power from 1989 – 2009.

17 *La Opinión* (Dec. 1977). 1. These accusations were particularly ominous in the context of the right-wing slogan that had been daubed on some walls in the city earlier in the year, "Be a Patriot - Kill a Priest".

18 In Mar. 2009, Mauricio Funes of the FMLN, the party of the former leftist guerrilla group, became the first elected President from the left since the 1992 peace agreement. On Mar. 24, 2010, to mark the thirtieth anniversary of Romero's death, President Mauricio Funes unveiled a mural of Romero. This was the first time that the state officially marked the anniversary. In the name of the state, Funes asked for pardon for the death of Romero and others who died in the civil war. He said: "I know that it is a relief to society, that it is a balm for a country that is tired of violence and that seeks the reconciliation of spirit."; cited by Elisabeth Malkin (Mar. 24, 2010). "El Salvador Leader Apologizes for Archbishop's Assassination", *New York Times.*

constant criticism within the church. During his years as Archbishop he worked with a sharply divided Bishops' Conference – in which he and Bishop Rivera y Damas were invariably minority voices. His diary records the pain that he experienced as a result of divisions in the conference and the personal toll that they took on him.

In light of these attacks, Ricardo Urioste points to a suggestive link between Romero and Christ. He says: "And as Jesus, he was crucified" (cited by Miglierini 2010). Interpreting Romero's death in this way can serve as an important reminder that work for meaningful reconciliation is rarely easy or comfortable. Romero's commitment to reconciliation did not rest on a theology of "cheap grace" but of solidarity with those who suffered most. He tried to reach out to all sides, but he did not seek to distance himself from the conflict and speak from a safe place. Instead he stood in solidarity with those who most needed his support. Because of this he exposed himself to the same violence that they faced in their daily lives.

There is a famous photo of the procession which accompanied Romero's funeral. At the front of one of processional columns a white-robed cleric carries a large crucifix, which shows Christ on the cross with his arms fully outstretched. The crucifix is a graphic reminder that the common physiological cause of death on the cross is from overstretching and asphyxiation. When a victim's arms are outstretched and above his head, the victim is unable to breathe normally when hanging in the resting position. As the crucifixion progresses and breathing becomes more difficult the victim has continually to raise himself enough into an elevated position for a gasp of breath before slumping back down again. This is a painful and prolonged process, it can continue until physical exhaustion eventually makes breathing impossible, unless death from some other physical cause such as loss of blood or anaphylactic shock occurs before then.

The unbearable stress of crucifixion is a powerful image for Romero's work of reconciliation and the price he paid for it. In his ministry Romero courageously tried to reach out to, and hold together, the polarised divisions in the church and in wider society. This struggle against violence became a cross of death.

4. Conclusion

A few days before his death, Romero said: 'If I die I will rise again in the Salvadoran people' (Romero 1980, cited by Brockman 1989: 248). Thirty years after his death, his three years as Archbishop in a bitterly divided society deserve close attention by those articulating a theology of reconciliation today. Although Romero did not speak explicitly of reconciliation, its significance is clearly implicit in his strong desire for unity in the church and in society at all times in his life. Had he used the language of reconciliation, it would in all likelihood have been understood in sacramental and apolitical terms. Because genuine unity and true reconciliation require justice, Romero expressed the need for justice in the language of liberation that was available to him. However, now that more vibrant political theologies of "reconciliation with justice" are being articulated, it is a good time to revisit Romero's life and writing as a political and religious activist from this perspective. In many ways Romero deserves to be remembered and admired as much for his commitment to reconciliation as for his commitment to liberation. It is only when the complementarities of these two concerns are understood that the full significance of his witness is appreciated.

As an example of wider processes within the church, the Salvadoran church under Romero is an interesting illustration of some of the features of the Catholic Church described in the first half of this chapter. The argument was made that the Catholic Church in Latin America is usually located to the right of the political spectrum, but when extreme right-wing parties and military dictatorships assumed power in many Latin American countries in the 1970s there were two significant consequences for the church. First, it was 'shifted' to the left of the government, even though in practice it did not move and usually remained right of centre. In such cases, the Catholic Church's sense of social inclusivity and its sense of its historical role to society could offset its natural conservatism and caution, and put it in opposition to extreme regimes. The church's very conservatism could become the basis of its resistance to the hard-right. Second, the polarisation of wider society often exacerbated divisions within the church, and 'stretched' its right of centre political position in both directions.

These twin dynamics – shifting and stretching – are a useful framework for understanding Romero's own role as a church leader. His own personal instincts were conservative, and his vision was the traditional vision that the Catholic Church was a church for all. Yet in a situation of violent division and polarisation this belief was far more radical than it might otherwise have been. Essentially moderate, even quite conservative, theological principles were the grounds for his prophetic witness to an alternative to destructive confrontation, and his willingness to stand in solidarity with those most in need of protection whilst seeking to reach out to everyone.

Romero sought to hold both society and the church together, so that a new and more just society might be built through peaceful means. His life is a dramatic reminder that this prophetic commitment to reconciliation is not an easy option; on the contrary, it is difficult and demanding and may even be dangerous. Christ's suffering on the cross is a resonant image for Romero's time as Archbishop, and a reminder that the church's ministry of reconciliation may come at a high personal price.

References

BROCKMAN, James R. (1989). *Romero: A Life.* Maryknoll, NY: Orbis Books

COMBLIN, José (1986). "Otema da Reconciliacáo e a Teologia na Américan Latina" in *Revista Eclesiástica Brasileira.* Volume 46. Fasc. 182. 272–314. Translated as MacLean, Iain (2006). "The Theme of Reconciliation in Theology in Latin America". In: *idem* ed. *Reconciliation, Nations and Churches in Latin America.* Alderhsot: Ashgate. 135–170.

La Opinión (Dec. 1977). 1.

LÓPEZ VIGIL, María (2000). *Oscar Romero: Memories in Mosaic.* trans. Kathy Ogle. London: Catholic Fund for Overseas Development.

MALKIN, Elisabeth (Mar. 24, 2010). "El Salvador Leader Apologizes for Archbishop's Assassination". *New York Times.*

MIGLIERINI, Julian. (Mar. 2010). "El Salvador marks Archbishop Oscar Romero's Murder". BBC News San Salvador. URL: http://news.bbc.co.uk/1/hi/world/americas/8580840.stm. [accessed on Mar. 24, 2010].

ROMERO, Oscar (Feb. 10 1977). *Prensa Gráfica.* cited by James BROCKMAN (1989). *Romero: A Life.* Maryknoll, NY: Orbis Books. 4 and 11.

ROMERO, Oscar (1978 and 1979). *A Shepherd's Diary.* trans. Irene B. HODGSON (1993). London: Catholic Fund for Overseas Development and Catholic Institute for International Relations. esp. 51 (Apr. 26, 1978), 184 (Apr. 6, 1979). 241 (May 28, 1979).

ROMERO, Oscar (1980). *Voice of the Voiceless: The Four Pastoral Letters and Other Statements.* trans. M. WALSH (1985). Maryknoll NY: Orbis Books. Abridged from Spanish orig. La voz de los sin voz: la palabra viva de Monseñor Oscar Arnulfo Romero. Cardenal, R./Martín-Baro, I./Sobrino, J., ed. (1980). San Salvador: UCA Editores.

United Nations (1993). Truth Commission for El Salvador. *From Madness to Hope: The 12-Year War in El Salvador.* New York. 127.

ZAMORA, Rubén (Mar. 5, 2005). "Requiem for Romero". BBC Radio 4.

Matthieu de Nanteuil

Violence and Modernity

Reflections on the Present Situation in Colombia[1]

For this accumulating horror is not the essential. One can list the details interminably. Yet one cannot recount the meaning of a day, starting with waking up at four-thirty in the morning and ending with a curfew. The harrassing work, perpetual hunger, the permanent lack of sleep, the bullying of the *Capo*, latrine fatigue, blows by the SS, working in assembly-lines in the munitions factory, smoke from the crematorium, public executions, endless roll-calls in winter snow, exhaustion, and the death of friends can neither touch what is essential, nor reveal the glacial mystery of that experience, its sombre shining truth. The darkness on which we foundered was fated. What one founders on is fated for all eternity. Or rather, for all history.

Jorge Semprun, Literature or Life

This study proposes looking at the present Colombian situation both descriptively and normatively. In particular, we want to offer a more precise description of specific characteristics of Colombia's situation. But we will also critically examine the bond that ties Colombia to modernity – and especially the liberal aspect of modernity. The central thesis is: in order to understand the Colombian armed conflict one needs to analyse its role in a society that unceasingly claims membership in the liberal tradition. This happens in the dominant political regime as well as in the aspiration of its elites, even though they have not tried to lay the social foundations for such an aspiration.

More accurately, then, Colombia presents the case of a country that – today more than ever before – makes this claim, while letting armed violence systematically destroy the sociological foundations required to become "modern". Colombia also basically assumes a social ethic. Now, as European

1 This text originates in a conference on Nov. 26–27 2009, organized by CRHIA (University of Poitiers) and CIREMIA (University of Tours), on the following topic: "The Role of Art and Artists in the Colombian Peace Process". The initial title of the conference was: "Representing the body, reflecting on public space. Lessons from Colombia and elsewhere". This text takes up its principal elements. An introductory section was added, and certain developments in Colombian society were noted during a stay in Colombia, as invited professor between Jan. and June 2010 (Universidad Nacional and Universidad de Los Andes). This text was also used for a lecture at the Universidad del Norte, Baranquilla, on Apr. 26, 2010 on "Democracy and Violence. Reflections based on the Colombian Case". The author would like to thank Marie Estrépaut-Bourjac and Juan-Manuel Echavarria who allowed him to discover a part of Colombian artistic activity; Leopoldo Múnera for his always helpful comments on the specifics of national political life, as well as on political theory in general; Alfredo Gomez-Muller for his invitation to the colloquium in Nov. 2009; and, the students of the Universidad Nacional and the Universidad de Los Andes whose many suggestions provided incentives for reflection.
Translated by Maria S. Odendaal.

history has demonstrated, such an ethic can never be exclusively produced by liberalism. On the contrary, its original impulse is society's critical power, through resistance to State control *as well as* to commodification. Our reflection is dedicated to the absence of such an impulse in Colombia, while it claims to be liberal, a situation to which society pays a very heavy tribute.

In this paper, the conflict will, therefore, be widely interpreted as an ideal-type of those contradictions which are reflected throughout the whole modern Liberal tradition. The contradictions appear when the liberal tradition finally becomes self-referential, i. e., when it calls for the immediate applications of its own principles without building social foundations for the society as such. Karl Polanyi has shown, in an analysis of considerable scope, how the self-referential character of Liberalism opened the way to mass destruction on the European continent during the thirties (cf. 1944). In line with such a perspective, this study seeks to trace how Colombian society itself is full of different kinds of violence due to having failed to dissociate politics from strict parliamentary representation; for not having recognized the crucial role of social movements and popular autonomous groups; and for not having massively redistributed and encapsulated the free-market into steady social regulations.[2] One question, though, remains open: how can one reconstruct this society's logic?

From a traditional Liberal perspective, the claim to individual autonomy – associated with the spread of institutions that guarantee civil liberties – manages to ignore social connections which organise the practical mechanisms of equality and liberty, that is to say, the means of autonomy. Such a tradition also obliterates its own role in violence and, even more profoundly, in the multiple forms of subjection, that are supposedly "required" by the pursuit of well-being and the formation of a political framework based on property rights. Yet these forms of subjection go far beyond listing lasting social inequalities, essential as that may be. In fact, they are the clue to the problem of what Hannah Arendt calls "the banality of evil." On behalf of "systemic coherence", they justify the eradication of the other's experience, as well as the other's fundamental wish for a worthy life. They open up a largely instrumental understanding of political action, and abandon seeking the moral significance of those complex situations in which such issues may appear (cf. Arendt 1963: 169 – 173). Beyond Arendt, however, we shall consider that the demand for another modality of political action is not enough to terminate it.

On the strength of Marx's early writings, and the work of the sociologist

2 There are many definitions of modernity. We have limited ourselves to two reference works that offer a critical analysis of Liberal Modernity, and help us towards a more complete and complex definition of modernity. In the eyes of these analysts, modernity is characterised by the tension between rationality and subjectivity (Touraine 1995 & 1997); or between a Liberal tradition, socio-economic and cultural structures, and social movements (Hobsbawm 1962, 1975 & 1987).

Zygmunt Bauman (cf. Bauman 1989; Marx 1970, 1998, and 2007), it seems to us that what is at stake basically relates to the "division of labour" throughout society. It prevents society from thinking about itself as a common space that extends beyond the objective functions accomplished by society's individual members. That would reduce human beings to simple abstract entities. The anthropological limit that human life roots in embodied singularity would then be overcome. The search for "equal dignity" originates there.[3] Without such a limit, *ignoring then becomes the rule, not in the sense of someone ignoring what happens, but in the sense of a society not having the means to leave the situation behind. Such a situation is considered inevitable, because it is perceived as an essential condition of "progress."* The complexity of Colombian society, which reflects an increasingly heterogeneous modernity, however, requires considering the notion of "division of labour" within a pluralist perspective: a division of *criminal* labour through the distribution of roles which the war has imposed on all the armed agents; a division of *economic* labour, which increasingly enmeshes the Colombian economy in globalization, dominated by the rules of the market; and a division of *political* labour through the clash between a Liberal-authoritarian State and a fragmented society.

This forms a set of complex processes. These processes give expression to the anthropological dispositions, which – in the desire widely expressed by Colombian society to become "modern" – also count among the powerful anthropological factors that perpetuate the "state of war."[4] As Zygmunt Bauman emphasizes, it is not only "the war" that suspends morality. The suspension of morality is mainly due to multiple divisions of labour that privilege functional specialization, and, therefore, widely forget the issue of human singularity. Such divisions assimilate the other as the simple expedient of the market's self-producing dynamic, or of bureaucracy, which substitute "moral responsibility with technical responsibility."[5] Consequently, this type of collective organization promotes effacing a common moral sense, which all of society needs in order to constitute itself as a human society.

This is the paradox of the armed conflict in Colombia, beyond the images

3 For the latter term see Kis 1989. In a life's universal singularity, assuming the vulnerability of the flesh, a double prohibition is settled: the prohibition of murder and the prohibition of objectifying.

4 The expression "state of war" is also defined by the authors of the project Planeta Paz in a document that presents the Colombian situation to the European Union: peacemaking "does not simply mean overcoming the armed conflict by incorporating all combatants into civil life or by the military defeat of armed groups that are considered to be illegal. Rather, it means eradicating the state of war from the Colombian social life, in which the majority of Colombia's inhabitants live: the permanent uncertainty of obtaining the necessary means to guarantee a…dignified life as well as access to the possibilities of self-realization, which the contemporary world offers." Cf. Corporación Derechos Para la Paz (CDPAZ) – Planeta Paz 2009.

5 The expression "substituting a moral rationality with a technical rationality" originates from Zygmunt Bauman (1989).

and stereotypes, which are themselves caught in the play of media polarisation: it is rooted in the desire for modernity – for a partial modernity. The background of a self-referential Liberal tradition provides the means for a growing collective indifference; it also stresses the importance of the connection between military violence and other forms of violence. At the same time, it offers perspectives on transformation.[6]

Beyond analysing the most salient characteristics of Colombian society, this analysis then attempts to account for the internal divisions which the Liberal tradition accepts, without measuring their deathly potential. Following this approach, we will see that the paradoxical relationship between Colombian society and Liberal modernity is not inevitable. We will conclude with some perspectives that allow for *another vision of modernity.* It is an essential condition, if not for a complete cessation of hostilities, at least for Colombian society to be able to establish a reflexive relationship to itself, as a prerequisite for peace – a type of peace based on the search for justice (cf. Suárez 2009).

1. Colombia Today: Complexity, Co-existence, Critics

To understand the intention that underlies this essay, we must specify the nature of our objective. It is not difficult to get a clear impression of the political regime in place and the instruments at hand that reproduce their "bellicose logic," when we try to avoid propaganda that reduces the armed conflict to a simple "fight against terrorism."[7]

Evident and huge crimes against humanity are committed by military and paramilitary groups in response to a guerrilla, which has in turn distanced itself from its initial emancipating project and participates in atrocities.

6 This hypothesis is advanced by Projet Planeta Paz. See especially González Posso, Herbolzheimer and Montaña Mestizo 2010.

7 This expression frequently recurs in the discourse of former President A. Uribe with regard to the guerrillas (primarily the FARC). It belongs to the "axis of evil" rhetoric that former US-President G. W. Bush initiated after the Sept. 11, 2001 attacks, which, in turn, is part of a qualification of groups who use military and violent means, resisting strategies of territorial implantation by governments whose legitimacy is contested. It is, for example, the case with Palestinian Hamas, which likewise is reduced to the level of terrorists by Israel and the United States. Independent of one's judgement about these actors, one has to note that the qualification implies the *re-qualifying the armed conflict itself*, in order to extricate it from "constraints" imposed by the rules of war and by international humanitarian rules. This departure from the international legal frame allows using every military means at the State's disposal, in order to assure "security." The effects on the civil population are that they participate in a strategy that legitimizes an exceptional State on a large scale. At the time of writing this chapter, it seems most likely that this strategy is also pursued by the successor of President Uribe, Manuel Santos, though through different means. For peace initiatives cf. also V. Bouvier (ed. 2009) (note of the editor).

Likewise the most visible elements of the State apparatus (Ministers, members of the armed forces, the President, etc.) constantly justify the reinforcement of their influence on society in the name of a security response for peace. Further examples include the menace that threatens the organisation of victims' defence; the many limitations to, or obstacles for, the judiciary's functioning; and the political games that privilege power conquest over immediately exiting the war. They all emphasize that the justification of an authoritarian State which abandons the most vulnerable members of the population cannot find – on ethical or political terrain – any serious argument in their favour. "Colombian reality" is, then, fully explained when one adds to this that Colombia is intricately involved in the international division of labour; that it is characterised by one of the most significant levels of inequality on the continent, which is a structural cause behind the existence and development of drug trafficking; and, that its public sphere is marked by a recurrent menace threatening public goods, such as universities.[8] In line with such descriptions, the propaganda of those in power could be confronted with an accurate catalogue of oppression and complicity in oppression by the dominant interests, *though without making such a catalogue credible in the eyes of a large part of the population and of what is conventionally called the "international community"*. The reason is that such a catalogue cannot ignore several difficulties. Such difficulties can be accounted for by three notions: complexity, coexistence, and critics. We will consider them in the paragraphs below.

The first difficulty relates to what one can provisionally name *the myth of exceptional political violence*. The Latin-American "case" would be particularly convincing. Only by confronting it directly, can a diagnosis detract from the vision, largely present in Europe and the United States; of Colombia as the (violent) exception to the common rule (of civility). Similarly, in an extraordinary conjunction of factors that support the logic of war, and because of the extent of the violence and how it participates in the country's ordinary functioning, Colombia would be the worst student of a westernized class, won over to the idea of an objective alliance between Liberalism, peace, and social progress. Yet, such a mix of views causes a double problem. On the one hand, it smoothes over the general discredit of a country like Colombia in the eyes of the most modernised nations. It again "naturalises" the western idea that "there is nothing to be done." In a more sophisticated formulation, it avoids engaging critical reflection on all the causes that globally work to generate the Colombian armed conflict. On the other hand, such an approach risks dismissing the manner in which Colombian society responds to violence, and tries to establish an institutional network dedicated to it. This observation does not imply that Colombian institutions do not encounter huge problems; but rather that it is crucial to take into account a

8 For figures on these issues cf. Appendix.

certain level of complexity when looking at the Colombian situation. This complexity refers to being *in* the conflict and coming *from* the conflict at the same time.

Let us look at an example. More than a year ago (on 2 March 2010), the Constitutional Court pronounced against the option of organising a referendum that would allow the former President A. Uribe to stand for a third term. This option was deemed unconstitutional. At first glance, this "institutional resistance" to authoritarianism seemed to attest to a certain democratic maturity. Nevertheless, one could see during the parliamentary elections that followed (14 March 2010), that not only did the large majority support the President's party, but also that the chambers of Parliament were organised in a very asymmetrical way. The democratic Left was very weak there. Furthermore, it included representatives of a "new party", formed explicitly by political elements issued from paramilitary groups (PIN).[9] This time, the parliamentary institution revealed its vulnerability in the face of a state of war, with a functional imbalance the inevitable result.

The question is, thus, not whether or not Colombia has got institutions, but what type of normative principles, and what modes of concrete organisation, stand behind them. Comprehending Colombian institutional complexity presupposes, moreover, managing to understand the "interpretive systems" on which it relies – indeed the conflicting interpretations throughout – as well as their capacity to produce representations of the conflict which articulate different levels of analysis.[10]

The complexity in question characterizes not only the institutional level. It relates to "context" and "conflict" itself. Maria Paula Saffon and Rodrigo Uprimmy remind us of this in an important text about transitional justice. Regarding the context, the relevant complexity in their eyes arises from "the profound influence of the international community, especially the United

9 On entering the two chambers of Congress (Senate and Chamber of Representatives), this party obtained eight per cent of the vote. That places them fourth, behind the party of President A. Uribe (the U, 25 % of the vote) and the two traditional parties, the Conservative Party (20 %) and the Liberal Party (16 %).

10 One could think, based on the work of N. Luhmann, that the message of the Constitutional Court was addressed to the self-referential logic of Colombia's political system. Its "irritating" function was to push this system towards engaging with a new phase of adaptation within its new juridical context. The strengthening of the President's party in Congress could then be explained by the political system's self-perpetuating dynamic, as well as by its capacity to generate new specialized functions. It could translate the constraints of the Constitutional Court into a mix of action dynamics favouring the system's "flexible" reproduction. Yet this reading could not explain the "interpretive system" that prevailed for the Court to give out a specific judgement. That appears to be, in spite of everything, an important element hemming in authoritarian power. As we shall see, the genesis of diverse interpretive systems is important for understanding how to end violence or, more broadly, to induce institutional transformation. For a functional analysis of institutions see Luhmann 1997. For an analysis that effectively emphasizes interpretive conflicts, indeed "hermeneutic contradiction," as driving force for institutional creation, see Ricoeur 1974 and, more recently, Boltanski 2011.

States, the ambiguous nature of the political regime, and the extreme polarization of Colombian society." Regarding the conflict, they identify four factors: "This is one of the oldest conflicts in the world," along with the Israeli-Palestinian and Indo-Pakistani conflicts. Not two groups, but many groups oppose one another: State, guerrilla groups, and paramilitary groups. The last factor adds to the complexity "to the extent in which pro-system groups, who have never been opposed by the State, but have been illegally aided in the State's battle against the guerrillas" act. Because of its duration, but also its multiplicity, and the heterogeneity of the participants, it is difficult to qualify the conflict. Finally, complexity lies in the number of victims and their dramatic situation. This is especially true, since most victims, except for those who are kidnapped, come from the most powerless social strata (2009: 166–173).

The second difficulty is similar to the first, but it concerns Colombian society as such. A diagnosis, as we gave above, cannot comprehend the coexistence of political-military violence *and* the pursuit of well-being. More precisely, it cannot explain the perpetuation of violence *combined* with the continual rise in aspiring to material prosperity standards, which accompany modernity. One could respond that material well-being is reserved for urban upper and middle classes. Since they constitute an extremely small fraction of the population, the matter could not be significant for a description of Colombian society. This is true, but only partially. Urban centres or regional security zones are actually protected from the most obvious incursions of conflict. They exist alongside with the violence that takes place in the poorer quarters of large urban conglomerations, or just outside the perimeters of Colombia's protected political and economic life. But still, this has a major consequence: it does legitimate the aspiration of a large part of the population to live within the conflict, in spite of everything, and deploy a mode of life exactly like that of their western colleagues.

The co-existence of political-military violence with the pursuit of well-being seems to us to have two consequences. Acknowledging the ties between prosperity and political-military violence firstly allows one to avoid premature representations of Colombian society as consisting of two opposing worlds, that of extreme wealth and extreme poverty. Even if these two elements form part of Colombian sociology, it is important not to reduce the country's socio-economic situation to this dichotomy. In between there is a whole range of intermediate situations, particularly the urban middle classes, which in themselves are quite heterogeneous. This position also allows one to investigate the social and symbolic status of consumer practices. One already knows that these not only offer access to basic necessities, as is the case for a very large part of the population, but they also define a way of self-expression, a way of representing reality that has a commercial origin. This is seen in the elites' attachment to promoting public consumption, particularly where a tangible connection to narcotraffic exists. It is equally seen in how big urban centres are surrounded by top-scale commercial centres, which are secure and accessible to a large public.

This kind of arrangement materially supports the idea that *consumer normality exists in spite of the absence of any form of other fundamental normality.* It helps keep the spectre of violence and death at bay. George Bataille reminds us that consuming is a way of keeping death at a distance. It privileges the many diversions that the use of inert things offers. It also provides a chance to achieve "free consumption," that is, consumption disengaged from the constraints of immediate utility, without object or limit (cf. 1991). Yet all of this has a cost. It presupposes a captive population. In the absence of massive redistributive measures, it risks deepening socio-economic inequalities more and more. It also presupposes organising urban space geographically with "territorial markers," physical and symbolical boundaries that mark the frontiers between those that have access and the "others."[11] Criticising Colombian society's wish for large consumption is not our concern as such. We intend to study scenes which reveal the contradictions in this society, the state in which it is today. While everyone is trying to promote a kind of material normality, these scenes paradoxically remind one that those consumer practices are far from "normal." They occur in a context of harsh socio-economic inequality and are founded on one of the world's oldest conflicts. Although they act as "morally tranquilizing" powers – Bauman speaks of the "paralysing" character of modernity (cf. 1989) – they cannot entirely mask the reality, which is both more profound and more violent. Their very presence as a boundary mechanism at the heart of Colombian society is therefore significant.

The last difficulty is of a different kind, but no less important. One could summarize it in the following way: if one stayed with a strict ethical-political judgment that explicitly shows the forms of perversity which persist in the Colombian State apparatus, one could not account for the cultural creativity within Colombian society. It would then be impossible to account for *the existence of diverse social movements that contest the restrictive definition of democracy on which the ruling powers draw to justify and maintain a "security orientation."* In various forms, and for a very long time already, such movements have challenged the confusion between the democratic project and its misguided use.[12] Without leaving behind the demands of the democratic ideal, these forms of collective action more often try to rely on existing institutions to support claims in matters such as the right to truth and reparation (victims movements), or equality in living conditions (popular movements). They express a mode of broader engagement in the public sphere with a view to reappropriating it for themselves.

11 On the notion of "territorial markers," see Goffman 1956.

12 The confusion relates to, for example, how some institutions can accommodate the state of war, or more generally, that institutions lack substantial foundations.

It is, however, necessary at this point to remember another constant in Colombian public life: the criminalization of social movements. They are directly confronted with violent death. This dimension is a structural component of Colombian history, especially since the time called *La Violencia* (1948–1958). This aspect is frequently underplayed by official powers, though. Historically, the most serious case probably deals with the systematic elimination of the Patriotic Union (UP) cadres in the eighties and nineties. The UP was a democratic political party formed to lay the foundation for a strong democratic opposition, anchored in the left. It included the Communist Party, non-communist members of the left, and elements from the Armed Revolutionary Forces of Colombia (FARC). The planned disappearance of almost all its members, following a series of homicides carried out by paramilitaries with support from a fraction of the armed forces, is part of the sad memory of Colombia's Left (cf. Wolf 2005). It reminds us of the significant menaces that threaten all social movements, especially those that seek to defend human rights. Let us take another example. On Mar. 6, 2008 a national march against victims of State crimes was organized in response to a government march against guerrillas' victims. It led to the assassination of nine regional leaders.[13] Apart from the force of, and limits to, their claims, the fact that such movements directly risk death explains why they feel the necessity of investing in the public space primarily as a *place of memory*. It publicly exposes death in order to oppose its denial. It also publicly reveals the collective conditions for overcoming it.

Next, we will emphasize the importance of action by the social movements for the future of Colombian democracy, in spite of their difficulties in redeeming a very fragmented situation (cf. González Posso, Herbolzheimer, and Montaña Mestizo: 2010).[14] Such movements are upheld by collective forms of expression, which aim to re-articulate that from which the Liberal tradition more often tends to dissociate. They know the *general principles* that shape public space, and the demands made by a society based on its war *experience*. To that extent they precisely depend on the democratic project, and directly address the killing spiral, produced by the war state. Their real (through the assassination or forced disappearance of their members), or symbolic (through intimidation or their absence in the media) effacement then looks like a symptom of a more radical effacement. What is eradicated is the possibility of a different experience and, more importantly still, the possibility of a political subject formed through the logic of not competing for power. An *autonomous subject* then, as a measure of plurality and effective liberty (cf. Castoriadis 1998), is effaced.[15]

13 One could multiply the examples, including peasant movements and the experience of the "Peace Community." Compare numbers and sources in the Appendix.

14 On the problem posed by the fragmentation of social movements, see below.

15 For this definition of autonomy, see Castoriadis 1998.

Complexity, coexistence, conflict – without pretending to be exhaustive, these are elements that allow us to approach the set of problems attending Colombian society today. We must then propose an exploration of Colombian society, with its connection to armed violence, economy and politics, on the basis of numerous other conflicts. As indicated by Rodrigo Uprimmy and Maria Paula Saffon, Colombia has a profoundly "polarised" society. It is necessary to try and understand what this element adds to a Liberal-authoritarian State, which subscribes to a bellicose framework. Yet above all these are the dynamics that contribute to producing and reproducing polarisation. Following Zygmunt Bauman, we will consider how the possibility of seeing the other as "enemy" roots in indifference to others. It is not meant in the sense of simple cognitive or affective ignorance, but *in the sense of ignoring the other as he/she is, an embodied subject, with his/her own singularity, a member of a community with universal aims.* Not permitting such a fundamental recognition is caused by different kinds of "division of labour", which reduce the other to an abstract function, supposedly "required" for the maintenance of the system. This is where the suspension of morality begins. It gives people permission to avoid critical discussion of schemes, or "cultural" stereotypes which are assigned to other members of the community, and lead to racist, xenophobic, and bellicose expressions. Following a diagnostic sketch of Colombian society, we will devote the next sections to this working hypothesis.

2. In the Footsteps of Antigone: Considering Colombian Society

In a very thought-provoking publication on the "Colombian tragedy," the Swedish historian Roland Anrup describes the displaced populations of Choco. This is the Atlantic coastal province where many ghosts or worn-out actors haunt the stage of Colombian public life. Naked bodies lie exposed to the ever increasing sovereignty of power (cf. 2008: 13–41). He recounts Antigone's unforgettable cry. In her persistent demand for a grave for her brother, she opposes her father's law, that is, the violent affirmation of authority, supposedly upholding political and social order. Anrup writes:

> The Greek drama would appear like the drama of truth opposed to unjust political power. Political subjectifying is the capability to produce controversial scenes. They are paradoxical scenes that visualize the contradictions in the logic that postulates existence. It is also not existent or non-existent. Thus, Antigone appears in front of Creon as an equal, not as an inferior, but as a citizen. Yet, they are not equals. This means that she demonstrates the contradictions of an institution of citizens excluding their own kind. She shows that women are necessarily included in the people's equality, and at the same time radically excluded (ibid.: 46).

The Exceptional *in* Normality: Colombia as an Ideal-Type

In correspondence with Colombian reality, one could specifically recall Anrup's critique of the Liberal tradition. The figure of Jean-Jacques Rousseau is evoked with subtlety as one of the founders of democratic sovereignty – sovereignty *of* the people, and *for* the people. Anrup reminds us that Rousseau presents an "anti-bureaucratic" and "anti-centralising" democratic demand. It is bound to its "original" nature, and not "derived" from a general will. And it is intended to go beyond private interests and "willing what is common" (ibid.: 91 and 93).[16] The author similarly points out that Rousseau does not manage to overcome a certain mysticism, based on the construction of an idealised and homogenised portrayal of people. It is the source of many ambiguities in the Liberal State. Anrup examines the winding way of this foundational ambiguity, and proposes a critical interpretation of the political use of sovereignty, which has justified recourse to a state of emergency from Hobbes to Schmitt. He begins with what Derrida calls the "mystical foundation of right," which one could also designate as its transcending self-endowment for objectives fixed by the State.[17] In Colombia, the multiple mechanisms of the Liberal State's authoritarian character are not only a rhetorical matter. They are central to rational justifications of the State's growing influence on society. The doctrine of "Democratic Security," forged by former President A. Uribe, is in some measure the result of this long process, even though such an influence goes well beyond the single government party. It encourages most conceptions that shape Colombian politics today.

It would be wrong to limit the authoritarian practice of the Colombian State to a simple "police" attitude. As a collection of authors have shown, it is rather the capacity to introduce and maintain a number of emergency statutes, within a single jurisdiction, which permits the State to keep tight control of society. It also favours, by and large, the reproduction of bellicose schemes which feed the "war as a response to war." In the introductory article to a collection, Leopoldo Múnera calls to mind, amongst other things, that questioning the relationship between what is normal and what is exceptional allows one to go beyond the stereotypes which associate Liberal democracy with the "normal", and dictatorship with the "exceptional." Today, what lies between indicates the porosity between democracy and State violence, but also between politics and rights. Múnera is interested in the work of several critical political theorists as well as in the power of the "multitude" (society's self-government beyond established political forms) and writes:

16 On the idea of a general will as willing what is common, see Weil 1982.

17 More broadly, one knows that controversies over legal, but undue influence, on this sovereignty are at the heart of divergent interpretations of a State ruled by law.

However, on the threshold between normal and exceptional, law and politics, democracy and dictatorship are mixed up and delimited. Judicial becomes political, political is transformed into legal. Democracy acquires the form of a dictatorship to save itself, and dictatorship pretends to be the ultimate foundation of democracy. After 11 September 2001, and the tortures at Abu Ghraib and Guantánamo, Giorgio Agamben and Slavoj Žižek state that the world, dazed by the procedural democratic discourse, is living on a threshold that tends to transform the exceptional into the normal, the pure reason of State into global legal forms. Such a situation, limited to national space, has appeared in Colombia since the second half of the twentieth century. From another perspective, Paolo Virno has investigated the contemporary nature of the multitude as a power that, in spite of its ambivalent character, contains the elements necessary to subvert the dominant forms of political normality. Here may be an exceptional but constitutive origin, which contains the germs of new types of democracy (2008a: 14).

In the case of Colombia, the exceptional practise is not new. One of its major examples, paramilitarism, was put in place by legal means at the end of the sixties.[18] The initiative came from the two dominant parties on the Colombian political scene in order to protect armed elements of the population. Far from signalling the alarm, that parties function amongst themselves, and are lastingly cut off from the country's popular base, the initiative has served to provide a constant justification for recourse to violence by the State apparatus (armed forces and police) and its allies (paramilitaries) against the development of guerrilla groups.[19]

In 2000, the one clear case of producing an exception within judicial

18 Law 48 of 1968, adopted following legislative decree 3398 of 1968. For a reminder of the historical conditions for legalising paramilitary groups (first called 'self-defence groups"), see Movimiento nacional de Victimas de Crimenes de Estado (MOVICE) 2009.

19 Historically anchored in the peasant movement, the FARC (Fuerzas Armadas Revolucionarias de Colombia) was born in 1964, after the Valencia (1962 – 1966) government's decision to bomb the regions "under communist influence." This guerrilla group, against whom the armed fight is constantly carried out, today counts more than ten thousand members, but there are no reliable sources on the subject. The ELN (Ejercito de Liberación Nacional) was formed a little later, in 1965. Camillo Torres belonged to this guerrilla group. He was a national icon, a priest engaged in the armed struggle for "the interests of the poorest", who died in Feb. 1966. Likewise, this group currently numbers some thousand members. The "intellectual" guerrilla group, the M-19 (the Movement of 19 April) was established in 1970. It followed the elections of 19 April1970. These elections were won by President Pastrana Borrero (1970 – 1974), but in controversial conditions. They allowed the former President Lleras Restrepo (1966 – 197) to dismiss the candidate of the opposition, which was supported by ANAPO (Alianza Nacional Popular), knowing that part of the M-19 was made of young ANAPO members. M-19 renounced the armed struggle in 1989 in order to create the Democratic Alliance Party after President Belisario Betancur (1982 – 1986) started peace negotiations. Those resulted in merciless reprisals against occupiers of the Palace of Justice in 1985. Finally, the EPL (Ejercito Popular de Liberación), a Maoist guerrilla group, formed in 1967. They, too, have abandoned the armed struggle. Today they remain a small minority with a few hundred members.

normality was the "Justice and Peace" law, which came into effect in 2005.[20] We will not go into detail here, but only recall that it was presented as legislation which would allow the important demobilisation of paramilitary groups. Around thirty thousand people, according to official numbers, were in fact demobilized. However, it entailed reversing victims' rights, so that a number of specialists called it a mechanism for impunity rather than justice.[21] Rodrigo Uprimmy and María Paula Saffon recall a "manipulative use of transitional justice," which is explained by the fact that the ethical and the political base to end the conflict have never been united. In this sense, they speak of a procedure of "transitional justice without transition," which is, of course, a contradiction in terms (2009: 174 and 191).[22]

One finally remembers that there are other exceptional mechanisms that especially apply to the situation of displaced people. On this topic, a publication of the Council on Human Rights and Displacement (*Consultaria para los Derechos Humanos y el Desplazamiento* – CODHES) recalls the "unconstitutional state of things." Even when the Constitutional Court – the highest authority in the country – has since 2004 effectively decreed fairly precise obligations on displaced populations' right to protection, the blur surrounding precise State obligations makes their implementation exceedingly difficult. Beyond the problem of government sources which underestimate the numbers, the general mechanism to identify displaced people presupposes their self-declaration. In many cases, these people would really need to present themselves far from their homes, without transportation. Or, they would have to reveal their identity to local authorities who may have ties to those actors who caused the displacement. Moreover, one notices that many adults do not wish to register their children for fear of social stigmatisation.[23] At the same time, the juridical instruments which one would need, could not

20 Law 975 of 2005 called "Justice and Peace Law."

21 According to a recent publication, the main characteristics of the "Justice and Peace" Law are the following: it addresses all armed agents, but was really intended for paramilitaries, since the FARC and other guerilla groups rejected it. In exchange for laying down weapons, the law proposed the reduction of prison penalties, independent of the seriousness of crimes, and without victims gaining access to facts. It was conceived on a negotiation model between armed groups, protected by political power, but outside the control of any judiciary authority. Victims' complaints were not examined, thus opposing universal principles of justice, truth, not repeating extortion, and complete material and symbolic reparation. The "Justice and Peace" law really did not succeed in its anticipated aim. Reintegrating paramilitaries in civil life took place in an uncontrolled way. They were concentrated in urban or rural zones, where they substituted the police force. They preserved what they gained through violence and political opposition was irregularly muzzled." Cf. Nanteuil 2009: 198 – 199.

22 For a juridical and political evaluation a little after its coming into law, see Revista Pensiamento Juridico 2006. For a more recent evaluation, offered by one of the main victims' organisations, see Movimiento nacional de Victimas de Crimenes de Estado (MOVICE) 2009.

23 On these elements, notably the problem of underestimating the numbers involved in forced displacements, see Romero 2007. Likewise, see different documents that offer analyses by CODHES at www.codhes.org.

deal with the numbers of current displaced populations, covering a large part of Colombian territory. With more than four million people already estimated to be displaced, it becomes one of the most important cases of forced displacement worldwide. It signals the scope of the Colombian humanitarian tragedy. One could add all the victims, detained and disappeared, imprisoned, victims of homicide, "false-positives," and so on (cf. Appendix).

One understands, then, that the mechanisms for different kinds of exception are embedded in the juridical and institutional systems of Colombia. They constitute one of the problematical elements of Colombian politics. We referred to Leopoldo Múnera above, who points out that Colombia is not exceptional at all. The grafts of normality and exception have become the norm in a large part of the western world, especially since Sept. 11, 2001. Yet, Colombia is an exemplary case that gives birth to the structural foundations for exceptional politics and their most tragic effects. Furthermore, what is important is not only factually stating a situation. Also important is the manner in which this situation, in turn, stands in the tradition in which Hobbes forms a corner-stone. It defends the confusion between normal and exceptional as being *justified by the protection of people and the defence of their private interests.*[24]

Bare Life: Instrument and Mirror of Power

To grasp this phenomenon, one can recapitulate Giorgio Agamben's proposal, cited by Roland Anrup:

> When the *body* happens to be the central metaphor of the political community, like in Leviathan or in the Social Contract, it always maintains a close link with bare life. … The bodies of the inferiors, completely exposed to receive death, form the new political body of the West (2008c: 15).

In the name of defending the individual, basically understood in terms of ownership, the construction of State authority presupposes the existence of superfluous masses. They are mere reflections of the State's constitutive power. Múnera comments on Agamben's accurate analysis:

> The life of the *homo sacer* who can be killed by anyone but who cannot be sacrificed at the same time: its death is neither subject to any ritual nor to any legal matter. Bare life is not the simple natural life, but a politically unprotected life, permanently exposed to death or humiliated with total impunity for the sovereign power and for

24 The author, thereby, recalls Benjamin Constant's phrase, which is like a negative echo of the need for security: "The aim of the Ancients was to divide social power between the citizens of a single country. They called that liberty. The aim of the Modernists is the security of private possession" (Constant, cited in Anrup 2008: 81). For an analysis of the effects a "Hobbesian politics" has on Colombia, see Múnera Ruiz 2008c.

those who, as citizens, create it. … In contrast to Foucault, in this case it is not simply about letting live and killing, but about creating life through death, bare life. Consequently, sovereign power would contain, as a constituent element, a fundamental and unlimited capacity to dispose of the life of its inferiors, simply because of its sovereignty. Consequently, sovereign power would be bio-political from its origins, the power of death over the bare life that it is creating (2008a: 26–27).

This would be, according to Agamben, the practise of an exceptional State: exposing the subjective life, returning it to a biological state without social or institutional membership. Briefly, in depending on the sovereign, it is both instrument and mirror. One must, however, at this point suggest a somewhat different interpretation from that of Agamben. If one proposes, as he does, that the exercise of power happens well within the specific connection to the public status of the body, one should also consider the characterisation of an exceptional State.[25] Can this radical exposure of human life, reduced to the level of a biological given, entirely depend on power practises? Agamben defends this thesis also in *Means without End*, with his reminder that human life differs from biological life, in that it uses life forms, that is to say, all possibilities of existence, mediated by institutions. This permits human subjects to escape from a repetitive cycle (cf. Agamben 2000). Yet, it is necessary to return along the road that Agamben seems to have gone, to arrive at, and then investigate, the process that underlies this radical exposure. Can one not consider Antigone's cry as, not only an expression of asymmetrical confrontation between political power and bare life, but also as the result of a progressive exclusion from a sphere of integrated, socialized speech? For it is essential that her request finds no echo in the social organisation, that some members of society have more to do than concern themselves with the foundational law of communal life. Therefore, the problem is maybe not only Creon… but also the society of which he is the legitimate political expression.

What is at stake here functions on two levels. On one side, Antigone incarnates the reverse side of power. Her language is not the language of Creon. It is a language that refuses to extract itself from the reality of the human community but also to subscribe to the unworldly law of authority. Antigone's body thus rings with an insupportable challenge. Just with her presence on the visible stage of the political theatre, the complicity between *death and power* is

25 Corporality reveals itself here, against a chain of evidence, as the surface on which unlimited power is exercised. One can add that the Liberal tradition is endowed with a specific definition of body, through the notions of "sentiment" and "sensitivity," especially in Hutcheson, Hume and Rousseau. Yet utilitarianism, through the following enterprise, has ended the debate that took shape, by subjecting human experience to a principle of the general equality of pleasure and pain. What Agamben reveals, and before him Foucault, is that the body re-appears in the same margins of thought which wanted definitively to fix it to the "objective" task in a place and with an equivalency. On the question of the Liberal tradition's relationship to the body, see Audard 2009: 29–98.

criticized, and the *gender rule* is overturned (cf. Butler 1990). Pointing to a social life that cannot be simply "represented", she shows another relationship to the world than the one to which the master aspires. Something essential happens in the *crack of vision*, in the clear appearance of an intrinsic limit to the exercise of usual political domination. Finally, the presentation of the body in the power scene is the exposure of relationships, which unify them beyond power itself. The non-static, lively foundations of solidarity are presented.

Another side, however, is that Antigone's body also expresses her solitude. She suffers rejection and finds herself again dependent on the ruler. This sudden extraction from society thus has a history. It really needs to be preceded by an ordinary mode of organisation that, at no point, could assimilate the claim of a woman carrying a dead body. In her very isolation, Antigone is *placed* in a situation that takes away her subjectivity.[26] What does this show? As we indicated in the introduction, the hypothesis that underlies this work is that such an isolation process is not "natural." It is the result of multiple forms of division of labour throughout Colombian society, which prevent it from inventing a concrete solidarity, through which the other would not be reduced to an abstract function but considered as an individual, thus avoiding to be treated negatively by racist, xenophobic or bellicose expressions. From there, the "war" and the "war state" are reproduced – the collective characteristic that associates the other with an abstract individual and the idea of an "objective enemy."

In the next section, we will give an account of the registers in which different forms of division of labour are put to work. We can distinguish three: division of *criminal* labour, division of *economic* labour, and division of *political* labour.

3. Division of Criminal Labour: Diluting Responsibility and Promoting "Rational" Justifications of Extortion

In an article that exposes the "Hobbesian" roots of Colombian politics, notably through the "Democratic Security" doctrine's diffusion, Leopoldo Múnera recalls the way in which war agents themselves engage in carrying out violent acts. Contrary to many stereotypes on the subject, a *functional rationality* is at work. This author notes that

> ...the responsibility for human rights violations and violations of International Humanitarian Law is not homogeneous. So, for example, most kidnappings are

26 It is there, in that progressive disembodiment between subjective and social life, in a much older and more profound process of dehumanising, that the practical logic of Sophocles's tragedy, its true political significance for our times can undoubtedly be discovered.

caused by the guerrilla, forced disappearances by the armed forces and police, with paramilitary support, and most political homicides and forced displacements by paramilitaries (2008c: 3).

To this list, one could add other forms of extortion committed by different protagonists, but making a detailed list is not very interesting. What is important is how the protagonists develop their more or less "specialised" violent practices.

Such a specialisation does not mean that the practices do not overlap. They often do, be it as criminal practices, or factors at play in the genesis of some type of violation, like forced displacement. Yet, the concept of specialisation helps us to analyse the development of the conflict's main actors, what strategies they pursue in occupying territory, placing populations under supervision, and accumulating financial resources, as well as their "rational" quest for legitimacy, even in the brutality of war. Following the pioneer work of Orlando Fals Borda,[27] such an analysis allows for "demystifying" the violence above all, that is to say, for revealing its internal coherence. Moreover, refusing to use such an approach too often falls back on describing the conflict as a kind of constitutive irrationality – or as a "natural and unavoidable order." Our reflection leads to at least two sets of consequences.

The first is that, when violence forms part of a strategic global alliance and serves the dominant political-military system, it clears itself of its guilt.[28] In effect – and this has largely been the result of the demobilizing that accompanied the creation of the Justice and Peace Law or, more recently, the so-called parapolitical affairs – there is a division of criminal labour between State agents and paramilitary groups. It allows the State to preserve its legitimacy along with its apparatus for maintaining order in the service of the Liberal-authoritarian tradition. Likewise, the "Justice and Peace" Law, besides the criticism mentioned above, has focused attention on the paramilitaries alone, completely ignoring the direct or indirect responsibility of State agents for the practical organisation of violence, especially the armed forces or the Police. Similarly, "para-politics" is the tip of a larger iceberg. It pertains to the condemnation of the most visible people, accused of the most blatant corruption, so that they cannot escape some minimal punishment. At the same time, they are involved in preserving a large part of the dominant political apparatus, that is, they leave their capacity for survival more or less intact, and protect this kind of practice for the future.[29] More profoundly, the symbolic

27 Fals Borda was the founder of sociology in his country. See Fals Borda et al. 1962. Re-published by Taurus in 2007, this book marks a turn in the analysis of violence in Colombia. For the first time it offers a precise evaluation of the situation and an examination of its internal logic.

28 On the topic of pro-systemic agents, see especially Múnera Ruiz 2006.

29 "Parapolitics" designates how a large part of political decision makers (near the President, members of the government, Parliamentarians, etc.) clearly appear to have been directly supported by paramilitary groups during the second mandate of President A. Uribe. This scandal broke after one of the AUC leaders, Salvador Mancuso, declared in June 2005 that more than one

and ethical roots that justify State authoritarianism in the name of a Liberal tradition, centred on the defence of private interests, seem hardly shakeable at all.[30]

Secondly, by offering functional support for the implementing criminal practices, this division of labour opens up every "rational" justification for extortion. At the same time, it prohibits the analysis of the internal logic, possible gradations, and specific qualifications by International Law of those criminal practices. Under the cover of an indefinite conflict, "everything is allowed," to cite Hannah Arendt's famous phrase. All protagonists dismiss their own responsibility for the worse deeds and, at the same time, affirm their commitment to those very deeds. It would be wrong, however, to see in enacted violence a kind of passionate outburst, an "upside-down potlatch,"[31] in which one would need to give "more" unceasingly, and be engaged in a flight from violence to affirm one's power. Behind this hasty vision, a certain kind of rationality is at work. Every actor has "good reasons"[32] for practicing this or that type of extortion.

layer of Congress members are "his friends." In 2007, the Supreme Court decreed the arrest of more than thirty members of Congress, more than half of those who were suspect. In spite of international criticism, notably from US Democrats, paramilitarism has far from disappeared off the official political scene. The arrival of the PIN in the two chambers of Congress in the Mar. 2010 election tends to show, moreover, that they are settled at the centre of the country's political institutions. On this subject, see especially *Latin reporters*, Apr. 23, 2008. Due to the re-arrangement of paramilitary groups' political position in a new institutional context they now receive recognition.

30 Under a striking title the political campaign of President A. Uribe was interspersed with many insults to lawyers, intellectuals, or journalists engaged in defending human rights. Power could at the same time give different personalities the means of "official" protection. Yet the public disqualification which they regularly received transformed them into potential prey of paramilitary groups, or of the failure of common rights, preventing them from getting work. In such a situation, the legitimacy of the State apparatus stayed more or less intact, even if these people increasingly lived with the constant threat and/or fear of being killed.

31 "Potlach" refers to the logic of exchange in "archaic societies," according to Marcel Mauss. It is based, beyond any utilitarian relationship, on the triangle "give-receive-return." Under this name it points to kinds of dependence and reciprocity which precede the contract form, and bind the different protagonists to a social exchange and obliges them to give at least as much as they receive. In Mauss's eyes such a structure is endowed with a more compelling force than a contract. It also works within a non-monetary form of solidarity (cf. 2007).

32 This expression comes from Raymond Boudon. It is present in all of his thinking, from *Effet pervers et ordre social* (Paris: PUF, 1977) to *Essais sur la théorie générale de la rationalité* (Paris: PUF, 2007).Very broadly, it sets out from calling theoreticians of rational choice to order. In this precise instance, one can still discover its intrinsic weakness which can rigorously justify everything as well as its opposite. It emphasizes that explaining actions in this way cannot be a normative referent for reflecting on violence. Without another referential, it only provides a "rational" basis for the perpetuation of violence.

The Guerrillas: Between Kidnapping and Crimes against the Civilian Population

Kidnapping, mostly done by guerrillas, is neither new nor limited to Colombia. It has become commonplace in contemporary history. In Colombia its roots are in the end of the Cold War, but also in the transformation of the guerrilla groups and the development of an armed struggle, more and more disconnected from its own goals. After the disappearance of the EPL and the M-19, the FARC continued to reinforce their ultra-authoritarian practices with regard to their members. They formed themselves in an almost exclusively military way, and they disconnected more and more from objectives other than the perpetuation of the armed struggle.[33]

One must understand the practice of political kidnapping within this context. They are the only means – a violent option that includes assassinating prisoners when the military attacks – of entering the Colombian political game, of public existence, and of affirming oneself as influential in Colombia's internal politics. Paradoxically, the so-called "Democratic Security" doctrine, put in place by former President A. Uribe, partially justifies them. It seems like a functional product growing directly out of such military radicalization. The guerrilla effectively turns into a kind of "meta-reference" in national and international geopolitics. It also serves the hegemonic strategies of the Liberal-authoritarian State. As for economic kidnapping, they belong to a quest for new financing, which characterises the end of the Cold War. Kidnapping is not only employed by the FARC, and is widely used by ordinary delinquents. Thus, its rationality can be explained by the end of support from the former USSR but also by the relentless struggle to control drug trafficking and the regions where narcotics are produced. This struggle pits the guerrillas against paramilitary groups. Thus, they participate in a political conflict economy (cf. Romero 2007), which is also central to forced displacement practices.

A further consideration may be described as *spoils of war* – the kidnapping of police and military personnel. The goal, particularly for the FARC, is to claim its alternative military power over the State's military agents. They thus develop a logic of action which is that of war itself. In all of this, *political-military coherence* is part of this kind of action. It does not exclude any violation of International Humanitarian Law or committing crimes against civilians in the form of *"crímenes de lesa humanidad"* (crimes against humanity).[34] The violent claim of a political-military existence, associated

33 On the origins of this guerrilla group, see above. In 2012 the FARC proclaimed the end of the Kidnappings (note of the editor).

34 H. Valencia Villa defines the notion of "*crímenes de lesa humanidad*" as "serious crimes" against the human condition and, consequently, against International Law, which are under the jurisdiction of the International Criminal Court. According to Article Seven of the Rome Statute, the following eleven types of conduct are "*crímenes de lesa humanidad*" ('crimes against hu-

with a new financing economy, justifies the many criminal practices of which the civilian population is the primary victim: assassination of civilians allegedly serving the "enemy"; extrajudicial assassinations; participating in massacres; laying land-mines;, as well as the brutal control of networks for providing drugs; forced recruitment of youths; sexual violence, etc.

However, one must add that kidnapping is not necessarily a dead-end practise. The freeing of two of the oldest hostages, Daniel Calvo and Emilio Moncayo, held for twelve years, shows that it is possible to reverse the course of things. The hard work of Senator Piedad Cordoba, with the support of a group of Colombian politicians and academics (Colombianos y Colombianas por la Paz) brought it about. Moreover, the operation "Jaque" of July 2008 (mostly seen as the freeing of Ingrid Betancourt), the escape of long held politicians (Alan Jara, Luiz Eladio Perez), but also the desertion of some of their members reveal the faults in the FARC's organisation. These elements indicate, too, that *room for choice* exists for those who prefer a non-violent way of liberation – which happened in the case of freeing Clara Rojas – over a military attack. Today, however, uncertainty on this matter remains.

Let us now linger over a perfectly "modern" paradox: the media echo surrounding these freeings. The general media coverage of the freeing of some prisoners tells us essentially two things. The first, regards the illusion of a radical reversibility of choice. For the media, the freeings suggest that the conflict is not inevitable and that exits exist. Yet this runs the risk of limiting the whole of Colombian history to those moments when media constructs and emotions fuse. As though it were possible to wipe out, in a few moments and

manity'): murder, extermination, enslavement, deportation or forced population transfer, arbitrary deprivation of freedom, torture, sexual violence, persecution, forced disappearance, apartheid, or institutionalized racial discrimination, and inhumane acts, when they are committed as part of a widespread or systematic attack on the civilian population" (2003: 98–99). Homicides, arbitrary deprivation of freedom, sexual violence, or persecution also form part of crimes against humanity. We also need to consider the kind of debate which surrounds the FARC's case. First of all, it concerns an armed force whose subjective legitimacy depends on a structure of social and political inequalities. Therefore, FARC see their crimes simply as *war crimes*. That means that, from their point of view, they are crimes justified in the context of *armed conflict*, but also according to the code which applies to them as an armed actor. This justification is excessively problematic, since it is equally used by other adversary agents (armed forces, police, and paramilitary groups) to justify their oppression. In the second place, one must emphasise the differences between different kinds of imprisonment. If imprisonment of the civilian population (with a political and economic target) mocks International Humanitarian Law, founded on the principle of distinguishing between armed agents and civilian populations, the imprisonment of police and militaries are "governed" by the rules of war. That does not prevent its being a violation of fundamental rights, especially the right to liberty. Finally, the constant mingling of the guerrillas with the civilian population, added to forced recruitment, constitutes the systematic violation of International Humanitarian Law. Yet these don't go by the name of "crimenes de lesa humanidad". One notes elsewhere that this last aspect is a general characteristic of armed conflict. It also concerns adversary elements (paramilitary groups, armed forces, and police). See the figures in the Appendix.

on a planetary scale, the conflict's complexity – the complexity of its actors and its roots (political, economic, social, and cultural). Perhaps the media's role regarding these liberations has been to play with the idea of public engagement, without daring to account for the massive repression committed by other actors than the guerrillas. The media dare not attack the dominant ideology which deems it necessary to broadcast *those* events and not others, such as disappearances, or forced displacements, or collective massacres. Thus, the most problematic aspect is what one might well call *one-sided media coverage.* It is not the fact that the media reports events, which are highly significant for the families as well as the country, but that silence reigns concerning other aspects of the armed conflict. More serious issues in terms of escalating repression or horror are cleverly hidden behind the remains of a kind of post-Cold War guilt, which regards the FARC as the mere remains from a time driven by totalitarian passions. It sets them up as the obvious target of a Western consciousness in search of a "good conscience". Therefore, it is necessary to account for the extortions committed by other actors of conflict, starting with paramilitary groups.

The Paramilitary Groups: Multiform Terror beyond Forced Displacement

Here again, we touch upon a complexity inherent in the conflict, and, upon a particularly functional rationality. Even if it is extremely perilous in some ranks to make a pretence of restitution for paramilitarism's history in Colombia – and for its multiple ties with the big drug cartels, economic elites, local authorities, or the armed forces – it is still possible to briefly describe the dominant modalities of paramilitarism's role in what we have called the division of criminal labour. As Leopoldo Múnera pointed out, but also as numerous documents of the Counciltancy on Human Rights and Displacement (CODHES) indicate, paramilitarism directly participates in forced displacement (cf. Appendix).

This happens in different ways: (i) by surrendering completely to the logic of a war that, due to its territorial anchoring, forces civilians (especially peasants) to leave their land and flee from combat zones, (ii) by taking control of some regions or villages, pursuing those who oppose being violently resettled, trying to repopulate those new areas to the benefit of a local elite which the paramilitaries control, or guaranteeing work on the infrastructure, which earns them a public recognition usually due to the State; (iii) by investing in the control of significant agricultural or energy resources, which allows them to launder a large part of the funds produced by drug trafficking and to enrich themselves more and more legitimately, by establishing "mega projects", and exporting their "own" products on a grand scale.[35]

35 "Mega agro-industrial projects" are large-scale operations, located in rural areas, and aimed at

It is important to note that the implication of paramilitary groups in forced displacement does not go in one direction only. Forced displacement also results from the war between armed agents, legal or illegal, who force populations to flee and leave their places of residence. Above all, forced displacement reveals the conflict's political economy. The furious war with guerrillas on one side, State agents and paramilitaries on the other, creates a situation that takes the civilian population hostage, forcing it to "take sides", and to submit to the intensity of the bellicose logic. In a country where local and regional differences are considerable, and decide the parameters of war, *this mortal affront takes place in the silence of regional diversity*, in remote areas of the countryside (Caqueta, Putumayo, Nariño, Cauca), the mountainous regions (Antoquia, Boyca), or the coast (Choco, Cordoba, Sucre, Guajira), exactly where it is most difficult for international observers to keep track, where the most enlightened urban elites cannot go.

But that is not all. As forced displacement makes the Colombian theatre a tragedy of which the resolution seems to retreat further and further, it often also leads to a juridical dead-end. A new generation of rights arise in the face of assertions of massive displacements, without generating a political practice of going to the roots of those displacements at all. The functional rationality that guides paramilitary groups in their criminal practice is not halted (cf. Consultaria para los Derechos Humanos y el Desplazamiento 2009). Beyond their major implication in drug trafficking and corruption,[36] one cannot dissociate their mode of action from strategies aimed to terrorize regions or villages as they choose. More than their direct responsibility for political homicides, assassinations, forced disappearances in support of the armed forces – implying torture and assassination – the paramilitaries' terror strategies are based on crimes that are generally committed on a grand scale: massacres of villages and groups, using common graves, and accompanying sexual violence.[37] The category "crimenes de lesa humanidad" clearly applies to these crimes. Nevertheless, three elements "distinguish" them from those committed by guerrilla groups: the *extent* of criminal practices under such a category, their more systematically collective character, which often turns these practices into *mass violence*, as the common graves demonstrate, and finally, the *number of crimes* committed during decades of conflict.

specialising agro-industry in the intensive cultivation of export products. These operations can launder significant sums coming from drug-trafficking. They are generally accompanied by forced displacement, as far as they include brutal territorial re-arrangements imposed on local populations, mostly peasants. Their apparent economic legitimacy entails degrading the means of subsistence for the concerned populations.

36 This includes partial control of Congress. See below, on the problem of "parapolitics."

37 Rape is not only a characteristic of crimes committed by the paramilitaries. It is war itself, which often transforms women into "war spoils," as the work of the Fédération Internationale des Droit de l'Homme (FIDH) especially recalls in its *Résolution du Bureau international de la FIDH sur la Colombie*, May 2008.

For the period of 2007 – 2008, the recent publications of the Colombian Commission of Jurists (CCJ, Comisión Colombiana de Juristas) point out a larger participation of paramilitary groups, and/or State agents, in collective massacres, although guerrilla groups were also carried out such operations.[38] In a preface to Maribel Wolf's book, *Regresan siempre en primavera*, Maurice Lemoine points out that, in his view, "seventy per cent of crimes committed in Colombia were committed by paramilitary groups" (2006: 17). The figure is both a good indicator of the asymmetry of violence characteristic of the Colombian armed conflict, and an ambiguous indicator. The asymmetry in carrying out criminal practices amongst guerrilla groups, paramilitary groups, and State agents, is evident when one looks at the numbers in the Appendix. Nevertheless, one must guard against over-hasty conclusions. All depends on what the qualifyer "crime" means. If it is limited to the question of homicides "outside combat", it refers to the asymmetry between assassinations committed by the FARC, reprisals or forced disappearances committed by the armed forces and police, and homicides committed by paramilitaries, including their support for forced disappearances. The figures agree with those published by the Colombian Commission of Jurists. The Commission reminds one that the primary forces responsible for violations of human rights and International Humanitarian Law continue to be the paramilitary groups, "who originally, between July 1996 and June 2006, caused 71.06 % of out-of-combat deaths from socio-political motives" (Colombian Commission of Jurists 2006: 2). But if "crime" extends to population displacement, as it does in the definition of "crimenes de lesa humanidad," the numbers show the asymmetry in the global production of criminal acts. It also recognises that forced displacements are essentially tied to the acts of paramilitary groups, but that they equally depend on the "logic of war" in which the FARC directly participates.

That is why *the reflection on the asymmetry of violence needs to be tied to reflection that move beyond mere accounting*. Otherwise one risks obeying a strict utilitarian rule of crimes and victims, and displaces the analytical plan with a "rationalist" structure of conflict, justifying its indefinite reproduction. Therefore, one of the most interesting projects on the subject seems to be one which aims to qualify crime by social movements, particularly by victims' movements, as for example the reflection offered by the National Movement of Victims of State Crimes (Movimiento Nacional de Victimas de Crimenes del Estado, MOVICE) demonstrates. It goes beyond the basic qualification of

38 On the subject, see for example, Colombian Commission of Jurists Dec. 2009. On the topic of mass violence, see the reflections of Jacques Sémelin, particularly his definition of the term in an article in the *Encyclopedie en lignes de violence de masse*, as "phenomena, for which the causes are principally political, social, cultural or religious, which destroy humans collectively. … This idea refers not to recovering armed battles inherent in war, but rather to the totality of violence which directly affects civilian populations in times of peace as well as in times of war." The document is available at www.oemv.org.

crimes set out by International Penal Law. This movement is formed around the idea that the extent and the gravity of extortions cannot be the only criterion of differentiation. Their specificity has more to do with what one could call *their moral structure.* What distinguishes the guerrillas' crimes from that of "pro-systemic" groups (paramilitaries and State agents) is not the degree of horror, but the fact that the latter act in the name of the State. They act in the name of the very institution which, in modern democracies, is supposed to correspond publicly to the general interest. At the same time, there can be no question of "justifying" the crimes committed by the FARC, for any reason whatsoever.[39]

One of the clearest consequences of the terror strategies which paramilitary groups have developed lies in bringing entire geographical areas under their control. In this way, they create an adequate base for managing economic resources and for the armed struggle against the guerrilla. Controlling the whole country would be an impossible project, because of its political-institutional organisations is so complex , but also because of entire segments of the population's resistance to such a project . Without being able to secure control over the whole country, the paramilitaries never stop maintaining, or redeploying their presence through less and less visible acts. They are capable of anything, simply in order to affirm themselves as a "local army." From this angle, one can say that paramilitarism perpetuates itself in the sense which Michel Foucault called an anonymous practice of discipline and suppression. As for some famous leaders – they affirm their presence through a heterogeneous network of threats and actions. They avoid coherence but they never stop inserting themselves in those local societies where they reign with secret and menacing power.[40]

Without a doubt, one other element of differentiating between the paramilitaries and their principal guerrilla enemy is organisational. The FARC is formed on dispersed fronts, even though it has put in place a centralised and ultra-authoritarian organisation. The paramilitaries more often exist as small groups with patchwork organisation. They keep up an acute presence near political elites, or regional economic interests. This difference also applies to their power. It has allowed the paramilitaries to reconstitute after their demobilising in 2005. It has provided them with

39 One must underline the important work done by other victims' organisations, particularly Asfaddes (Association of Relatives of the Detained and Disappeared), who regroups the families of detainees-disappeared, crimes most often committed by State forces with support from paramilitaries, and Asfamipaz (Association of Families for Peace), an association of families of victims of economic and political kidnapping, most often committed by the guerrillas.

40 The "invention" of this new political anatomy cannot only be understood as a sudden discovery. It is more like a multiplicity of often minor processes from different origins and scattered localities which recover, repeat themselves, or imitate themselves, one supported by the other, distinguishable according to their realm of application, converging, and little by little outlining the draft for a general method"(Foucault 1989: 140).

important adaptive capacity under new war conditions, notably Colombia's increasing integration in the economic division of labour. They have also continued to evolve in the clandestine margins of power. Above all – and this is the most important aspect of their evolution, especially with regard to the older group of the Autodefensas Unidas de Colombia (AUC) – *they could avoid being identified as a central and homogeneous actor in the conflict. It is a great benefit to them today, engaged in the hidden threads of Colombian reality, that they are less condemned internationally than the guerrilla groups, even though their criminal acts are more extensive.* With some exceptions,[41] there is only a weak international conscience of the importance of this criminal division of labour, which permits the State to pillory certain historic figures, without attacking the roots of paramilitarism. It allows the latter to reconstitute in the very diversity of its regional embeddedness and of its ties to local authorities. Therefore, it is necessary to think, at last, about the specific role of State agents.

State Agents: The Symbolic and Institutional Construction of "Forced Disappearances"

Here again, it is not possible to accurately measure the entire historical significance of how Colombian political elites are structured, or the role the State apparatus plays in preserving their interests, as well as the structure of a "public sphere" in reaction to these practices (cf. Múnera Ruiz and Rodrígues Sanchez ed. 2009). For now, extending our reflections to the criminal division

41 In particular, the regular reports from Amnesty International, the FIDH, Human Rights Watch, or the UN High-Commisioner for human rights, taking the place of the Colombian Commission of Jurists. It is difficult to list all the publications on this topic. Here one can only mention some reports, amongst the most recent ones, which mention the criminal acts of paramilitary groups and which integrate them in a global analysis of acts violating Human Rights and International Humanitarian Law, war crimes and crimes against humanity committed by all armed agents, comprising the guerrilla and State agents. The Amnesty International report, *The struggle for survival and dignity. Abuses of human rights for indigenous people in Colombia,* particularly reveals the Human Rights violations against indigenous peoples (February 2010, available at http://www.amnesty.org/es). The 2008 report produced by the International Federation for Human Rights (FIDH) especially emphasises sexual violence by all the armed agents (Resolution by the International Office of the FIDH on Colombia, May 2008, available at http://www.fid-h.org). The FIDH report, *La demovilisacíon paramilitar, en los caminos de la Cort Penal Internacional,* points out the impunity paramilitaries enjoy and the limits of the demobilisation process (See: document nr. 481/3, October 2007). Human Rights Watch ("Paramilitaries' heirs. The New Face of Violence in Colombia") reveals the specific implication of paramilitary groups in the armed conflict (Feb. 2010, available at www.hrw.org/en/reports); The "Annual Report of the High Commissioner on Human Rights on the Situation of Human Rights in Colombia," presents a general view of human rights violations in Colombia, committed by all the armed agents (A/HCR/10/032, February 19, 2009). The feeble international awareness, especially tied to too little media exposure, contrasts the importance of national output on the subject.

of labour, we would like to make a relatively simple statement. As Leopoldo Múnera emphasises, State agents' involvement (mostly among the armed forces and police) in perpetuating the war does not happen only in the war itself, but also in their specific contribution to violently controlling the civilian population. Beside bloody repression, or planning massive reprisals and diverse acts of arbitrary detention; the practice of forced disappearance is one of the central elements of criminal labour.

Here, we touch on an extremely delicate point. Since acts take place that are directly carried out by the State apparatus, their origin and extent are difficult to evaluate. This is nothing new. It characterizes dictatorial practices that have often prevailed in Latin America, especially in the dictatorships in the South (Chile and Argentina, specifically). Nonetheless, it poses two difficulties. The first is that "forced disappearance" means, above all, brutally effacing human life. It is not surprising that this practice depends on institutional agents. It permits them to implement the power of their social position, for it clears them of their responsibility for crimes and permits them *to keep the image of their institution, the institutional power base, safe and sound.* The other difficulty is in some way its mirror-image on an international scale. It pertains to the *media's near-silence surrounding such practices, in Colombia as well as abroad.* In the Cold War context, disappeared Chileans or Argentinians benefited from marked international support.

How can this be explained? Besides relating to techniques for controlling public information, especially with the support of a well-controlled press, different elements can explain the process. First of all, there is the power that the Colombian Army enjoys, being close to the political and economic elites. In a country that is by definition "at war" and also a country where the rates of unemployment and poverty are particularly high (cf. Appendix), the Army figures as a beacon and protector of the population's interests. It also figures as an employer guaranteeing a future and some stability for a large number of young people, which none of them could dream of having otherwise (Arangure Romero 2010). This power, which blends explicit influence with a surface of symbolical legitimacy (among part of the population), is all the more striking since its reverse side, the involvement of sectors of the military in State violence (assassination of opposition leaders, acts of mass crimes) is not to be shown.[42]

One of the keys to the whole construct of the armed conflict and its indefinite perpetuation is the absence of an explicitly totalitarian State, a situation that one cannot qualify as "dictatorial." This emerges from the work of a number of historians. The notable exception is the last part of *La Violencia*, which saw five years of military dictatorship under General Pinilla

42 On the participation of the Armed Forces and Police in massive repressions against the civilian population, see Movimiento Nacional de Victimas de Crimenes del Estado (MOVICE) 2009.

(1953 – 1958).[43] Parallel to the exercise of violence, one can trace the continuation of a State under the rule of law in Colombia, most particularly in recent times, in spite of its limits and contradictions. In other words, the institutional game never stopped forming and reforming, articulating corruption and institutional violence, but also constructing and preserving some of the major institutions of democratic life, like public universities, or the Constitutional Court. As we indicated above, it is not possible to ignore the complexity of Colombian society and the relationships and benefits its institutions offer.

A whole struggle organises itself around those institutions. Some look like ambiguous occasions for practical politics. They allow impunity to intrude into large parts of the Colombian judicial system, but they also allow complaints, condemnation, and their own transformation into public objects. They allow corruption to infect the whole body of national life, but they also allow some local and national responsible people to consistently oppose corruption. They allow political action to be confronted with constant problems of legitimation and application, but they also enable shaping "more inclusive" social politics, although those are held back by hindrance and limitation strategies. That is why it is less effective to suppress these institutions than to control them. It is not a struggle for, or against institutions, which characterises the hidden side of Colombian public life, but *a struggle within the institutions*, in order to make them profit some secret interests or, to the contrary, to use their more honest elements to develop the primacy of public interest (material in the struggle against corruption, for health, victims' rights, etc.). Thus, one can better understand the interpretation of forced disappearance as State violence. Violence must preserve the institutional dynamic of the country, as well as guarantee Colombia's international legitimacy with the United States and the European Union.

Therefore, ties between State agents and paramilitaries, in their alliances but also their internal conflicts, are of crucial importance. The legitimation for an institutional power base, and for the idea that the State functions in spite of everything as a "State under the rule of law" is hidden. The epithet of "State under the rule of law" is as surprising as it is powerful in view of the lawless areas throughout Colombian society. Emphasising this paradox is essential for a more accurate idea of the State violence's internal logic. For the criminal division of labour, which concerns the highest levels of political life, allows the military and police institutions, if not to subcontract the "dirty job" (they already practice forced disappearances), at least to dilute responsibilities, to distribute roles and functions, to plunge State violence into a mire of complex and intellectual rationality ... and so *to preserve the idea that the State is not itself directly responsible for violence.*[44]

43 On the "recovery" from this period by the Frento Nacional, see below.

44 In a parallel way this element explains how the criminal labour division, which we have pre-

Behind the functional rationality of crime and the interplay of pro-systemic actors, who together, yet in different ways, serve the interests of the dominant political system (cf. Múnera Ruiz 2006), is the central figure of the State under the rule of law. It guarantees the protection of the "people's" interests. This is what is at stake in the social organisation of violence. Exceptional regimes seek their reflection in social action which allows them to uphold the pretense of the rule of law. They preserve the belief that the civil basis for society remains independent of war. Once again, we must differentiate among criminal practices. By uncovering violent strategies one can analyse the effective responsibilities, the causalities that link them, as well as their relative coherence and the justifications that uphold them. Such an approach returns to naming what is really at stake. It implies thinking critically about the conflict's contemporary sociology. At the moment, the problem is perpetuated, but in-depth analysis could open ways to end it. For the main objective of such an analysis leads to no other result than denaturalising war on the symbolic level of deconstructing the justifications offered by some actors in support of their choice. On the juridical level it assumes the need to analyse responsibilities, which is a necessary condition for a politics of justice, truth, and comprehensive reparation.

In the meantime, there is really a logic of horror, not in the sense of a series of macabre and relentless events, but as Foucault and Bauman most carefully said, in the sense of a kind of rationality inherent in modernity. This logic measures the degree of shocks, accompanied with a strategic intelligence that divides responsibilities, that separates shade from light in the visible regime in order to extend legitimate power. Therefore, it concerns *an explicitly modern violence*, which demands, well beyond the simplistic alliance of official propaganda and simplistic protestations. It unmasks the appeal to a modern Liberal vision as the single escape from the way things are. For it is precisely the hard promotion of such a vision which, when added to the divisions produced by war, leads to the development of "false-positive" practices. They seem literally aberrant but practically relatively logical.[45] Properly speaking, there is no limit to violent practices, and their rationalisation, in the war game in a country where terror practices have never stopped at all, a country where the bellicose logic does not interrupt the rhythm of daily life on the other side of an invisible frontier which separates large urban centres from regions defeated by great poverty. The role of A. Uribe's government, under which such practices arose, was to make people believe that these were just signs of

sented here, must not be considered too rigidly. We are, above all, dealing with a complex intermingling of responsibilities, which does not allow assigning criminal practices exclusively to any specific agent of conflict, most particularly to paramilitaries and State agents.

45 The practice of false-positives appeared, it seems, in 2008 when armed elements chillingly assassinated marginal civilians, before clothing them like members of the guerilla to inflate the statistics in the "struggle against terrorism." This act was officially condemned by the UN in June 2009. Yet there is no definite proof today that it has stopped.

exceptional pathology. Yet, in fact, they were profoundly coherent with the very doctrine of "Democratic Security" which aimed to establish war as a legitimate strategy for defending the interests of the "people." For if war was the sole response to war, how could one prevent such practices? One observes that this only fulfilled what the President himself asked for, namely acknowledging the utilitarian value of war booty, and installing a politics of monetary incentives for denouncingor assassinating "enemies" of power.[46]

Civilisation is at stake today in Colombia. This situation calls for thinking and being *modern in another way*, for overtaking the division of labour, which has made not distinguishing between normal and exceptional and mass violence the "new legitimate system." It calls for reflection on how to exit the conflict with a different reading of Colombian society's possible destiny. This is true on a criminal level but also on an economic level.

4. Division of Economic Labour: Poverty, Inequality and International "Success Story"

It is fitting to spend some time over what one could call the "political economy" of Colombian society. The intention here is to restore, though in a necessarily restricted and fragmented manner, the way in which the economy – in the general sense of the term – in turn has brought about an anthropological "formatting," that is to say, a modification of society's relationship to itself, but also of relationships between people. It would be less effective to describe the "economy" as such through a series of signposts, than to understand the socio-anthropological transformations induced by society's material base. The reflections by Marcel Mauss or Karl Polanyi, for example, cast some light on the matter. As in the case of analysing the criminal or political division of labour, the general idea is to emphasize the effects of the separations underlying society's organisation, which claims to achieve some degree of economic development, particularly, through its ever more successful anchoring in the international division of labour. Likewise, it can be shown how division and integration hide an analysis of material conditions of existence from a large part of Colombia's population (the labour-force or peasantry, but also more exclusive sectors). Our interest is clearly not only to determine profound social inequalities in the country's recent development. It is also to emphasize how, by assimilating the "social question" to a simple appendix of economic development, the organisation of the economic field *hides the moral problem. It is the concrete experience of indignity for many*

46 The most famous case was the paramilitary who, on television, brandished the hand of a guerrilla member, whom he had assassinated, in order to claim his reward in the shortest possible time.

Colombians for the sake of "successfully" integrating the national economy in the global economy. We will reflect on some historical particularities of the evolution of the Colombian economy. An increased interconnection – practical more than conceptual – has developed between the market and armed violence. Whereas the magnitude of the national social question is drowned out by the country's increasing economic integration in the international division of labour.

Some Historical Particularities ...

For those few who are interested in the country's recent economic history, let us say during the last twenty or thirty years, one must first state that Colombia has not complied with a succession of modernisations, crises and restarts that seem to have characterised the cycle of its Latin-American neighbours. So, for example, the Colombian historian Ricardo Arias Trujillo notices that Colombia has not, on an economic plane, participated in what many call the "lost decade" (the decade of the Eighties), which applies to most countries on the subcontinent, with the exception of Chile. The parallel with Chile is striking to the extent that the economic development, there as here, continues on the basis of systematic political violence, although it implies a different kind of state force. How should one understand this?

According to the aforementioned historian, it is above all necessary to point out that the beginning of the Sixties – the period in which the *Frente National* was formed – was accompanied by a phase of economic take-off in which one particularly held on to the birth or consolidation of Colombian industry:

> Colombia's economy also experienced significant changes and, as we have mentioned already, those explain the increasing importance of the cities with regard to its demography and economy. Generally, economists point out to an unprecedented accelerated and sustained growth. This development is not only due to coffee, which continues generating a good part of the State resources, but also to industrial development. Whereas the country depended on agricultural activity almost exclusively until then, other economic activities gained more importance from the mid-century on: transport, public services, communications, finance, and, especially, industry. The height of this last mentioned activity did not bring about conflicts with the coffee union (Trujillo 2006: 351 – 352).

Yet this typical phase of modernisation, the progress made by a country leaving a decade of violence, was nourished by immense poverty. It served as pretext for a principle of intrinsic limits to state intervention. It was the birth of a market for industrial goods that did not exist earlier. In other words, the recent evolution of Colombian industry happened at the same time that the political elites, reconstituted and stabilised by the *Frente Nacional*, agreed to the principle of free-exchange as a condition for tangible, even though very limited, economic progress. Consequently, Colombia's first post-war economic expansion corresponded to the discovery of the market's "virtues." At the same time Western Europe experienced the diametrical opposite. The Sixties were the most important moment of growing State influence, which depended on Keynesian growth policies. The State's "retreat" from the nervous centre of an emerging industrial market had a double effect on the Colombian political crisis, born at the beginning of the Seventies: on the one hand, an unheard of increase in violence; on the other, a terrain more and more favourable to implementing an economy in tune with war. Armed conflict discovered a novel occasion for recycling, or reorganising, its own financing in an emerging and weakly regulated economy.

A War Economy? Competitive Market and Army Violence

Therefore, Colombia at this time looks like Chile under Pinochet: political violence accompanies progressive economic growth. Different from Chile, however, where masking inequality presupposes eradicating political opposition and dismissing thousands of Chileans who clamour for decent working conditions, the Colombian State has maintained itself by discarding the market and instilling itself as an agent of war. That is to say, it has allowed the war to select the "good" and the "bad" players of a competitive economy, physically by eliminating "adversaries," or symbolically by refusing, in the name of a permanent conflict, to invest more in settling the social question. For, in fact, at the end of the twentieth century, the Colombian economy truly has developed on the basis of permanent confrontation between armed actors, *as well as between labour representatives and capital, represented by the war logic.* So, the Guerrilla presents a feeble but legitimate reason for the elites' incapacity to take charge of the "small people," while paramilitarism excels in opposing the left: trade union leaders and peasants who claim their rights are the preferred target of paramilitarism's murderous logic.

Even today one cannot avoid mentioning the extent to which this violence is embedded in the market economy, and is more relevant than ever. Colombia has, for several years, held the sad record for the highest number of assassinations of trade union representatives in the world.[47] One then understands that when neoliberal ideology permeates international institutions, it finds in Colombia a political-economic system willing to accept its terms. Any contesting forces have been decimated through the armed conflict.

47 See the important report drafted by the Escuela Sindical Nacional (ENS), with support from the European Union, the Colombia-Europe-United States Co-ordination, and the United Labour Confederation (CUT): G. Correa Montoya, "2515 o esa siniestra facilidad para olvidar. Veintiún años de asesinatos sistemáticos y selectivos contre sindicalistas en Colombia (1986–2006)", in: *Cuarderno le derechos humanos.* Nr. 18. Medellín (June 2007).

The capital-labour asymmetry is one of the most prominent on the sub-continent. This ideology has been accepted widely enough by successive governments, specifically that of President A. Uribe. Nevertheless, one sees a different strategy on Uribe's, at once subtler and more rational, with regard to trade unions.[48]

It is really under these successive principles that the global growth of Colombian economy was broadly increased. This provides a practically incontestable argument for legitimacy. Even beyond giving the job market greater flexibility, however unprotected, and increasingly opening the market for export, *the scope of capital's mobility* (technical development, energy, and "people") *retrospectively seems to be one of the key principles of the political economy that supports the war.* Logically enough, it is accompanied, not only by the "para-political" scandal, but generally by securing important routes, by developing "mega-projects," by intensifying forced displacements, and by worsening poverty in rural settings. It intends, within its own construct, to free capital from the fetters of a society, which refuses war. It uses capital's increased mobility to the detriment of labour. Here, we are brought to the heart of the economic division of labour: eloquent macro-economic indicators, at least on the level of recent history, based on achieving inequality of unprecedented proportions.

The National "Social Question" and the International Division of Labour: A Political Economy of Denial

The "social question" is not limited to seeing Colombia as a uniformly poor country. During these last years the country has known – we will return to this point later – a sustained economic development, unknown in its recent history. That has been due, in particular, to significant growth in some sectors, prompted by international demand. Most importantly, Colombia's economy could reconstitute, organise, and modernise itself – while exhibiting one of the most significant poverty rates in the sub-continent and a continuing increase of its inequalities. This "modernisation" unfolds in the following context:[49] In spite of a decrease in the urban population below the poverty threshold[50], the rural population below the poverty threshold has remained at a very high

48 Homicides and the percentage – compared to the world-wide situation – diminished in 2000 and 2005, in spite of a drastic rise in 2001. This relative decrease is accompanied by a drastic drop in the number of union agreements in the period (cf. Table 2, Appendix). At the same time, the proportion of trade unionism went from from 6 % in 1996 to 4.93 % in 2002 and 4.6 % in 2005.

49 According to the figures from the last major research carried out on the subject, the Gran Encuesta Integrada de Hogares (GEIH), of the Departamento Administrativo Nacional de Estadísticas (DANE). This research was carried out by the Misión para el Empalme de la Series de Empleo, Pobreza y Desigualdad (MESEP) in Nov. 2009.

50 40.3 % in 2002, 37.4 % in 2005, and 30.7 % in 2008.

level[51] . The evolution of destitution in villages[52] is equally important. It has experienced a new increase in the country, after an initial decline[53] . For the whole period it shows stagnation. In other words, *in recent years the social divide has been coupled with an intensifying geographical composition.* A third of the rural population experiences poverty and hunger. Poverty, added to destitution, names a situation marked by the inaccessibility of elementary public benefits (health, school, etc.). Today it even affects nearly two thirds of the rural population. Victims of armed conflict are the first to be affected (cf. Appendix).

When labour market figures are collected, they are primarily preoccupied with this principal reality. There again, one must account for the complexity of Colombia's situation. The change in unemployment rates saw a regular decrease between 2002 (15.5 %) and 2009 (12 %). Yet we know that the way this rate was measured changed and tended to emphasise the decrease.[54] The rate of under-employment[55] applies to more than one third of the active population (from 34.8 % in 2002, 31 % in 2005, to 29.7 % in 2009). It maintains a particularly high level in the informal sector (60.5 % in 2001, and 60 % in 2009). Despite the statistical reduction of the rate of unemployment, the reality is marred by a real economy which essentially remains on the periphery of legality. There again, rising assets are coupled with hiding what is not listed among the working population at the risk of worsening the inequality between the two "worlds." This duality is not merely a matter of intangible data. With regard to mounting social vulnerability and increasing uncertainty in France, Robert Castel already wrote a few years ago: "Unemployment is not a growing blister in labour relations which can be cured. It is becoming clear that employment insecurity and unemployment are part of the current dynamics of modernisation. … It is the structure of salaried relationships itself which risks being put in question" (1995: 400 – 402).

The social base of the Colombian economy is really characterised by a long "uninterrupted" chain, a collection of various structural weaknesses.[56] They go from a particularly low minimum wage,[57] to the near-absence of social coverage for the great majority of workers, through the existence of more and

51 69.3 % in 2002, 67 % in 2005, and 66.2 % in 2008.

52 9.4 % in 2002, 7.4 % in 2005, and 6.8 % in 2008.

53 32.5 % in 2002, 27.4 % in 2005, and 32.6 % in 2008.

54 The unemployment rate is measured in proportion to the active population. See figures in the Appendix.

55 "Under-employed" is defined by the GEIH 2009 study as a professional situation characterised by one or more of the following criteria: insufficient income, too few working hours, a kind of disqualification (someone with a medical degree becomes a taxi driver, for instance). The rate of under-employment is measured in proportion to the employed population.

56 To use the famous expression Robert Castel "popularised" in this book.

57 In 2010 it was $515 Colombian dollars a month (minus $ 200) for a bread-winner at the head of an average family (a couple with two children). The last GEIH 2009 inquiry shows that this allows people to leave the threshold of need, but not poverty.

more weakened labour union agreements. In addition, union representatives or politicians who try to oppose the disastrous social practices of some firms are subject to repeated threats ... or also banishment and expropriation. All of this describes a series of violent elements aimed at weakening labour as well as consolidating the country's capitalistic structure. It reinforces the capital-labour asymmetry in an undefined way and completely dilutes it in a new macro-economic growth. These inequalities take many forms. Poverty corresponds to serious statistics regarding infant mortality, illiteracy, the absence of social coverage, or exclusion from the education system.[58]

Nonetheless, as we said before, one cannot explain the perpetuation of this whole problem without alluding to the country's macro-economic strategy. Far from having chosen the "low" road of corrupted power, incapable of guiding the country rationally, the governments that have followed one another since the *Frente Nacional* have, on the contrary, shown a remarkable ability to choose international economic integration. This has been put in place progressively by opening the market, by international specialisation, and by reconstructing a global economic legitimacy. This is shown, for example, by the high level of education in economy and administration throughout the country's universities. As Ricardo Arias Trujillo recently points out, the fact that Colombia has avoided sinking in the "lost decade" is not only tied to the importance of the illicit economy and recycling money from drug trafficking. It also refers "to the responsible and prudent behaviour of the ruling class, who has avoided excessive debt and supported exporting non-traditional goods, which has given a decisive impulse to economic growth during the Eighties" (2006: 335). This new economic reality has likewise integrated the international dimension. Colombia has participated in the great economic changes of the Neoliberal era, "going to look for its principle clients outside and breaking its too great dependence on an internal market, by definition of little power (ibid.: 351). Above all, it lacks the smallest wish for Keynesian revival.

The existence of an extremely rich sub-soil, which is also one of the reasons for forced displacements, has done the rest. From supporting figures one discovers *a real strategy of international specialisation* around carbon, petroleum products, bananas, and other agricultural products of prime necessity. They make Colombia an indispensable economic partner of the big international donors, the United States and the European Union. In spite of an ever more pronounced dependence on the first, the recovery of the country's international legitimacy is about to reach a decisive stage when the Free Trade Agreement between Colombia and the European Union is signed.[59] In view of

58 In 2008, the GNI index, which indicates the rate of concentration or distribution of wealth, rose to 0.587, the highest on the Latin-American sub-continent. 0 indicates a completely equal distribution, 1 a situation in which a single person owns the whole wealth of a nation.

59 The global volume of North American investments rose to 11,847.8 million US dollars from

the EU's international image, a medium range economic agent with a relatively strong image of respecting human rights, the economic "coup" seems clear. It allows the problem of the social question to disappear behind the mirage of a prosperous economy, capable of signing and respecting international agreements on a high level. Thus one sees the appearance of what one could call *a political economy of denial* in Colombia on the very basis of economic growth, and the skilful steering of the national economy.

Overlaying the reflections of Marx on the structure of inequality in Capitalism with those of Levinas on economy (cf. Marx 1992; Lévinas 1971: 109–200), one can consider how the whole contradictory change succeeds, *nolens volens*, by negating the practical experience of the majority of Colombian people. The majority is given no face, or subjectivity, considered only a lifeless cog in the work output and accumulation of capital. Even more radically, Colombian economic power reveals its specificity around denying the other, where he/she is most vulnerable. What is especially serious in this seemingly implacable logic is not only those who are "excluded from progress." The moral conscience, which from the nineteenth century surged to the centre of the European industrial society to see in poverty and inequality a universal attack on human dignity, is about to disappear behind the national economy's tangible progress.

Yet, what is a national economy, which ignores the majority of its members, other than, a fetishized construct? For it quite works on that level. In a country that experiences an increasing gap between town and country, it becomes more and more difficult to make the intrinsic violence of a lastingly unfair capital-labour structure visible. This applies especially to the deliberately isolated or decimated social movements and opposition parties. The subjectivity of the other – worker, peasant, various faces of those "excluded" and swallowed by the spiral of conflict – is neutralised by the symptoms of "successful" internationalisation. Yet this seems to be more and more ignored by objective economic thinking. If the life of another person constitutes a responsibility, as Lévinas always maintains, and if this responsibility cannot be considered separate from its material base, which remains one of the most important legacies of Marxist thought, why should this damage to Colombian society not be seen as a damage to its proper moral identity?

One recognises, therefore, that for reflection to take place, it must be liberated from rationalising human labour under market constraints and not

Jan. 2002 to Sept. 2009. It is 42 % of all foreign investments, against 6, 349.4 million US dollars for Europe, 23 %. That being so, the economic ties with the European Union continued to strengthen during the last years, going from an exchange volume (import/export) of 4,046 million US dollars in 2003 to 9,802 million US dollars in 2009. While imports mostly relate to machines, equipment goods, chemical products, metallurgy and the automobile industry, exports essentially concern carbon (53.7 %), bananas (11.7 %), coffee (9.2 %), petrol and derivative products (5.9 %). (Source: Ministro de Comercio, Industria y Turismo. Direción de las relaciones internacionales, Feb. 2010. See figures in the Appendix.)

counting the costs in terms of human life. This prejudice constantly amplifies the industrial division of labour on a national and international level. As we will have occasion to repeat later on, this process works as a mechanism to ensure the weakening of the moral conscience for the sake of a largely idealised "global" growth, which economic Liberalism considers the surest sign of well-being. What Colombian society is called to imagine, then, is not a scarcity economy, but one, which bases its development on an unbreakable respect for social rights. It has to invent solidarity mechanisms – especially with regard to health, education, agrarian reform and income distribution – and implement a growing non-market sector (to express public intervention and a Third Sector). This will allow for *the legitimation of a "domestic economy" in which the other would not interminably be returned to basic invisibility.*[60] It remains to be seen if the political field, caught in its own difficulties, can achieve this.

5. Division of Political Labour: Popular Classes, Territoriality and Social Fragmentation

Doubtlessly, one of the most profound but also most difficult and controversial aspects of Colombian society still needs to be addressed: its relationship to "power" in general. Here, Michel Foucault guides us once more. He emphasizes the continuous relationships, which express how a political system crystallises in the figure of the "State" with multiform extensions into society. This foundational position allows Michel Foucault to show modernity's new power economy, which takes place in the silent shape of exclusion

60 The notion of "domesticity" has various sources. One finds the term in the book by Boltanski, Luc, and Thévenot, Laurent (1991). *De la Justification. Les économies de la grandeur.* Paris: Gallimard. It points out one of the forms of justifying economic action when it refers to tradition, to the continuity of ties, and to reciprocity. This term also echoes K. Polanyi's reflections on the principles of a "non-monetary" economy. It is set in a socio-political network from where it draws its meaning, capable of responding to the population's needs by freeing itself from the market's self-referential logic. This "domesticity" interrupts the utopia of the "self-regulating market." And it can re-establish itself in the form of a "pluralistic economy," expressing redistribution (mediating State intervention) and solidarity (based on the existence of a commons). On the subject see especially Polanyi, *The Great Transformation.* Yet, this term also has roots in the economic thinking of Emmanuel Lévinas, especially his reflections on residence, tools and work. In his eyes, economy (the rule of the house) has its phenomenological roots in the specifics of living. On the ethical plane, economy defines itself not as the effacement of the other person, but as the recognition of that presence in the world, fraught with ambiguity and separation: ambiguity, because the embodied subject takes possession of the world and participates in its reality through work, separation, for economy gives a specific place and thereby introduces a particularity, a distance from others. On the subject, see Emmanuel Lévinas, *Totality and Infinity.* These different orientations urge us to think about the economy in another shape than industry (rationalisation) or capitalism (accumulation), and to establish the rights of a subjective life in the cycle of material production.

(lunacy), of disciplining (detention), and more widely, surveillance (generalised), as well as different schemes for new "governmentality." Beyond that, a central discourse juxtaposes the Liberal cause's emancipating power and underhand violence at work in those disciplinary institutions, which uphold the practice of Liberalism. It is necessary to prevent many recoveries between power, State, and society. In Foucault's posthumous texts one discipline is a figure announcing the network which links power in society. The State is only one instance in which it takes shape, although it acts as an essential authority (cf. 1977).

Within the frame of our analysis and traceably under the influence of Marx's early writings, one can nevertheless state that ties between state and society do not only concern those silent and anonymous extensions. To use a term from the *Criticism of Hegel's Philosophy of Law* (cf. 1970), it also plays out in the political division of labour, that is to say, in how the State feeds its hegemonic power in society, and is bound to defending its particular interests. In this division of labour the State appears to be the only trustee of general interest, and is thus seen to be invested with an imaginary power. It is appointed umpire, the exclusive guarantor of what it considers relevant for the will of all. Maybe one can describe the political division of labour as a double process that, on the one hand, accentuates society's many divisions and, on the other, shows how to divide the roles between State and society, to construe the former to the detriment of the latter.

It goes without saying, that it would not be simply a question of "overtaking" the division of labour and dreaming of a kind of communal fusion in the political field. In history this dream has often been expressed by installing some kind of totalitarian power. What matters, beyond official institutions, is that the role distribution, which draws its practical logic from a society struggling with incessant divisions, cannot be thoroughly examined and criticized. For there again, as in the case of a limitless extension of market logic, the "other" is reduced to a pure abstraction and placed under the control of a hegemonic power strategy. Its function makes it just one cog in a kind of communal life. In the Colombian case, this double movement of the divisions in society and their instrumental use by the State is highly questionable. What forms do these elements take in present-day Colombia? It seems important to us to mention three aspects.

Political Parties, Social Movements and Common People: The Question of Representation

The first aspect pertains to what one could call the relationship between political parties, social movements, and the common people, transcending traditional bipartisanship. It is commonly known in Colombia that the period of the *Frente Nacional*[61] was essentially ambiguous: on the one hand, it ended a violent decade (the period called *La Violencia*, "inaugurated" with the murder of the Liberal Jorge Gaítan in 1948), rehabilitating traditional party politics, and returning a "decent" appearance to Colombian politics. Yet, on the other hand, this reorganisation of the political field was accompanied by the formation of a political oligarchy. It was viewed as a stabilising power against division, yet it fully controlled the national political agenda. It led to a more and more marked separation from the Colombian population, especially the general public. Consequently, members of the general public saw themselves as deprived of representation mechanisms that could give them hope for social transformation through the political game. Thus, the paradox (and its complexity) is particularly characteristic of Colombian society.

At the same time, a political class regrouped in Colombia, lending some moral legitimacy by its ability to end civil war. However, this recovered stability appeared to the large majority of Colombians as a disguised form of domination. It permanently discredited – until this day – any possibility of expressing ethics and politics. More broadly, this situation denied the Colombian political game any chance to endow oneself with legitimacy other than on purely instrumental grounds, tied to the conquest and preservation of power. It is, then, not astonishing that this period should also be the one that saw the formation of guerrilla groups, especially the FARC and the ELN. Their common aim was, in spite of many sociological and political differences, to denounce the exclusionary concept of politics, and to install an alternative power with arms.

One can nevertheless add that, in Colombia's case, the inherent paradox of the *Frente Nacional* is nothing new. Ricardo Arias Trujillo comments on the years in between and points out that this situation forms the background for a first peace process, but also for the legality given to paramilitary groups, as in the 1991 Constitution. The 1991 Constitution could not stop the violence, "even if it opened political spaces like never before in the country's history" (ibid.: 2006: 337 and 341 [on the Betancourt presidency] and 315 [on the 1991 Constitution]).[62] In Europe, the alternation between violence and autonomy

61 The *Frente Nacional* refers to the period from 1958 – 1974 when Conservative and Liberal Presidents alternated and Congress was divided to the almost exclusive benefit of these two parties.

62 In an unpublished UCL document, Leopoldo Múnera Ruiz states that, needing or wanting to give status to belligerent agents, the 1991 Constitution was internally constructed around a hypostasised concept of positive rights, as well as on a partial sociological basis. This situation provoked the retreat of the Guerrilla, the FARC especially, when they precisely should have been integrated into the new political process in order to exit violence. On the same day as the election for the Constituent Assembly, the Government bombarded the Casa Verde, one of the FARC's general seats and the symbol of peace negotiations. It revealed the ambiguity of this project and the failure of a political process disconnected from society. (cf. Múnera Ruiz 2008b: 34).

presents classical political behaviour. Max Weber undoubtedly saw it more clearly than others.

One of the most problematic, not to say dramatic, consequences of the lasting breach between Colombia's political elite and its social base, still is the *systematic eradication of any form of democratic opposition.* The assassination of Union Patriotica (UP) leaders has caused a kind of paroxysm, which calls one to conclude that the national political space has made the formation and recognition of a stable opposition practically impossible. A stable opposition could be a legitimate counterpoint to dominant political actors who have evolved from the Centre to the Conservative Right. Now, the need for such an opposition is not required only to enable alternative political action and, on occasion, in terms of the more and more urgent need for a politics of redistribution, agrarian reform, and restoring public welfare. It also pertains to the possible modification of the general power equilibrium. In the tension between opposing political parties, the space for representation gets larger and opens a way to civil society as a full political subject, no longer prisoner of the capture and division strategies implicit in political charges. From this perspective, the collapse of the Left opposition in Congress in March 2010 disquietingly continues the past. Whatever face the elected President has, this situation raises the problem of the country's democratic future, which supposes that society is given the chance to exist in, and by the game of, political-ideological differences, and to look at and regulate its own internal divisions differently (cf. Lefort 1986).

It is also important, apart from problems posed by bipartisanship, to question what one could call *the culture of Colombian political elites with regard to society – and particularly its common urban and rural layers.* Lacking institutional support oriented towards rebalancing the whole political game, this culture consists of permanently disqualifying the "people" – even when it pretends, at least in the words of many elites, to serve specific interests. Certainly, this contradiction would not exist, if one could ignore modernity's way of legitimizing political action. Its power is drawn from an idea, which reduces civil society to a collection of egoistic individuals, for which the market or the State provides the only legitimate means of collective organisation. One must say, however, that in Colombia's case the situation is exacerbated by the structural mixture of poverty, and the armed violence extolled by guerrilla groups. Enough schemes help spread disparaging judgements and credit the idea that only an elite group, which could survive society's jolts, is able to lead the country in any way. Afterwards, the appearance of paramilitaries, their implication in violent outbursts, and the development of drug trafficking lead to a systematic depreciation of the general public. This happens at the moment when the State's permissiveness regarding paramilitary actors reinforces the "need" for vigorous power, like a game of communicating vessels.

The problem of the relationship between elites and society is two-fold. On the whole, it exposes a characteristic trait of Liberal modernity. The relationship aims to devalue society's political autonomy, at least its attempts to constitute itself as *full political subject, which* works to produce universal elements capable of surmounting divisions, but which also disputes the State's legitimate monopoly on the issue. This problem also applies to the split which exists in Colombian civil society today between its most integrated elements (middle and upper classes, NGOs, political and associative movements, etc.) and its most disrespected elements (the large majority of peasants and working classes, but also victims of violence, particularly displaced populations). These disrespected elements are denied a minimum of institutional support (schools, hospitals, etc.). Since they do not own any symbolic capital, through which they could claim their rights, they are *found at the periphery of society even when they make up its huge majority.*

One can add that the deliberate break between the working classes and the political elite forms one of modernity's sociological plots, especially in the West. Yet, when this problem was taken on by the trade union movement in Europe, the middle class structure grew as did "Social Democracy," even if in very different forms. These elements do not have a tangible existence in Colombia, particularly because the trade union movement has been criminalised. Ever since, constructing a lasting connection between political elites and civil society remains a major problem. And that, in a country that claims to belong to the Liberal tradition. It is remarkable as far as organising free elections and growing legitimation for the principle of representation are concerned. Yet, it does not completely discard the political analysis of society, which allows it to face deficiencies, which have always characterised the Liberal tradition in different areas. *Apart from corruption, Colombia's case appears very different from a simple exception: it reminds us that such massive problems are always possible in a country that refers to a limited vision of modernity, without giving itself the proper means to tackle the human cost that, inevitably, accompanies such a vision.*

This does not at all mean that civil society is not dynamic or that its popular segments are incapable of engaging in the social struggle to claim their rights and to propose alternative political programmes. As has already been noted elsewhere, social movements in Colombia offer a particularly dynamic tradition, heterogeneous, organised, and creative. Doubtlessly one sees a "response" there, which society always looks for, answering its own violence. The problem is, however, much more profound. Organic ties between political parties and society's self-organising dynamics have never really existed. Therefore the social movements have always been suspected of causing polarisation and war, even when they have sought to eliminate such constant perversion.

This situation does not only reflect the conservative Right's arrogance towards the working classes. A party like the *Polo Democratico* often discovers the real difficulty in thinking that its discourse and its practice could be supported on a "communitarian" tradition, scattered afar amongst peasant and indigenous backgrounds, but also amongst a few *barrios* (large urban neighbourhoods). They think that by referring to them, popular movements or victims' movements could in some way serve as recommendation. A part of Polo's own membership shares the vision of Colombia's political life as a jungle of knocks and opportunities. The last years have shown how difficult it is for this party to abandon such an imagination and to shore up its power conquest with popular deeds. One knows nevertheless – and we have said it in the introduction – they bring "practical knowledge" to light in the test of war (cf. Bourdieu 1998; Certeau 1990; Dejours 1993: 47–70). Far from being merely local, this knowledge contributes to the design of justice and peace practices which are *in phase* with problems communities encounter in their *real* relationship to violence.

Inversely, it is not at all surprising that populism should have developed under the two mandates of former President A. Uribe. The Ultra-Right has always established a party for its political legitimacy, using those disappointed by the traditional Left. So it is endowed with "popular" energy. This was the case in Europe during the Thirties, when, in Germany and Italy, for instance, the imminence of war and recourse to nationalistic arguments propelled a part of the working classes into the arms of Fascism, furthered by divisions in the Social Democratic party. Yet this has also been the case much more recently in France (especially with the extreme Right's entrance for a second vote in the presidential election on April 21, 2002). The divisions of the French Left, associated with ambiguous socio-economic measures, helped a good number of workers and employees switch to the radical Right, disappointed by the absence of credible perspectives on social transformation.

Finally, we discover a form of congruence between various levels of social disqualification, specifically regarding society's most vulnerable members. Not only are they trapped by armed conflict, they really are the principal victims of a war which constantly mocks the principle that civilian populations (all the intimidation, territorial conquests or terror by armed actors is behaviour targeted against the civilian population, underlining society's complete "nakedness" in the face of war, to repeat an expression used by Roland Anrup above) should be protected. They are further disqualified by the dominant political system, which is invested in emphasising its growing connection to the Liberal tradition. Such a situation, which one could call a "double penalty," at the same time lays out a future road to renewal. The link between political parties and the working classes needs new consideration, with special reflection on the key role of social movements. This will nonetheless not preclude limitations or contradictions.

Multiculturalism, Forms of Violence, and Territoriality: Geography and Fragmentation

We must now approach a second aspect linked to the organisation of Colombia's political life. One might call it *the logic of its internal divisions.* One could offer a critique of the political oligarchy. Likewise one could criticise the absence of permanent mechanisms to free civil society from its dependence on political games and return the working class to political life, through a specific media group. It would, furthermore, be appropriate to look at how society is organised, and how it defines itself politically. In this regard, three characteristics merit attention.

The first concerns Colombia's multi-cultural tradition in which the 1991 Constitution presents a key moment. In this regard, Ricardo Arias Trujillo writes:

> Beyond measures to strengthen democracy and extend rights and liberties, which already represent a significant change of the state's orientation, the new constitution recognized and gave value to the Colombian nation's plurality. It emphasized and defended its social, ethnic, religious, political, and sexual diversity. If, on the one hand, equality was rated very important, the National Constituent Assembly (ANC), on the other hand, considered the right of differentiation as fundamental, because respect for the "other," that is to say, tolerance, was deemed a basic principle for harmonious coexistence (2006: 355).

This is not the place for a long and extensive discussion of the relationships between multi-culturalism, redistribution, and Liberalism. One knows that with supporters of a *communitarian criticism of Liberalism* (Taylor, Walzer, MacIntyre), the multi-cultural affirmation goes along with deconstructing the Liberal project, at least its pretension to a unique model, which equalises existential conditions, and/or denies the autonomy of cultural qualifiers. However, the significance of the relationship between multi-culturalism and redistribution remains quite indeterminate. Left Liberalism (the "universal basic income", supported by Van Parijs, and Vanderborght) demands a radical modification of those conceptions underlying the redistributive project. Nancy Fraser goes even further. She heavily underlines the risks in hiding the social question. She connects them to people asserting their cultural membership more and more pronouncedly, knowing that a large-scale redistributive strategy forbids one to stop at any one sense of identity since this would *de facto* limit the impact of the assertion (cf. Fraser 1997).

However, this discussion is not our main aim. We are more interested in the political significance of suddenly formulating a multi-cultural norm in a country characterised by the co-existence of modernity and war, but also by a diversity of violent practices and identities. So, claiming to recognise the other's otherness in a general way is in itself not enough. The claim cannot hide the social conditions that produce otherness, that is, the whole material and symbolic process by which "the other" has already been constructed in society. Thus, it seems very perilous to evoke the other in a-historic terms. It is, for that matter, largely idealised to ignore the other as in some way pre-fabricated by existing organisational structures such as the armed conflict, but also the perpetuation of a class society, the rural and urban segmentation, and difficulties in promoting public benefit. Recognising an ethnic difference for example, in the sense of identical components that together mark the singularity of a social group, cannot disconnect the accompanying modes of recognition or of low esteem, which already exist at a larger scale. In more conceptual terms, the statement's context is a component of the statement's performativity (cf. De Munck 1999).

Problems in Colombia are caused not by the question of otherness *in general.* It is rather the lack of a central process of social integration to articulate the particular and the general, even if that articulation were to be questioned in the course of generations or struggles. For, "the other" has existed in Colombia before the 1991 Constitution ... as it does today. Yet, it has remained (and still remains) subject to the power of society's internal divisions, the result of decades of juxtaposed violence which contribute to making "the other" an abstract member of the system, indeed the "objective enemy." *Multiculturalism offers only a limited response to this question.* If it gives cultural communities the means of a stronger affirmation in the public space, and if, from this angle, it contributes to the autonomy of political subjects, it merits high praise. Yet, it does not really address the problem, which we pose. Otherness, when it does not rely on the strength of connection, or membership, can actually be an apology for difference, which, in turn, expresses rejection or separation. Its critical power is much rather linked to its capacity for creating obstacles to standardizing social means of integration, notably generated by the market (as a key-dimension of the United States' regulation model), or by State bureaucracy (which serves the ideology of Republican homogeneity in France). Modes of shaping difference are radicalised by war. Superimposing the multi-cultural claim on such modes really contributes to playing the general game of allowing no differences, *since a communal referential that allows affirming the other as neighbour, identical to oneself, no longer exists.* Here one falls into the trap of subjectivism, disconnected from the universal ambition which inspires otherness (cf. Nanteuil 2009). One finds this aspect in social movements as well.

We cannot here relate the tragic epic of Colombian social movements, or of their creative power. We would only like to pause at one point which is like the crossroads of their power and their difficulties: their relationship to armed conflict. We have already indicated, since the introduction, how their proximity to violent death forms one of their characteristics. It must, of course, also be seen along with their amazing determination. Above all, the strength of the social movements is that they have never abandoned the idea of a society constructed from "below." They always hold onto the option of political proposals coming from society itself, especially from its most vulnerable segments. One might add that the social movement's problem is not its existence as such, but its disconnection from political rationality, or Colombian party politics. In other words, it has immense difficulty keeping a hold on public space through a mix of organised and durable intermediaries. How the movement is marked by war and by a class society is certainly a structural component of its history and development. We could not leave at that, however, for such a vision presupposes that the vast majority of these movements would only be simple social actors trapped by structural determiners which they cannot change. Such a vision quite contradicts their wish to overturn a given state of the world, especially as far as war is concerned, as well as their perseverance. One could rather see their own logic and underline the fact that they are confronted by a double centrifugal movement: the first is the *polarisation of violence* (especially for victims' movements), the second is the *increasing territorial organisation of the conflict and of society* (especially for the popular movements).

It is quite pointless to return to the violent behaviour enacted on Colombian territory, since we have mostly listed it above. The problem which we wish to expose here is the following: due to their obvious and complete participation in denouncing human rights violations which have characterised Colombian society for decades, the movements defending victims give voice to those crushed by war, but also build their principal identity on this basis. Such mediation remains an essential universalizing element. Yet, they are just as much shaped by claiming the dignity due to victims, as by constructing an identity linked to that humiliated identity. One can understand it. The nature of the atrocities, but also their public denial, must sometimes be overcome with moral grandeur, which cannot successfully rise above a single identity. One can also never emphasize the political function of such movements enough. It helps victims to leave their state of victimhood, and become social actors as full political subjects. Yet, from that very perspective, the problem continues.

Within the scope of our reflections one could qualify it in the following manner: in spite of themselves, these movements belong to the division of labour which characterises the Colombian political field. They in turn participate in defending a specific category of interests and values. In other words, they see themselves trapped in some kind of relationship to society and the political system. The idea is basically that they have every reason for particularity, but not for generality. Once again, this is not a problem of the intrinsic value of their actions, but of their mode of organisation and how it structures identity. For the facts reveal, not only does it allow the State to throw oil on the fire by playing off tensions amongst victims' organisations,[63] *but it also reinforces the idea that the inclination for general interest would only come from State structures, and not from the social movements.* Raising consciousness for this situation has started several years ago, with the development of many networks of smaller organisations on collective platforms, regional and national, networks of networks, etc. This movement is undeniably one of the most adequate responses to the difficulties in Colombian civil society with regard to the criminalization of its most active members. Yet, we are still only at the beginning of a long process. The underlying socio-affective and symbolic dynamics will necessarily take a long time to change.[64]

The conflict's territorial dimension adds to this first statement. It has a direct effect on the organisation of popular movements (unions, peasant movements, indigenous movements, etc.). State agents, or paramilitary groups, criminalize trade unionism and strike the social movement at its heart. It is all the more troubling, since Colombia clearly belongs to the current dynamic of economic globalisation, mostly of the market, through which it achieves new international legitimacy. Opposing such a situation, popular movements tend towards deep territorial anchoring. This element is an essential condition for making the claims linked to a territorial logic of conflict, but also to the territorial distribution of resources. We have indicated above that it is the case, and, how the absence of agrarian reform keeps a large part of the country in the hands of local power, large landowners and multinationals, run on a neoliberal model, as well as drug trafficking networks and political-economic clientele. *In this context, the territorialisation of popular movements is also their weakness.* In a country where the relationship of demographic forces between countryside and town reversed two decades ago, where rural areas are places where problems overlap (front line war, poverty, resource control, violence, etc.), insisting on such territorial dimensions gain a double implication: ignoring it is part of a firm denial of Colombian reality, but it does not in itself provide means to achieve the causes for which such movements struggle.[65]

The idea of society's self-government, inherited from the Enlightenment, in Colombia clashes with a number of complex structural factors. The problem

63 Most particularly by construing the figure of the "good victim," those kidnapped illegally, whose families benefit from special juristic (and media) treatment.

64 It is not possible to cite all the networks here. One can note that today there is no longer any communal platform for all victims together, which would really allow "uniting" victims of guerrilla groups with those of paramilitaries or State agents. That being so, one should not t ignore the fact that many people engaged in these movements are starting up local initiatives in this direction.

65 For an extensive portrayal of Colombia's social movements, see Archila Neira, *M. (2005). Idas y venidas. Vueltas y revueltas. Protestas sociales en Colombia. 1958 – 1990.* Bogotá: ICANH/CINEP. See also M. Palacios, M., and Safford, E. (2006). *Colombia. País fragmentado, sociedad dividida.* Bogotá: Norma.

of criminalising the social movements, stigmatising them, but also their fragmentation belong to this situation. This clearly illustrates the transfer as well as the perpetuation of what we have called the political division of labour in a country where the political game has throughout the past decades remained attached to the idea of the indisputable superiority of political decisions or the State apparatus over every other practice for social change. It cannot be said that Colombian political practice has never known change. On the contrary, the multi-cultural affirmation of the 1991 Constitution, but also a push towards decentralisation, which has handed many powers to governors and mayors, attest to important transitions central to Colombia's political model. Yet, such an evolution does not succeed in changing the structure of the political field and the logic of its internal divisions. In particular, it can never – willingly or unwillingly – allow social movements to pierce the armour of the dominant logic and recognise that human subjectivity fully participates in political action. Now, this generally poses *the problem of society's anthropological status in forming public space.* That status remains remote from the initiative for change and, at the same time, its identity as a political subject is quite under-estimated, indeed denied. Yet, without this basic recognition, without this possibility of acceding to a political identity disentangled from the logic of the State apparatus or political competition, one does not precisely see how an alternative tendency could establish itself. It is done in the name of "progress," which is considered indisputable, and in the name of a Liberal modernity, which saturates the "rational" outlook.

Another relationship to the other …

During a European conference, Leopoldo Múnera presented a brief synthesis of the situation in which Colombia's social movements find themselves. He emphasized how the organisational problems in the political field were reflected in the field of official historiography. He wrote:

> A good part of Liberal and Conservative historiography is constructed on the voluntary or involuntary forgetfulness of popular sectors and movements. This selective amnesia is not only characteristic of historians, but also of Colombian governors, for whom *the popular other* only appears when it reaffirms the *institutional self,* but never as a real other that is so absolutely heterogeneous that it cannot be reduced to official history (2007: 2).

This author very accurately "places" the problem. *It is in regard to the idea of a relationship to the other or a model of otherness that Colombia's future is at risk.* Recognising the other presupposes that one recognises the other's real existence, with its socio-historical and socio-cultural singularity, in the singularity of its own body-shaped subjectivity. The problem is, then, not only the existence of institutions, but the relationship between institution and society, between the objective forms of the dominant political logic and the structures of the living world (*Lebenswelt*). The social movements vividly recall the existence of those structures, in spite of their own temporal contingency. Similarly, the question is not whether modernity exists in Colombia – it is doubtlessly more present than ever – but whether it can think about its relationship with human subjects, which daily establish their otherness. For this is what Liberal modernity stands for: its incapacity to recognise the process which threatens society down to its foundations in society's divisions, and which undermines the very promise on which Liberalism unceasingly backs up its justifications; the promise of an individual *in* the world, rational and autonomous, protected from abuses of central power, capable of deciding freely on her, or his, fate, and that of their fellows, by means of parliamentary representation. Ignoring foundations for such a promise leads Liberal modernity to consider the rest of the world as a "thing" – Bauman says a "garden" (cf. Bauman 1989) – that has to be rationally maintained. It promotes civil rights and liberties without questioning social and historical conditions to achieve them. It frames a social anthropology based on the apology for a lonesome and calculating individual – but an individual disconnected from real power, tied to an existential solitude only overcome by an everlasting growth in material gains. Therefore, it allows violence to spread throughout the country, to offer supposedly "rational" justifications and to transgress basic anthropological barriers, such as human life and human dignity *at no cost.*

Conclusion

This text has not primarily tried to open "practical" ways about the question of what must be done to leave the current situation behind. In some way, the choices are only too clear. From the humanitarian agreement to the (re-) construction of a political opposition, articulated by the social movements; through the affirmation of victims' right to justice, truth, and complete reparation, the struggle against poverty, the endless drug trafficking, white-washing and corruption, but also the consolidation of public goods, combined with reinforced solidarity: it is not difficult to offer perspectives which could allow Colombian society to rearticulate and realize justice and peace, and so to define itself *beyond* conflict.

This text has another ambition. Above all it wants to investigate *the reasons why such choices did not and still cannot take place.* Said differently, it wants to reflect on the matter of sociological mechanisms, which underlie the project of Liberal modernity. In Colombia, a large majority, not only its elites, aspire to such a modernity, though the country has never developed the proper mechanisms of self-regulation which always oppose Liberalism but form strong social ethics and give society a certain consistency, at least in the Western tradition where this ideology is wide-spread, excepting Europe of the Thirties.[66]

In the coming decades, Colombia needs to free itself from restrictive definitions of economics and politics in order to constitute society as a mix of rights and collective rules, with the social gains of a welfare State and cultural counter-forces. Similarly, one must insist that nothing is more illusory than affirming, in a kind of post-Cold War historical rationalisation, that the Western tradition is essentially *the* model of *Liberal democracy*. This view is a caricature that rests on a particular trick: to deny the intrinsic contradictions of a single model, and to ignore the weight of history which determines precisely that reality is never shaped according to only one single point of reference. Certainly, regarding these different questions, we stand at the dawn of a new phase, particularly in Europe and in the United States.

Bibliography

Agamben, G. (2000). *Means without End. Notes on Politics.* Minneapolis: University of Minnesota Press.

Anrup, R. (2008). *Una tragedía a la colombiana.* Bogotá: Ed. Buena Semilla.

Arangure Romero, J. P. (Mar. 4, 2010). La militarización de los cuerpos jóvenes: reflexiones de los prcesos de tránsito hacia la vida civil. In: *Conferencia en la Universidad Jorge Tadeo Lazano.*

Arendt, H. (1989). Le cas "Eichman" et les Allemands. In: Abensour, M. ed.: *Ontologie et politique. Hannah Arendt.* Ed. Tierce. 169 – 173.

Arendt, H. (1963). Eichmann in Jerusalem: A Report on the Banality of Evil. New York: Viking Press.

Arendt, H. (1958). The Human Condition. Chicago: University of Chicago Press.

Arendt, H.(1951). The Origins of Totalitarianism. NY: Harcourt, Brace.

Arias Trujillo, R. (2006). "Del Frente Nacional a nuestros días". In: *Historia de Colombia. Todo lo que hay que saber.* Ed. Taurus Pensamiento. 311 – 366.

Audard, C. (2009). *Qu'est-ce que le libéralisme ? Ethique, politique, société.* Paris: Gallimard.

Bataille, G. (1991). The Accursed Share. Vol. 1: Consumption. New York: Zone Books.

Bauman, Z. (2001). *Community. Seeking Safety in an Insecure World.* Cambridge: Polity Press.

Bauman, Z. (1995). *Modernity and Ambivalence.* Cambridge: Polity Press.

Bauman, Z. (1989). *Modernity and The Holocaust.* Ithaca: Cornell University Press.

66 K. Polanyi notably retraced the genealogy of this precise situation in the cycle of a new phase of the liberal model's self-referentiality (cf. Polanyi 1944).

BOLTANSKI, L. (2011). *On Critique. A Sociology of Emancipation.* Cambridge: Polity Press.

BOURDIEU, P. (1998). *Practical Reason. On the Theory of Action.* Oxford: John Wiley & Sons.

BUTLER, J. (1990). Gender Trouble. Feminism and the Subversion of Identity. New York: Routledge.

BOUVIER, V. M. (2009). Colombia, Building Peace in a Time of War. Washington US Institute of Peace Press.

CASTEL, Robert (1995). *Métamorphoses de la question sociale (From Manual Workers to Wage Labourers: Transformation of the Social Question).* 400–402.

CASTORIADIS, C. (1998). The Imaginary Institution of Society. Cambridge, MA: MIT Press.

CERTEAU, M. de (1990). *L'invention de quotidien.* Vol. I. Paris: Gallimard.

Columbian Commission of Jurists (Dec. 2009). *Situacíon de los derechos humanos y derecho humanitorion en Colombia 2007–2008.*

Consultaria para los Derechos Humanos y el Desplazamiento (CODHES) (2009). *Desplazamiento Forzado. Hasta cuándo un Estado de Cosas Inconstitucional?* Bogotá: Ed. Ántropos.

Corporación Derechos Para la Paz (CDPAZ) – Planeta Paz (2009). *Observatorio Nacional de Paz. Documento de presentación hacia la Comisión europea.* Bogotá: documento no publicado.

DEJOURS, C. (1993). Intelligence pratique et savoir pratique: deux dimensions méconnues du travail réel. In: *Education permanente.* Nr. 116. 47–70.

FALS BORDA, O.et al. (1962). *La violencia en Colombia* Bogotá: Universidad Nacional.

FOUCAULT, M. (1989). *Surveillir et punir. Naissance de la prison (Discipline and Punish: The Birth of the Prison).* Paris: Gallimard. 140.

FOUCAULT, M. (1977). *Discipline and Punish: The Birth of the* Prison. New York: Random House.

FRASER, N. (1997). *Justice Interruptus: Critical Reflections on the 'Postsocialist' Condition.* New York: Routledge.

GIRARD, R. (2007). *Achever Clausewitz.* Paris: Carnet Nord.

GIRARD, R. (1987). Things Hidden since the Foundation of the World. Stanford: Stanford University Press.

GIRARD, R. (1977). Violence and the Sacred. Baltimore: Johns Hopkins UP.

GOFFMAN, E. (1956). The Presentation of Self in Everyday Life. Edinburgh: Univereity of Edinburgh Press.

GONZÁLEZ POSSO, C./Herbolzheimer, K./Montaña Mestizo, T. (2010). *La vía ciudadana para construir la paz. Más allá de la derrota o de la negociación.* Bogotá: Indepaz Ed.

HOBSBAWN, E. (1987). The Age of Empire, 1875–1914. New York: Pantheon Books.

HOBSBAWN, E. (1975). The Age of Capital, 1848–1875. New York: Scribner.

HOBSBAWN, E. (1962). The Age of Revolution: Europe 1789–1848. London: Weidenfeld and Nicolson.

Kis, J. (1989). *L'egale dignité. Essai sur les fondements des droits de L'homme.* Paris: Seuil.

Kristeva, J. (2001). Female Genius: Life, Madness, Words. Vol. 1: Hannah Arendt. New York: Columbia University Press.

Lefort, C. (1986). Essais sur la politique. XIXe–Xxe siècles. Paris: Seuil.

Lévinas, E. (1969). Totality and Infinity. An Essay on Exteriority. Pittsburgh: Duquesne University Press.

Luhmann, N. (1997). Die Gesellschaft der Gesellschaft. Frankfurt: Herder.

Movimiento nacional de Victimas de Crimenes de Estado (MOVICE) (2009). *Sin Justicia y Sin Paz. Verdad Fragmentada, Reparación Ausente.* Bogotá.

Marx, K. (2007). Economic and Philosophic Manuscripts of 1844. New York: Dover.

Marx, K. (1998). *The German Ideology* (1845 – 1846). Amherst, NY: Prometheus Books.

Marx, K. (1970). *Critique of Hegel's Philosophy of Right* (1843). J. O'Malley, A. Jolin ed. Cambridge: Cambridge University Press.

Mauss, M. (2007). *Essai sur le don. Forme et raison de l'échange dans le sociétés archaïques.* Paris: PUF.

Movimiento nacional de Victimas de Crimenes de Estado (MOVICE) (2009). *Sin Justicia y Sin Paz. Verdad Fragmentada, Reparación Ausente.* Bogotá.

Múnera Ruiz, L. and Rodrígues Sanchez, N. ed. (2009). *Fragmentos de la Público-Político. Colombia siglo XIX.* Bogotá: La Careta Edítores.

Múnera Ruiz, L. (2008a). Normalidad y exceptionalidad en la politica. In: Luis Múnera Ruiz, L. ed.: *Normalidad y exceptionalidad en la politica (Schmitt, Agamben, Zizek y Virno).* Bogotá: Universidad nacional de Colombia. 13 – 49.

Múnera Ruiz, L. (2008b). Démocratie, mouvements sociaux et Université (1991 – 2011). In: *Démocratie et droits humains en Colombie. Quelle place pour les mouvements sociaux et la société civile?* Texts written for an Inter-disciplinary Project Target (PIC). UCL. 34.

Múnera Ruiz, L. (Mar. 2008c)."Colombia: El grado cero de la politica". *Communication au Grial*, Université catholique de Louvain. unpublished.

Múnera Ruiz, L. (Apr. 2007). "Genesis de los movimientos populares en Colombia", *Communication à la conférence "Colombie: des chemins vers la paix".* Université catholique de Louvain.

Múnera Ruiz, L. (2006). Proceso de paz con actores armados ilegales y parasistémicos. Los paramilitares y las politicas de reconciliacíon en Colombia. In: Pensamiento Juridico 17.

Múnera Ruiz, L. (1997). *Relations de pouvoir et mouvements populaire en Colombie (1968 – 1998),* Louvain-la-Neuve: Académia Bruylant.

Nanteuil, de M. (2009). *La Démocratie insensible, Economie et politique à l'épreuve du corps.* Toulouse: Erès.

Polanyi, K. (1944). The Great Transformation: The Political and Economic Origins of Our Time. New York: Farrar & Reinhart.

Rangel Suárez, A. ed. (2009). *Justicia y Paz. Cual es el precio que debemos pagar?.* Bogotá: Intermedio Ed.

Revista Pensiamento Jurídico (Nov.–Dec. 2006). Bogotá. Colombia No. 17.
ROMERO, M. (Apr. 2007) "Desplazamiento forzado: entre la guerra y la economia politica del despojo". *Communication à la conférence "Colombie : des chemins vers la paix"*. Université catholique de Louvain.
RICOEUR, P. (1974). The Conflict of Interpretations: Essays in Hermeneutics. Evanston: Northwestern University Press.
TOURAINE, A. (1995). *Critique of Modernity*. Oxford: Blackwell.
TOURAINE, A. (1997). *What is Democracy*? Bolder:Westwiew Press.
UPRIMMY, R./SAFFON, M.-P. (2009). Usos y abusos de la justicia transicional en Colombia. In: RANGEL SUAREZ, A.ed.: *Justicia y Paz. Cual es el precio que debemos pagar?*. Bogotá: Intermedio Ed. 161–236.
VALENCIA VILLA, H. (2003). *Diccionario de los Derechos Humanos*. Madrid: Espasa. 98–99.
WEIL, E.(1982). *Philosophie et réalité* Paris: Beauchesne.
WOLF, M. ed. (2005). *Regresan siempre en primavera*. Barcelona: Icaria.

Appendix

Human Rights

One can evaluate human rights in two ways:

- diachronically, listing all human rights violations during a specific period;
- synchronically, presenting the various types of violation at a given time.

Diachronic evaluation

We can henceforth say that within thirty years, from 1975 to 2001, the actions of the Guerrilla, the paramilitaries, the armed forces, and the Police caused more than 100000 political homicides, two and a half million displaced people, or more exactly "exiles," sixteen thousand prisoners, and five thousand disappeared persons. Sources: Colombian Jurists' Commission (CCJ), Asfaddes, CODHES, País Libre, listed in Luis Múnera, "Colombia: El grado cero de la politica" (Communication in the GRIAL, Catholic University of Louvain, Mar. 2008, unpublished). The differences from recent figures (see below) are related to the fact that forced disappearances end in homicide. Both categories tend to be grouped together when bodies are found. The same applies to detentions: people can be freed or murdered. They then enter another category (see below).

Synchronic Evaluation

These numbers need to be updated with recent changes to present a synchronic reading.

- Between July 2002 and June 2006, 11 292 non-combatant *detainees-disappeared persons* were murdered. Source: Colombian Jurists' Commission, "Colombie 2002–2006: situation des droits humains et du droit humanitaire" (2006 : 2). In this document the Commission adds that the data for 2006 contain only the figures of the first semester, because listings were unavailabe when the synthesis was made. The data thus under-represents reality. Altogether, we have to notice that the main responsibility for these kinds of violations continue to lie with paramilitary groups. Originally, between July 1996 and June 2006, they accounted for 71.06 % of deaths for socio-political, non-combatant motives. Source: Colombian Jurists' Commission (ibid.: 9).
- More recently, between July 2007 and June 2008, 1, 470 *persons lost their lives "out of combat."* 1,344 were homicide victims, fifty bodies of forcably disappeared people were found (likened to homicides), of 126 forced disappearances no bodies were found. Amongst these were 105 women and 61 children. The Colombian Commission of Jurists attributes these deaths, according to the figures they report, as follows: 32.4 % of homicides (913 people) by known authors were committed by the State agents, 50.4 % by paramilitaries, 17,2 % by guerrillas. As for forced disappearances, the bodies of 126 people were never found. 40.7 % could be directly attributed to state agents, 53.1 % were carried out by paramilitaries, 6.2 % by guerrillas. Source: Colombian Commission of Jurists, "Situación de derechos humanos y derecho humanitario, 2007–2008" (3–4).
- All in all, the figures which prompt a global evaluation of the number of *forced disappearances* vary between 30,000 (FIDH 2008) and 50,000 (MOVICE 2009). In an aforementioned document the Colombian Commission of Jurists estimates the number of persons reported missing between 1996 and 2002 at 20,000 (CCJ, on 2006). We note, however, that there is always uncertainty as to the exact evaluation of forced disappearance cases. The actors are not always known and when they are known and bodies are found, as already mentioned, the forced disappearances fall under the category of homicides. Sources: Movimiento Nacional de Victimas de Crimenes del Estado (MOVICE), *Sin Justicia y Sin La Paz. Verdad Fragmentada, Reparación Ausente*, (Bogotá: 2009); International Federation for Human Rights (FIDH), *Résolution du Bureau international de la FIDH sur la Colombie*, (May 2008); Colombian Jurists' Commission, "Colombie 2002–2006: situation des droits humains et du droit humanitaire" (2006).

- As far as *massacres* are concerned, the Colombian Commission of Jurists raises the figures from the last listed period (between July 2006 – June 2007 and July 2007 – June 2008). During the first time-period, 17 massacres claimed 82 victims. During the second period, 126 persons were killed in 25 massacres. 22 % were committed by State agents, 66.2 % by paramilitaries, and 11.7 % by guerrillas. Source: Colombian Commission of Jurists (ibid.: 4). The same document analyses recent changes in *extra-judicial executions* carried out by the armed forces and police. The number of extra-judicial executions has risen constantly, from 127 (July 2002 – June 2003), to 197 (July 2004 – June 2005), till 274 (July 2007 – June 2008). Source: Colombian Jurists' Commission (ibid.: 7).
- For *the victims of forced displacement or "banishment"*, the most reliable results are supplied by *Consultoría para los Derechos Humanos y el Desplazamiento* (CODHES), the non-governmental organization which carries out a systematic follow-up for this population sector. According to this organization, the annual average of displaced people between the first half of 1999 and the first half of 2002 was 328,880, whereas the average reached between the second half of 2002, and the second half of 2005 was 289,813, a 22 % decrease. In absolute terms, we observe the following changes: 412, 553 persons were moved in 2002; 207,607 in 2003; 287,581 in 2004; 310,387 in 2005; 221,638 in 2006; 305,966 in 2007. It is, furthermore, necessary to specify that there are numerous regional variations of such figures. So, in 2007, the departments in which forced displacement was most significant were the following: Bogotá, Nariño, Antioquia, Valle del Cauca, and Santander. Generally, one can assume that around four million displacements were reached by the end of 2007. This places Colombia at the head world-wide. Source: Codhes (http://www.codhes.org/index.php?option=com_docman&task=cat_view&gid=55&Itemid=51).
- On the other hand, *kidnapping*, which constitutes a violation of human rights and International Humanitarian Law, showed a slight decrease, even if it did not disappear. The statistical data of the *Fundación País Libre*, a pro-government organisation, registered the following changes: 3,138 detention victims between 1998 and 2001; but 1,810 between 2002 and 2005; and 604 between 2006 and 2007 (the yearly average). This decrease can be explained by the military and political turn to which the Guerrilla was forced under the pressure from the armed forces and paramilitaries. Between 1996 and 2007, 28.9 % of detentions were committed by the FARC; 22.8 % by the ELN, 16.5 % by criminal bands, and 4.97 % by paramilitaries. In twenty-two per cent of cases, those responsible could not be identified. Source: Múnera Ruiz 2008c; Fundación País Libre (http://www.paislibre.org/images/PDF/informe%20secuestro1996 m1_2007 m12 %20_2_.pdf). In its May 2010 newsletter this organisation considered it impossible to give a precise assessment of detention figures in Colombia. (http://www.paislibre.org/

alfa/index.php?option=com_content&view=article&id=1060&Itemid=31&lang=es).

Trade Union Situation

Tab. 1 – Rate of Unionising

Year	1947	1965	1974	1984	1996	2002	2005
Rate of Unionising	4.7	13.4	12.5	9.3	6	4.9	4.6

Source: Escuela Nacional Sindical (ENS)

Tab. 2 – Homicides of Union Members: World-wide and in Colombia

Year	Number of Homicides World-wide	Number of Homicides in Colombia	%
1999	140	80	57
2000	209	137	66
2001	223	197	88
2002	213	186	85
2003	129	94	73
2004	145	96	66
2005	115	70	61

Source: Escuela Nacional Sindical (ENS) – Cuaderno de Derechos Humanos No.18.

Tab. 3 –Violations of the Rights to Life, Liberty, and Integrity for Colombian Trade Unionists

Kind of Violation Year	2000	2001	2002	2003	2004	2006	2007
Homicide	137	197	186	94	96	72	39
Death Threat	180	234	190	296	445	244	224
Attack with or without injury	13	24	17	20	6	5	11
Forced Disappearance	17	12	9	6	7	5	2
Violation of Domicile	1	1	–	12	3	2	4
Arbitrary Detention	37	8	11	49	77	16	19
Harassment	2	13	19	54	17	22	16
Confinement	24	41	27	7	5	5	0
Forced Displacement	155	70	2	91	33	7	101

(Continued)

Kind of Violation Year	2000	2001	2002	2003	2004	2006	2007
Torture	2	1	1	–	1	4	2

Source – Escuela Nacional Sindical (ENS)
Actualized in the Human Rights Quaterly, No. 2
NB – The notable increase in numbers of forced displacement is tied to the ENS' concentrated focus on this matter. One knows, that previously they were seldom declared, for different reasons, among which, fear of reprisal. Between 1991 and 2006, 496 trade union leaders were assassinated, between 12 and 65 per year. In this case, 285 can be attributed to paramilitary groups, 147 to guerrilla groups, and 21 to State agents, the rest to common delinquency.

Tab. 4 – Number of Collective Agreements

Year	2000	2001	2002	2003	2004	2005	2006
Number of collective agreements	648	483	700	284	628	360	141

Source – Escuela Nacional Sindical (ENS)Socio-Economic Numbers

Tab. 5 –Direct Foreign Investment (Jan. 2002 – Sept. 2009)

Region	Jan. 2002 – Sept. 2009
North Ameria	11847.6
Europe	6349.4
Antilles	4635.4
Central America	3999.8
South America	1390.1
Asia	157.4
Rest of the World	146.3

In million US$; Source – Ministerio de Comercio, Industria y Turismo, Dirección de relaciones comerciales (Ministry of Trade, Industry and Tourism, Directive on Commercial Relations), Feb. 2010.

Tab. 6.1 & 6.2 – Exchange Volume with the EU and international specialisation

Year	2003	2004	2005	2006	2007	2008
Commercial Exchange Volume (import-export)	4046	4648	5706	6887	8446	10090

In million US$; Source: Ministerio de Comercio, Industria y Turismo, Dirección de relaciones comerciales (Ministry of Trade, Industry and Tourism, Directive on Commercial Relations), Feb. 2010.

Tab. 6 (continued)

Principal Exports	2009 (%)	Principal Imports	2009 (%)
Coal	53.7	Machines and equipment goods	52.5
Bananas	11.5	Chemical Products	24.4
Coffee	9.2	Metallurgy	5
Petrol and Petroleum derivatives	5.9	Automobile Industry	4.1
Ferronickel	5.4	Paper	2.4
Flowers	2		

NB – In 2009 the EU was both the second largest foreign investor and the second largest source for Colombia's imports.

Tab. 7 – Employment, Under-Employment and Informal Sector Figures

Year Indicators	2001	2002	2003	2004	2005	2006	2007	2008	2009
Employment Figures	14.9	15.5	14.1	13.6	11.8	12	11.2	11.3	12
Under-employment Figures	31.7	34.8	32.3	31.8	31.9	33.9	35	29.1	29.7
Figures for the informal Sector	60.5	61.3	60.6	58.6	58.7	58.5	56.6	55.9	60

Source – Misión para el Empalme de la Series de Empleo, Pobreza y Desigualdad 2009 (MESEP)

NB – Under-employment is characterised as: insufficient income, insufficient working hours and/or being over-qualified (for example, a qualified doctor working as a taxi driver).

Tab. 8 – Figures of destitution and poverty (urban/rural areas)

Year Indicators	2002	2005	2008
Figures of poverty			
Urban	40.3	37.4	30.7
Rural	69.3	67	66.2
Figures of indigence			
Urban	9.4	7.4	6.8
Rural	32.5	27.4	32.6

Source – Misión para el Empalme de la Series de Empleo, Pobreza y Desigualdad 2009 (MESEP)

Mariana Chacón/Witold Mucha

Indigenous Voices in the Andean Region

A Comparative Perspective on the Transitional Processes in Bolivia and Peru

Introduction

During the last decade, the political landscape in Latin America has been characterized by a shift towards left-wing oriented governments staying in or taking over political power. Inaugurations of presidential candidates like Luiz Inacio Lula da Silva in Brazil, Michele Bachelet in Chile or Tabaré Vazquez in Uruguay instantly raised expectations among those segments of societies which had historically been marginalized and discriminated against: the indigenous peoples. Their call for genuine participation, empowerment and socio-economic as well as political access became the 'loudest' voice in the run-up as well as aftermath of the respective elections. Hence, polarizing leaders like Hugo Chavez in Venezuela or Evo Morales in Bolivia learned to make use of that cultural-ideological instrument by further cementing the Manichean rift between the so-called indigenous and non-indigenous people. The question whether this 'indigenous rise' has effectively stabilized the democratic culture, system, and legitimacy in various Latin American countries remains to be resolved. The present article analyses to what extent those indigenous movements can be considered as such and whether they have initiated and marked a genuine transitional process.

This paper will give attention to the Andean region. Being a region with an abundance of a variety of natural resources, the five Andean countries (Bolivia, Colombia, Ecuador, Peru, and Venezuela) are characterized by a multitude of governance problems. Although varying from country to country, these include political instability, frequent constitutional reforms, presidential crises, and a volatility of democratic institutions and violence. Out of these, Peru and Bolivia are selected as empirical case studies. This is due to both countries' common characteristics, such as their colonial past, democratization process as well as socio-ethnic composition. More concretely, according to the prevalent time series values both countries qualify as lower-middle-income economies (World Bank Atlas 2010). Second, Peru has traditionally been dependent on minerals and metals; Bolivia's external sector of the economy relies more on energy and fuels as well as ores and metals and accounts for almost two-thirds of its total exports (ECLAC 2007). Third, Bolivia's ethno-social composition generally resembles the Peruvian equivalent by consisting of one large indigenous group (Bolivia: Quechua and

Aymara 55 %; Peru: Amerindian 45 %), a mestizo one (30 resp. 35 %) and a white group (both 15 %) (CIA World Factbook 2010). This composition has always included a vast number of indigenous people that have traditionally been discriminated against and lived in the peripheral margins of both countries' social structure. Paradoxically, the indigenous population has been at the centre of important political changes and social turmoil in both countries. However, the role of indigenous movements, where existing, has varied in each country.

This article elaborates to what extent the transitional processes in both countries have been determined by indigenous movements or, in other words, what role does the indigenous 'voice' play. It is structured as follows: It will present an overview of both Bolivia's and Peru's history and traditional conflict patterns. Then, their transitional actors and institutions, with respect to the significance of the indigenous identity and its reinforcement, will be cursorily depicted. Finally, we will look at the current state of the indigenous population in both countries.

Bolivia 1985 – 2000: "Democracia Pactada" and "Nueva Política Económica"

Before delving into the recent developments of the Bolivian transitional process since the inauguration of the first indigenous president Evo Morales in 2005, it is important to give a brief overview of the major structural patterns of the Republic of Bolivia that was established in 1985.

After decades of chronic political instability since 1952, the inauguration of the Victor Paz Estenssoro government in 1985 introduced a phase of democratic stability which was characterized by two major features: the "Democracia Pactada" (Pacted Democracy) and the "Nueva Política Económica" (New Economy Policy), which led to the strengthening of the political center-right, and the party system got concentrated on three parties which sustained the Bolivian reform agenda throughout the first 15 years of democracy. Until 2005 these three parties, the "Movimiento Nacionalista Revolucionario" (MNR – Revolutionary Nationalist Movement), the "Acción Democrática Nacionalista" (ADN – Nationalist Democratic Action), and the leftist "Movimiento de la Izquierda Revolucionaria" (MIR – Movement of the Revolutionary Left), which continuously formed parliamentary power alliances and alternately participated in the government coalitions, provided the president (Alenda 2004: 4). That party-political convergence enabled the implementation of structural adjustment policies according to the 'Washington Consensus' approach and thus simultaneously weakened the labor and peasant organizations. The historically evolved corporatist conflict pattern between the military on the one hand and the labor unions on the other was superseded by the institutionalized cooperation between political parties (cf. Zilla 2006: 8).

The implementation of the structural adjustment policies represents the second crucial feature. At the end of Aug. 1985, the Paz Estenssoro government initiated the "Nueva Política Económica" due to pressure from international financial entities such as the World Bank and the International Monetary Fund (IMF), which made loans dependent upon the respective measures. "The [Nueva Política Económica] consisted of the usual recipe of reducing the fiscal deficit, reforming the monetary system, rationalizing the bureaucracy (through mass dismissals), liberalizing markets, promoting exports, and reforming the tax system" (Salman 2007: 116). Indeed, Bolivia had been the first Latin American country exerting a structural adjustment program (SAP) under democratic rule. Compared to other countries in the region, this SAP stood out due to its fast pace and broad reach which successfully reduced hyperinflation and thus was given the poor people's consent (cf. Wolff 2004: 41). However, the "Nueva Política Económica" did not result in macroeconomic success; instead it facilitated the laundering of revenues deriving from drug-trade – i.e. through investment in sectors such as construction, public utilities, banking etc. (Vellinga 1998: 21). Irrespectively of the multitude of measures against narco-dollar dynamics – e.g. coca leaf eradication or coca substitution programs –, the social costs of that initiative were huge: the coca growing regions were militarized. The policy of voluntary compensated crop eradication was substituted by forced eradication through armed security forces which led to massive human rights abuses against peasants. In turn, the peasants joined together and organized themselves in order to defend their communities and crops (cf. Gordon 2006: 16).

In summary, the first important steps of democratic transition in the Bolivian Republic were primarily shaped by two basic principles: First, the political stability of the Bolivian Republic's first 15 years of democratic consolidation between 1985 until the end of the 20th century was safeguarded by the consensual politics of the "Democracia Pactada" and the structural adjustment policies ("Nueva Política Económica"). Importantly, the comprehensive consensus sustained by the three major parties led to the substantial weakening of labor and peasant unions. As will be depicted below, that development bore relevant repercussions on the role of the indigenous 'voice' within those unions (cf. Goedeking 2003).

Second, the massive coca eradication programs led to tensions between coca growers and the respective Bolivian governments. However, analogous to the stabilizing effects of the party-political convergence, these tensions did not erupt into large-scale violence. This is due to the fact that the coca growers did not solely depend on coca production, given that the respective regions (e.g. Chapare) were able to diversify their production to legal crops instead of the coca leaf (cf. Toledo 2007: 65). Furthermore, the absence of armed group formations, such as the Sendero Luminoso in Peru, has been crucial. The coca growers, deprived by the income losses coming along with the eradication programs, indeed opposed these measures. But unlike the Peruvian case, they made use of rather informal political articulation strategies like roadblocks and protest marches, which were supported, by the corresponding political parties and social organizations (cf. Interview Espinoza 2008; Graubner 2007: 18).

Hence, the democratic consolidation developed along relatively stable coordinates during the first 15 years of the Republic of Bolivia. Yet at the end of the 20th century, the negative long-term side-effects of the "Democracia Pactada" became apparent, when conflict escalations erupted during the so-called "Guerra del Agua" (water war) in Cochabamba (1999 and 2000), the "Guerra del Gas" (gas war) in La Paz (2003 and 2005) or recently the violent disputes in Pando on the consequences of the Constituent Assembly (2008).

Whether post-2000 Bolivia accounts for a "*País Rebelde*" (rebellious country) and what role the indigenous communities have played during that period, these issues will be elaborated on in the following sections.

Post-2000 Bolivia: "*Un País Rebelde?*"

More than a hundred people were killed between 1999 and 2009 as direct consequence of demonstrations, protests and street blockades in Bolivia. Scholars, civil society activists and political observers have depicted several crucial factors responsible for the conflict escalations: In line with a deep recession between 1999 and 2004, there were "the collapse of conventional party politics (...); the decay of a number of key institutions (...); unemployment rising much faster (...); and very high levels of politicization (...) (Mosley 2007: 1)." In the following, three major conflicts since 2000 will be cursorily depicted and analyzed with respect to the indigenous communities' role.

"Guerra del Agua" (1999 and 2000): In Apr. 2000, the Bolivian city of Cochabamba erupted into protests organized by the "Confederacíon Sindical Unica de Trabajadores Campesinos de Bolivia" (CSUTCB – Unitary Union Confederation of Bolivian Peasant Workers) over attempts to privatize its drinking water and sewerage services under Law 2029. The then so-called "Guerra del Agua" took on national relevance, in particular in various parts of western and central Bolivia, as tens of thousands of people went on the streets to demonstrate against the price increases (up to 275 %). Although the government declared a state of siege, in the process of suppressing these blockades, four people were killed, at least one of them by the military. Ultimately though, the mass mobilized protest forced the government to rescind the concession previously made to the foreign-owned company "Aguas de Tunari" (Perreault 2006: 150).

Irrespective of the lessons learned within this context – e.g. weakening of the political establishment's legitimacy; emergence of horizontally organized protest coalitions –, it is important to put on record that political instability had derived from political flaws respectively the authorities' poor governance (cf. Dangl 2007: 69). The protesters went to the streets, fearing economic grievances they would endure in the near future when the water prices would increase. "First, protestors demanded procedural justice, calling for greater participation and transparency in decisions over the management of natural resources. Secondly, [they] demanded distributive justice, calling for more equitable distribution of the benefits deriving from [these] resources" (Perreault 2006: 154).

With respect to the 'indigenous' dimension of the "Guerra del Agua" in Cochabamba, the episode reveals no causal relationship, due to the heterogeneity of the social as well as ethnic composition of the movement. Given the large-scale impact of a possible water price increase, almost everybody joined the protests: These included the local population, Cochabamba's neighborhood associations, the coca growers from Chapare, the middle class, and even the Catholic Church. The same holds true for the ethnic perspective: the heterogeneous composition of the protest movement did not align along ethnic lines. Significantly, the (predominantly indigenous) rural areas worked together with the urban (predominantly mestizo) ones (cf. Crabtree 2005: 28). Hence, the movement did not go on the streets due to ethnic-cultural inequity or aspirations for financial gains and profit but due to equitable access to water.

"Guerra del Gas" (2003 and 2005): The "Guerra del Gas" in Oct. 2003 constituted one of the most critical phases of Bolivia's democracy since democratic rule was re-established in 1985. "The second administration of then -President Gonzalo Sánchez de Lozada, which was ultimately evicted in October by the popular revolt, killed more people in 14 months than did [General] Hugo Bánzer's seven-year military dictatorship" (Arze and Kruse 2004: 23). Tens of thousands of protesters participated in violent demonstrations against the De Lozada government. These were caused by the government's intention to export natural gas via a Chilean sea port in the Pacific. The prospect of making the country's exports dependent on Chile would be difficult to sell to public opinion, given that Bolivia had lost its coast – i. e. the maritime province of Antofagasta – to Chile in the War of the Pacific in the 1870s, which had made Bolivia a landlocked country (cf. Perreault 2006: 161). "As every schoolchild knows, recovery of the lost department is a duty, and the country's armed forces have long seen this as their mission" (Crabtree 2005: 99). As reaction to the protests the government responded by using military force against the demonstrators, which resulted in around 70 fatalities and 200 wounded. Being repudiated by large sectors of the population, De Lozada resigned and fled to the United States. Carlos Mesa, then vice-president, constitutionally succeeded him (cf. Ames, Pérez-Liñán and Seligson 2004: 9).

From a perspective of conflict resolution and similar to the "Guerra del Agua", the flawed governance of the De Lozada administration is striking: The government responded to protests by the use of military violence. Furthermore, the grievances felt by the protesters were not based on one certain group being socially, politically, and economically deprived. Again, a multitude of heterogeneous (and often antagonistic) social actors built up one protest movement against one single adversary: the government. This included, amongst others, a variety of Aymara peasants from the Altiplano, miners, workers, urban protesters from the poorer sectors of La Paz, and middle-class people from La Paz tired of the state violence (cf. Webber 2005: 39). No ethnic groups fought against each other, and indigenous actors acquired a leading role in the protest movement. In particular, the Aymara campesinos from the Altiplano played a major role in spearheading the protests against the De Lozada administration (cf. Hylton and Thompson 2004: 15). Significantly, their previous demands over indigenous autonomy and dignity within the so far exclusive Bolivian state had merged with the overarching call for the government's resignation (cf. Webber 2005: 39). Hence, the ethnic affiliation held a cohesive function within the protest movement, though it was not a founding one.

The gas issue became important again in summer 2005. At first, Mesa's succession of De Lozada had temporarily eased the national crisis in Bolivia. Indeed, as announced at his inauguration, he had submitted the contested gas issue to the public by calling for a national referendum in which voters were asked to give their opinion on the future of the country's oil and gas reserves in July 2004 (cf. McNeish 2006: 221). The referendum's outcome was the approving of the export of gas, albeit under stronger state control. Despite that tactical victory, Mesa was ousted in June 2005 in the context of new large-scale road blockades and protests of the same actors demanding the nationalization of the gas reserves. Given the threat of violence escalation and growing secession demands by the eastern provinces, this time Mesa did not order the security apparatus to intervene. He rather resigned, and the Congress agreed on the president of the Supreme Court of Justice, Eduardo Rodriguez, as interim president (cf. Salman 2006: 163).

Despite several similarities, the "Guerra del Gas" 2005 bore different characteristics from the "Guerra del Gas" 2003. First, in 2003, the protest movement was geared primarily against De Lozada himself, while Mesa enjoyed broader legitimacy among the public and the different social actors. Second, unlike his predecessor, Mesa did not respond to the demonstrations by making use of the security apparatus as rigorously as it had been the case in

2003. Third, the protest's organizational 'success' was due to the experiences made in prior revolts such as the "Guerra del Gas" 2003 (Dangl 2007: 191).

Again, the flawed governance of the political decision-makers – i. e. the Mesa administration – was crucial. Furthermore, similarly to the conflictive episodes depicted above, the protesters went on the streets due to proximate processes changing the socio-economic as well as political status quo. While the left-indigenous movement, predominantly based in El Alto, showed civil unrest for fear of 'grievances' from increasing water rates, the eastern departments were not willing to waive their political influence and economic wealth. Importantly, both actors protested neither due to their poverty nor unequal economic development. On the one hand, the western highlands had constituted the poorest part of the country for decades, its popular mobilization groups did not go to the streets because of their poor economic state but because of their adherence to the October Agenda that had emerged during the protests in 2003. Mesa's politics seemed to put that into question. Thus, the movement re-articulated its demands for a more 'nationalist' policy with respect to the gas reserves; implicitly, this included the political restructuring of the nation by the means of a Constitutional Assembly (i. e. power distribution and political participation). On the other hand, the eastern provinces, in particular Santa Cruz and Tarija, did not press for regional autonomy for reasons of poverty or unequal income distribution. De facto, these provinces belonged (and still do belong) to the wealthiest of the country. Their protests were driven by their opposition against Mesa's announcements to consider the alteration of the pre-existent hydrocarbons legislation and constitution, which both had always favored the eastern departments. Thus, poverty and income inequality played a relevant role among the (primarily Aymara) "alteños". In sum, the Altiplano actors rebelled due to their fear of being 'sold out' to foreign companies in the wake of further neoliberal politics and the "cruzeño" actors feared their loss of the political and economic status quo – i. e. gas nationalization and a Constitutional Assembly (Interview Condo 2008; Dangl 2007: 189–191).

The 'second' "Guerra del Gas" in 2005 has revealed a strikingly powerful role of the indigenous communities. Prima facie the indigenous pattern seemed obvious: The indigenous western highlands against the 'white' "cruzeño" elites. Indeed, this cleavage holds true for some instances (see below): "The bourgeois ideology of the *cruzeño* discontent is characterized (…) as that of the 'free market, foreign investment, racism, etc.,' which pits the 'modern', 'whiter' Santa Cruz elite against the short, dark-skinned, backward, and anti-capitalist Aymara and Quechua peoples of the western region of Bolivia, especially within the department of La Paz (Webber 2005: 41. Emphasis by the author)." However, despite this pattern's undeniable reality, in the case of the "Guerra del Gas" 2005 both groups primarily protested against the government on the basis of two different motives. This holds even more significance considering the fact that regardless of the respective political proposal – gas nationalization vs. the status quo regarding hydrocarbons legislation – Mesa was perceived as being in favor of one or the other. In addition to that, the heterogeneous anti-gas privatization movement did not define itself according to ethnic characteristics but rather on a left-based ideology, namely as a social class. Moreover, only during the episodes of severe crisis (e. g. "Guerra del Gas" 2003) the different divisions worked effectively together, while most of the time each of these groups rather stuck to its local or regional concerns (cf. Interview Condo 2008 ;Webber 2005: 40).

Hence, the (conflictive) protest movements during the "Guerra del Gas" in 2003 and 2005 were upheld by indigenous actors of the western regions. However, their indigenous identity was rather cohesively 'used' for an overarching common purpose; the ousting of the governments.

Constitutional Reforms (2008): The election of the country's first Aymara-Indian president, Evo Morales, in Dec. 2005 did not bring the climate of instability to a halt. This became apparent in sectarian rioting between miners in Oruro in Oct. 2006 (16 dead), demonstrations in Cochabamba in Jan. 2007 (2 dead) as well as in clashes between opponents and supporters of Morales' reform proposals in the northern department Pando in Sept. 2008 (approximately 30 dead). In terms of political architecture, the Dec. 2005 elections had produced three paradigmatic shifts: First, the traditional political parties had almost completely disappeared (see above). However, this shift by no means meant the stabilization of a new political party system. Second, although Morales had received a political legitimacy not seen before, his government faced an opposition capable of blocking major political initiatives. Third, the formal introduction of the direct prefect election was a first step towards political decentralization (cf. Jost 2006: 7–11).

Despite concerns about conflictive issues regarding the transfer of presidential power, the handing over was carried out in peaceful manner (International Crisis Group 2006: 3). Being inaugurated on Jan. 22, 2006, Morales announced that he would proceed apace with three major campaign pledges: the nationalization of the hydrocarbon sector; the implementation of the land reform; the establishing of a Constituent Assembly to rewrite the pre-existent constitution (cf. International Crisis Group 2007: 1). Indeed, during the first months of presidency no tensions arose in the country. For instance, the hydrocarbon sector was nationalized by decree on May 1, 2006, thereby straining bilateral relations with Bolivia's main recipients Brazil and Argentina (cf. Rochlin 2007: 1331). However, since then, the relevant political and social forces increased their critique on Morales' politics; in particular, the rivalry between the government and the eastern lowlands began to form around the prevailing contested issues of the Constituent Assembly, land reform, and regional autonomy (cf. International Crisis Group 2006: 32). Accordingly, already in Jan. 2007 the International Crisis Group stated: "The political opposition and economic elites equate each proposed reform with a threat to their way of life and seek to use every means available to defeat rather than moderate it. (…) The degree of polarisation is nearing that which led to the premature ouster of Morales' three immediate predecessors in five years, and it potentially threatens national unity" (International Crisis Group 2007: 1). That rivalry between the eastern provinces and the central government would define the future conflict pattern of Bolivia under Morales.

Irrespective of the latest major incident's course of escalation in Pando in Sept. 2008, there are several aspects worth to be mentioned regarding the changes induced by the inauguration of Morales in 2006. His administration has exhibited an authoritarian governance style (e.g. Constituent Assembly voting procedures; disregard of regional autonomy referendums). However, unlike in clashes during previous governments, the military has not been a major violence fuelling force. The recent crisis has rather shown the following conflict pattern: The "cruzeño" elites strive for regional autonomy, in order to maintain their economic and political status quo. Thus, they aim at dismissing the current government against Morales supporters who aspire the redistribution of the nation's wealth to the formerly unprivileged (indigenous) majority. Hence, the 'duelling referendums' which these two camps continuously apply, in order to subdue the other side can indeed be identified as a violence fuelling mechanism (cf. International Crisis Group 2008: 1). In particular, the lowland departments' elites have repeatedly called for civil unrest due to the political and economic grievances they potentially fear in the wake of a new constitution. Thus, their call for regional autonomy was a reaction and means against indigenous mobilization.

As far as the 'indigenous' dimension is concerned, due to Morales' Indian ancestry and its use as cohesion instrument for the indigenous electorate, ethnic polarization has become a more relevant component than had been the case in the prior conflictive episodes. The pre-existent western/"alteño" vs. eastern/"cruzeño" rift has deepened even further, due to the fact that both camps effectively instrumentalize the ethnic question (cf. Romero 2009). Whether this strategy was in support of a genuine indigenous transitional process in contemporary Bolivia will be discussed in the concluding section.

Indigenous Voices under the New Constitution

In the context of field research in Bolivia in 2008, indigenous development worker Freddy Condo questioned the assumption "from abroad" with respect to a coherent indigenous identity: "(…) [There] are at least 36 ethnic groups in present Bolivia. Apart from these 36, there is a multitude of different groups within these 36. (…) There is no such thing as the 'indigenous' Bolivian. This is a concept from abroad. For instance, if you go to the communities near San Julian [i. e. town in Santa Cruz department], there are villages where indigenous peasants live. These would rather call themselves as belonging to their home village than to one specific ethnic group" (Interview Condo 2008). Except during severe escalations – e.g. the "Guerra del Gas" –, the ethnic groups Aymara, Quechua, Mestizo, and European do not represent cohesive characteristics. Neither do the supposedly deprived Aymara and Quechua work together, nor do these groups intrinsically exhibit collective identities themselves: the individual communities identify themselves pursuant to their village rather than to any form of a collective 'indigenous' group (cf. Interview Condo 2008; Interview Arrueta 2008).

Despite such indigenous heterogeneity, today's Bolivia under Evo Morales bears potential for political instability when two factors are challenged: First, new conflicts might arise when future projects – i.e. particularly the implementation of the new Constitution – are piloted without a majority consensus among the influential (non-)parliamentary opposition and its supporters from the eastern lowlands. Second, the escalation becomes even more likely when the redistribution politics – e.g. land reform, hydrocarbons nationalization – affect those which see their current political and socio-economic status quo at stake. Although the considerate reactions of both political camps to the Pando escalations in Sept. 2008 have shown that there is still sufficient potential for political consent, the changed actor-constellation will remain highly conflictive in the near future. It seems unlikely that the formerly 'untouchable' political and economic elites from the prosperous eastern departments will accept the redistribution of the nation's wealth at their expense.

The latest political developments in Bolivia seem to point to two significant political trends:

1.) As far as the majority consensus is concerned, in the Dec. 6, 2009 elections Morales and the congressional candidates from his "Movimiento al Socialismo" (MAS) headed to clear victories. On the basis of strong majorities in both chambers of the legislative assembly and electoral gains in departments formerly dominated by the opposition, today the Morales government possesses a substantial political legitimacy. This legitimacy will open the way to deepen the already commenced pro-indigenous policies (cf. Nueva Crónica 2009/52: 3).

Analogous to the conclusions made above, Morales' expanding political power is supported broadly but not unanimously among his primary voters – that is, Bolivia's indigenous majority. While radical groups such as the "Ponchos Rojos" (Red Ponchos) praise the outcome of the elections as a revolutionary process of change, others such as René Joaquino, an indigenous candidate opposing the MAS, are concerned about the future of political decisions: "No one knows what will happen if a government attains absolute power" (Romero 2009). Opponents from the political left-wing such as the Aymara leader Felipe Quispe focus their critique on the president himself:

"This government exists to spend money on (...) [his] campaigns at the expense of the rest of us. (...) [He] is an Indian dressed in fancy clothing, surrounded by white men and mestizos" (Romero and Schipani 2009). Hence, the broad electoral legitimacy seems to have stabilized the present political architecture. However, the government's dominance might lead to inner-party rivalries which could add a further destabilizing factor setup, besides the prevailing lowland departments.

2.) In terms of the "alteño" / "cruzeño"-polarization, the election results have strengthened Morales' position. In particular, in the two gas-rich (and therefore recalcitrant) areas Tarija and Santa Cruz his party gained further ground which thus enables him to easier redirect petroleum revenue in order, to increase the promised social spending to the rural indigenous sectors (cf. Romero and Schipani 2009).

Nevertheless, the lowland departments' opposition remains influential for the political decision-making in La Paz. For instance, the new Constitution is regarded with skepticism, due to the duration of presidential terms. The eastern departments fear that Morales, who has already served four years and is formally limited to one additional five-year term, might attempt to remove term limits, as President Hugo Chávez did in Venezuela (Romero and Schipani 2009). Hence, the departmental and municipal elections in Apr. 2010 hold enormous political significance to the democratic architecture of the Republic of Bolivia. Three major results can be summarized: On the national level the MAS seems to consolidate its parliamentary power, due to the opposition's weak electorate support. However, on the communal level the oppositional groups have gained strength and (re-)articulate their local demands in a more cohesive manner towards the MAS-ruled government. Significantly, former MAS party members and middle class segments slowly turn away from the government party. This is due to the increasingly authoritarian governance style applied by Morales as well as the break with the strongest political ally – i. e. the "Movimiento sin Miedo" (MSM – Movement without Fear) (Buitrago 2010: 4 – 7). However, the present vertical power division between the central government – i. e. Morales administration – and the regional opposition – i. e. lowland departments – might redefine the potential for pro-indigenous reforms in the years to come (cf. Nueva Crónica 2009: 3).

Irrespective of the current political actor constellation, the previous analysis has shown that ethnicity indeed has played a role in the transitional process in Bolivia. However, its cohesive power applied in several different conflict contexts reveals a strikingly volatile nature. During the "Guerra del Agua" and the first "Guerra del Gas" the crucial collective 'bargaining chip' had not been configured along ethnic lines. In contrast to that, the ousting of Mesa in 2005 and the clashes in Pando in 2008 bore the signature of ethnic instrumentalization.

This optional and to some extent arbitrary use of the category 'identity' does not only reveal the enormous mobilizing power of ethnicity in Bolivia. One important finding seems to be that the direction of that mobilization – be it left/ right, indigenous/ not indigenous etc. – remains secondary. Hence, major political changes are inevitably influenced by indigenous demands and discourses. To put it in succinct terms, in any case the indigenous 'voice' is listened to in Bolivia.

Peru and Its Indigenous Population: A Story of Misconstructions

As it happened in other Andean countries, the story of the relationship between the state and the indigenous population in the Peruvian territory has been marked by the prolongation of the colonial structure that, since the 16th century, condemned the so called "indios" to the paradoxical situation of being second-class citizens in their own land (Pajuelo 2005: 111). However, the results of this complicated relationship were not the same in all Andean countries: Peru did not have indigenous movements similar to or as strong as the ones that have emerged in Bolivia or Ecuador, albeit having a population with a predominant indigenous origin (cf. De Ferrari 2008). Ever since 1821, the year in which the Peruvian Republic was founded, a political system of apparent legal equality that actually excluded the indigenous population from the political public scene was established (cf. Quijano 2006: 18; Guerrero 1997: 100).

This situation changed in the second decade of the 20th century, when new social groups emerged and started to question the hegemony of the dominant oligarchy. What prompted this new scenario? Indigenous mobilizations around the end of the 19th century (cf. Pajuelo 2005: 112) and the birth of "indigenismo", a cultural, political and anthropological current of thought, concentrated on the study and revaluation of the indigenous cultures, and the questioning of the discrimination mechanisms that affected the indigenous peoples. These factors, among others, were responsible for drawing attention to what was labelled "the indigenous problem".

There was also an institutional and judicial response to these new developments: the 1920 Peruvian Constitution recognized the legal existence of "indigenous communities" for the first time and stated that the Peruvian state would protect the "indigenous race" and enact laws that would promote their development and culture in harmony with their needs (1920 Peruvian Constitution: art. 58). Whatever the reasons, the first institutions dedicated to guarantee the indigenous "race" appeared, although with a clear paternalistic overtone (Landa 2006: 130). The *Sección de Asuntos Indígenas* (Berau of Indigenous Affairs) was created, alongside the Patronato de la Raza Indígena (Indigenous Race Board); the *Día del Indio* (Day of the Indio) was proclaimed and President Leguía (1919 – 1930) called himself Wiracocha: the "Apu", main

Andean divinity and protector of the indigenous communities (Astuhuamán and Daggett 2006: 26). This had much to do with Leguía's desire to expand his political popularity and little to do with his conviction about the need to enforce the rights of the indigenous population.

The *Instituto Indigenista Peruano* (Peruvian Indigenous Institute) was founded in 1946 and its goal was to elaborate state policies to achieve the "integration" of the "indio" to the "national society" (Sánchez 2001). The objective of this initiative was to institutionally promote the assimilation process, i. e., to encourage the conversion of the "indios" into "citizens" who would resemble the dominant culture rather than the indigenous one; this approach to the "indigenous problem" lasted for decades (Pajuelo 2005: 112).

Though these measures represented a change from the previous indifference towards more attention for the situation of the indigenous population in Peru, they were still built on the idea that being a citizen necessarily meant leaving the "indigenous identity" behind and to stop being an "indio". Hence, while administration after administration focused on that effort, the slow and silent process of the emergence of a new concept of "peruanidad" (i. e., that which is understood as being Peruvian) within the population was ignored: since 1940, hundreds of thousands of indigenous migrants abandoned their rural communities and increased the population in the cities –mainly Lima–, thus completely transforming the social and economic order in the country during the second half of the 20th century. However, the "indigenous problem" was given special attention under the military and authoritarian government of General Juan Velasco Alvarado (1968 – 1975). The most far-reaching initiative undertaken by the Velasco administration was the implementation of the land reform. The conditions that prompted it were (a) the massive migration from rural to urban areas, which generated "poverty belts" around the cities where the migrants established themselves, (b) recurrent and massive manifestations of peasants who wanted to vindicate their rights, a lot of which ended in the taking of land that belonged to private landowners, (c) the extreme concentration of land property in the hands of a few wealthy families, (d) poverty and extreme poverty in rural areas, and (d) the need to expand the market for an emerging industry that could not develop in a rural context with such characteristics (cf. Eguren 2006: 1).

The land reform was one of the most radical of South America. 71 % of all irrigated cultivation land was expropriated and adjudicated; the same happened with 92 % of all dry-farmed crops (dependent on rain) and 57 % of natural pastures (cf. Matos Mar 1980: 171), eradicating traditional landowners. The land reform was followed by other reforms aiming at the recognition and revaluation of the indigenous culture. The indigenous languages were recognized –quechua was declared an official language– and, for the first time, programs were designed to incorporate it into the national educational system. At the same time, the legal status of the so called "indigenous communities" changed, from then on they were "peasant communities", and the Amazon "native communities" were recognized as well (Pajuelo 2005: 113). All these measures were carried out in the context of an intense campaign of social reform and mobilization that used the image of TúpacAmaru II as a symbol, which was named "Plan Inca" by the government. On the other hand, the National Agrarian Confederation was founded in 1974 (CNA) with the objective of structuring an organized social base in rural areas. Ever since its creation, it shared and disputed political rural scenarios with the Peasant Confederation of Peru (CCP), a communist organization created in 1946. These two associations achieved national presence and led an intense process of unionizing and fought for the land, even after the land reform, during the 1970s and 1980s. The struggle continued, in order to pressure the government to quickly implement the general measures taken nationwide and to respond to the former landowners that resisted the land reform.

In 1975, a military coup overthrew Velasco Alvarado. Francisco Morales Bermúdez became president and the "second phase" of the military regime began, but it actually dismantled what had been promoted during the Velasco administration. In fact, several of the reforms implemented by Velasco were deactivated. Due to several national strikes and protests between 1977 and 1978, the military government had to call for elections for a Constituent Assembly, which started the return to a democratic regime.

After "velasquismo" was over, the CNA chose to defend the land reform, while the CCP gathered peasants that, although agreeing with the land reform, were unhappy with how it had been implemented. This organizational process was led by left wing parties in both CNA and CCP during the decades of 1970 and 1980, which prompted the consolidation of a strong peasant class consciousness that almost completely excluded ethnic or cultural demands from the agrarian struggle (cf. Pajuelo 2005: 115). This path did nothing but reproduce the old tradition of contempt against everything "indio" that accentuated the socio-economic and political differences between the dominant class and the peasants: being "indio" had become a synonym of being a "servant" or "illiterate".

1980 – 2000: Internal Armed Conflict and Authoritarianism

On May 17, 1980, in Chuschi – Ayacucho, a small village to the centre south region of Peru, five armed and hooded individuals burst into the office in which the electoral ballots for the national elections that were taking place the next day were kept and burnt all of them. The event did not receive much attention from the media in Lima –Peru's capital city– but it was the symbolic launch of the armed struggle by the Peruvian Communist Party – Shining Path (PCP-SL), led by Abimael Guzmán, against the Peruvian State (cf. Reátegui 2008: 97). This single act of violence and rebellion marked the beginning of a conflict that would profoundly and negatively affect the Peruvian state and society.

It is not a coincidence that PCP-SL chose Ayacucho as the place where their armed struggle would begin, since it was mainly based on a social tapestry of indigenous peasants from the poorest rural departments of the country: Ayacucho, Huancavelica and Apurímac. The members of PCP-SL initially recruited by its leaders were poor mestizos from different provinces as well as professors, teachers, and students from universities and secondary schools. The Shining Path's expansion to other regions of the country would eventually allow them to diversify their strength and recruit members of pre-existing left-wing parties, but their composition would always be based on the participation of mestizos and indigenous people (cf. Escárzaga 2005: 202).

However, PCP-SL did not incorporate the indigenous identity of its members to its discourse, nor valued, respected or vindicated their cultural features: The Truth and Reconciliation Commission found that the PCP-SL supported the Maoist thesis and turned the rural areas in the main scenario of the conflict (cf. Final Report 1). Nevertheless, they did not take into consideration the needs and economic aspirations of the peasantry, of their own organizations or cultural specificities; on the contrary, they turned the peasants into a "mass" that had to subordinate themselves to the will of the party. Individual dissidence led to assassinations and selective annihilations; collective dissidence often resulted in massacres and the destruction of entire communities. (cf. Reátegui 2008: 436)

Even when there was total disregard for the necessities of the indigenous population, the PCP-SL took advantage of their particular characteristics and of the ethnic and cultural polarization that existed in the country to intensify the conflict: it used their social networks to provide for food and for members; it also used the quechua language and their ancestral war symbols as an effective way of communication, in order to incorporate them into the organization, maintain the cohesion within the organization, and frighten its enemies; finally, it stimulated "anti-white" racism to intensify the conflict and the confrontation with the dominant criollo groups (Escárzaga 2005: 203).

Therefore, despite the knowledge and initial assimilation of the Andean world, the Shining Path, like other actors before, acted with a racist attitude towards the indigenous population. It used its initial social support for its own purposes and considered them incapable of making autonomist decisions. It established a clearly vertical and authoritarian relationship, where the peasants often found themselves in the middle of confrontations between members of the PCP-SL and government forces, turning them into casualties in the war against capitalism.

Regretfully, these trades were not exclusive to the PCP-SL. The Peruvian police and armed forces were also involved in this damaging cycle. Since the Shining Path did not wear any uniforms or distinctive symbols on them, basically anyone could be one of their members. In that sense, the indigenous population, mainly in the rural areas, found themselves right in the midst of the conflict and was often attacked by the armed forces in the belief that they might be members of the Shining Path.

This disregard of the life of peasants, mainly quechua-speakers is revealed in all its cruelty, when the subversive groups "take the conflict to the cities. According to testimonies gathered by the Truth and Reconciliation Commission, the average size of the groups in which people executed by the State died is 5.7 bigger in the rural areas than in the urban ones (21.2 vs. 3.7)". In the latter, the strategy was more selective. "In the rural areas, as the numbers indicate, the repression was more indiscriminate" (Reátegui 2009, 72).

As the Peruvian Truth and Reconciliation Commission concluded, the indigenous and peasant population were the main victims of the conflict. In fact, out of the total number of victims reported, 79 % lived in rural areas and 56 % worked in agricultural activities. These numbers stand in contrast to the ones obtained by the 1993 general census: 29 % of the Peruvian population lived in rural areas, and 28 % of the economically active population were occupied in the agricultural sector. Furthermore, 75 % of the victims had quechua or another native language as their first one; once more, this numbers contrast eloquently with the fact that the population that shares this characteristic constitutes only 16 % of the Peruvian population, according to the 1993 census (cf. Reátegui 2008: 434).

Consequently, the economic and social structures of the indigenous population living in the rural areas were seriously compromised, if not destroyed:

> "[The] internal armed conflict paralyzed the process of development in the rural world and left grave consequences for the productive structure, on social organization, on educational institutions and on the ambitions of the affected populations. Adding these repercussions to those [...] [produced] by the loss of human capital and by the ransacking and destruction of the community assets, it is possible to conclude that the process of violence left a desolate economic panorama with a huge number of affected people, to whom society and the State owe a debt of reparation" (Reátegui 2008: 409).

By the end of the 1980s, the conflict had escalated and reached Lima and other main cities of Peru, inflation was ravishing the economy due to erroneous decisions made by former President Alan García Pérez (1980 – 1985 and 2006 – 2011), such as the nationalization of the banking sector and the express refusal to pay the Peruvian external debt, which was already unmanageable. This context was propitious for a rather unknown candidate with no political background or traditional party support to gain momentum and win the 1990 elections: Alberto Fujimori.

Fujimori applied an "economic shock" – during his campaign, he had promised not to do it, since it was his opponent's (Mario Vargas Llosa) proposal – to stabilize the hyperinflation and open the ground for neo-liberalization to enter. The adoption of this measure marked the beginning of an authoritarian government that would soon manifest itself openly: on Apr. 5, 1992, Fujimori announced the closing of the Parliament and the intervention into the Judicial Power. The excuse for this act was that the Congress was an obstacle to every legislative initiative that the government presented to it for consideration (cf. Pajuelo 2005: 119). Fujimori took advantage of the discredit that the traditional political parties and the Congress experienced and installed a civil-military dictatorship that was supported by a large number of the people even until the last years of the 1990s.

The armed conflict continued intensely, parallel to the first couple of years of the Fujimori government. During those years kidnappings and selective killings were carried out by a special military group, designed to combat silently and, most of the times, illegally, the PCP-SL. However, it was not an illegal act what made the Shining Path to begin its withdrawal: PCP-SL was, as we have stated, an extremely hierarchical organization. Hence, a few people – the Cúpula Directiva (Leadership Group) – and, among them, the head of the party, Abimael Guzmán, made all the main and most important decisions regarding their activities. Therefore, on Sept. 12, 1992, and after a very careful and detailed intelligence operation by the Police Forces, Abimael Guzmán was captured and the organization lost its most important leader, causing its influence to decrease.

The intensity of the conflict decreased and it eventually ceased, which gave Fujimori a huge popularity almost through his entire government, although he institutionalized corruption, controlled all the media, tapped private phones and accentuated the tendency to dismember social and organizational structures, which, in turn, expanded the identity crisis (cf. Pajuelo 2005: 121). The peasant organizations and unions lost presence amongst the population, as the "classist" discourse lost credibility.

Towards the end of the Fujimori regime, a new political actor, who was openly opposed to Fujimori and would eventually become the next president, emerged: Alejandro Toledo. Toledo was an educated mestizo with indigenous features and, gathering the opposition around him and against Fujimori, he used symbols from the Andean worldview and identified himself with the Inca Pachacutec, considered to be the founder of the Inca Empire (Tahuantinsuyo), to reach a portion of the population that had been historically neglected through his discourse. Toledo did not win the 2000 presidential elections; Fujimori did, in the midst of serious accusations of fraud. However, his third period as president would not last. A video in which his closest advisor paid off an elected congressman to join "fujimorism" surfaced and confirmed the corrupt nature of the government. Fujimori left Peru and sent a fax with his resignation from Japan.

Vindicated rights? Indigenous Population in Post-Conflict Peru

On Nov. 22, 2000, Valentín Paniagua, President of Congress, was appointed as interim president after Fujimori resigned: a democratic transition began. The transitional government started a rapprochement policy towards the indigenous population. The Mesade Diálogo y Cooperación para las Comunidades Nativas (Negotiating and Cooperation Table for the Native Communities) was created, composed by representatives from the government and from the indigenous Amazon organizations. The Mesade Diálogo developed an action plan for subjects with priority, which included several urgent measures to strengthen the rights of the indigenous population, with agreements and established execution dates. However, the transitional character of the Paniagua administration proved to be a problem, since the creation of the Mesa was published only a few days before Toledo (who had won the 2001 presidential elections organized by the transitional government) took office. The Mesa de Diálogo lost its initial force and, although it has not been dissolved, the measures it contained have not been carried out. It has turned into a forum that is mostly active when a conflict between native and indigenous communities and the government surfaces.

Another extremely significant act by the transitional government was the creation of the Truth and Reconciliation Commission (TRC) on June 4, 2001, to investigate and disseminate the truth about what happened during the years of armed conflict in Peru. Nevertheless, the TRC's creation was not a result of the claim or uproar of a vast proportion of the Peruvian population. It was rather the result of the constant work and political pressure of civil society: nongovernmental organizations, associations of victims and families of victims, among others.

The TRC delivered its report on Aug. 28, 2003. As part of its recommendations, it presented the need to recognize and integrate the rights of the indigenous population and their communities into the national judicial system; they even proposed specific measures to achieve this goal (cf. Balarín 2008): a just and legitimate judicial protection as legal persons and the reaffirmation of diversity and plurality of the Peruvian nation (cf. Truth and Reconciliation Commission 2003: 118). Therefore, among other recommendations, it proposed the definition of Peru as a "multinational, multicultural, multilingual and multi-religious state" and that, consequently, the indigenous languages should be official, so that government personnel were obliged to learn it. It also mentions the importance of developing bilingual intercultural education and providing intercultural health. Finally, it recommended that the indigenous peoples should be recognized as legal entities, acknowledging their organization. This is closely related to their lands and traditional territories, since they are, according to the 1993 Constitution, inalienable, non-lapsable and not subject to expropriation. Most of these recommendations have not been implemented due to the lack of political will to do so, both from the government (Toledo and García) and from the opposition groups in Congress.

An important part of the TRC's recommendations was directed towards the creation of the Plan Integral de Reparaciones (PIR – Comprehensive Reparation Programme) that they developed. In the PIR, the word reparation is understood as "a gesture and an action that recognizes and reaffirms the dignity and status of peoples" (TRC, volume IX, part four, chapter 2, 2003: 139). It is not necessarily a payment that responds to a contractual obligation, but rather: "to perceive the reparation as a tool to consolidate the 'feeling' of being a citizen (…) despite having being a victim in the past" (Guillerot 2003: 9).

The PIR requires the solidarity, common effort and political will of the state, civil society, private companies, and NGOs that has not been present yet (cf. Balarín 2008). Actions are being implemented very reluctantly and are receiving a lot of criticism. Collective reparations –primarily for the indigenous population–have been implemented to some extent, but individual reparations, have not been awarded at all. According to the latest report (Sept. 2010) issued but the Reparations Council – state entity in charge of implementing the reparations – 76,382 have been registered as victims so far, out of which 39,007 are considered as beneficiaries (family of the killed and disappeared or people who were victims of sexual violation or were injured and have now a disability) of the economic reparations that the state gives since 2011. Although discrimination against the indigenous population has somewhat decreased in the last decade, it has not disappeared, nor did the traditional way to approach communication with them, which is tainted by a paternalistic tone. This became apparent in the tragic events of June 25, 2009 in Bagua, a province in northern Peru with a large number of native inhabitants. The government had emitted two legislative decrees with the objective of facilitating private investment in the Amazon region, without consulting the native population: it was a trigger for violence. A group of native citizens blocked the highway to prevent commercial products to go by. The government sent police forces, and a brutal confrontation between police forces and the natives left 35 persons dead and 87 wounded.

However, the relationship between the indigenous population and the state improved. Even though indigenous movements are not as strong as in Bolivia or Ecuador, a notable change has been recognized in the last decade: the formation of new organizations that not only vindicate their indigenous origins, but who aspire to the articulation of social movements nation-wide, actively participating on the local political scenarios (cf. Pajuelo 2006: 20). At the same time, the state has shown more concern about the –no longer called– "indigenous problem": it created the Instituto Nacional de Desarrollo de los Pueblos Andinos Amazónicos y Afroperuanos (INDEPA) (National Institute for the Development of the Andean, Amazonic and African-Peruvian Peoples) in 2004, which substituted the Comisión Nacional de Pueblos Andinos, Amazónicos y Afroperuanos (CONAPA) (National Commission of Andean, Amazonic and African-peruvian Peoples), which was created in 2001 by Alejandro Toledo. INDEPA was created by law and has autonomy within the government structure. It has a cross-sector composition and enjoys economic, administrative, and political autonomy within the government structure. This allows it to make institutionalized and binding decisions for the state and indigenous groups

Another element that stands out is that, among the Andean countries, Peru is the only one in which indigenous persons have been elected as congress representatives. Even more, they have decided to publicly vindicate their identity using their language (they insisted in being sworn into Congress in quechua), clothes or customs. This does not mean that racism has been overcome: we're far from it. Many people do not take the elected indigenous congresswomen serious and see them merely as decorative elements in Congress. Nonetheless, one of them has been appointed head of the Educational Commission of Congress in Aug. 2010. The difficulty to process the presence of indigenous congressmen and congresswomen reveals the subtle and intricate ways in which predominant racism manifests itself in the Peruvian society (cf. Pajuelo 2006: 81).

Indigenous organizations exist and are working towards vindicating their rights on the basis of real representation and public participation. However, it is still discouraging that they are (most) visible – either because they are more active and organized or because the media and government pay more attention to them – only when social conflict emerges. These conflicts are mainly related to the exploration and exploitation of the indigenous communities' land.

The government has established institutions such as INDEPA, which design programs directed towards promoting native and indigenous peoples' rights, and a greater part of the population is now more aware of the existence of racism and the risk of extending it. However, none of these initiatives will succeed unless the larger problem is tackled: the structural problems that allowed for 75 % of the victims of the internal armed conflict to be indigenous and poor.

It is a matter of having a different approach that enables the indigenous population to truly become citizens and speak for themselves in the public arena, which has not really happened in Peru: most of the times, there have been (necessary) intermediates, such as NGOs, that have "spoken for" the indigenous peoples. It is also necessary that the consciousness of the importance of this matter is raised among every citizen and in government offices. Government offices are responsible for designing, developing, and implementing public policies to, first, listen to the indigenous representatives and, then, work together to reach common goals, so that they become agents of change instead of reproducing a paternalistic relationship that has proven to be fatal for our country and our neighboring Andean countries. If not, this tragedy –not only the conflict but the constant and permanent discrimination against the indigenous peoples– will not be addressed, no matter how many Truth Commissions are formed:

"(…) Peruvians have (a weak historic memory) about the years of violence we suffered. The national public opinion does not present an active memory of the tragedy that it represents; despite the fact that it was the gravest confrontation between Peruvians in all republican history" (TRC 2003: 102, cited by Balarín 2008).

Conclusion: What Kind of 'Voice'?

The analysis has revealed several results that put the assumption of the so-called 'indigenous movements' in Latin America and their potential transitional power in question: indeed, there is no uniform 'indigenous movement' as such in the Andean region, for each has its own characteristics that are determined by the social structure that precedes them as well as by external influences providing or inhibiting crucial 'windows of opportunity' for change – be it economic crises, regional interest constellations or the like.

On the one hand, in Bolivia the janus-faced instrumentalization of the indigenous identity by different adversaries (i. e. lowlands vs. highlands) has proven strong cohesive power for collective action that resulted in several violent clashes. On the other hand, the homogeneity level of those groups remains volatile, given the actions' spontaneous and irregular character. In a nutshell, the 'indigenous voice' has clearly been a driving actor in Bolivia's transitional process particularly since 2000. The crucial question of the future will be whether these groups will use their 'voice' – so far articulated by semi-formal measures such as demonstrations, road blockades etc. – within the formal political decision-making processes. The indigenous population's use of their strongest democratic instrument, the referendum, suggests a first formalizing step towards the acceptance of the current democratic political system. Hereafter, much will depend on the performance of the MAS majority in parliament; given that future outcomes will ultimately bear witness to the stability of the political and inevitably social architecture of the Republic of Bolivia.

Furthermore, indigenous movements in Peru have not been as strong as the ones that emerged in Bolivia, though both countries' social structure seems to be similar. Nevertheless, one characteristic common to both scenarios is that the indigenous population has been discriminated in the past and been treated as people with no autonomy. In the Peruvian case, there have been some movements that have tried to vindicate the indigenous population's rights. However, such movements have not been the result of a nationally wide and massive organization that had the indigenous peoples rights' and interests as its objective; the political changes rather came "from above" or were the result of the pressure of intermediate actors that took upon themselves to speak for the indigenous population. This dynamic, in which the indigenous peoples were seen as "objects" instead of "subjects" helps to explain the birth and growth of an armed conflict that affected Peru for twenty years and that left, as the TRC found later, a vast majority of poor indigenous people living in rural areas as victims and their social networks even more weakened.

The Peruvian TRC identified and exposed this tragic outcome and openly stated that it had been possible given the indifference towards this sector of the population's well-being. Therefore, promotion and reinforcement of coordination among indigenous movements is necessary, so that their "voices" are directly heard without any intermediaries. Their role in the transition process should not only have been that of victims claiming for their rights through third parties, but of subjects directly approaching the government in an organized and direct manner. A change in the way the society as a whole sees the indigenous peoples, not as equals but as second class citizens, is also necessary and urgent. This needs intercultural educational and health programs that promote the revalorization of the indigenous culture.

Hence, the politically relevant (and thus scholarly interesting) question on the 'indigenous voice' in the Andean region should be directed towards possible measures for political, socio-economic, and cultural integration rather than towards its conflictive bargaining power. For instance, the non-linear driven transitional processes in that region may benefit from alternative perspectives on collective decision-making, subsistence economy or even basic health care, applied by indigenous communities

Empirical reality gives us the following picture: So far, the Bolivian case shows that the 'indigenous voice' has made itself heard after the inauguration of Evo Morales in 2006 and even more so since the elections of Dec. 2009, when the MAS government gained a two-thirds majority in the Senate and a close to absolute majority in the Chamber of Deputies (cf. Buitrago 2010: 1). On the one hand, the numerical gain in senators and deputies of indigenous descent might provide a substantial means to further introduce 'indigenous' issues into the political decision-making process. Indeed, several legislative proposals bear that so-called 'indigenous' signature – e. g. official language, local judiciary. However, on the other hand, a legislative that exclusively makes policies in favor of certain segments of society (i. e. indigenous groups) will automatically provoke resentments among the neglected segments (i. e. the former economic and political elites); a political custom that had been despised by the MAS members and votaries themselves in the pre-2005 era. Hence, a whiff of 'politics of revenge' might compromise the transitional window of opportunity (cf. Interview Urioste 2010).

In order to consolidate the 'indigenous voice' within the formal political sphere in today's Bolivia, two mutual processes will have to begin: For one thing, the benefits of indigenous/ rural expertise (e. g. alternative health) to the entire society will have to be communicated in a manner that mitigates reservations among non-indigenous/ urban people. Furthermore, the indigenous peoples themselves – particularly within the MAS-led government – will have to display a comprehensive understanding of their role as being a citizen within the Bolivian state: A citizen that is characterized by his or her equal rights as well as equal civil duties in a multinational society.

References

Alenda, Stéphanie (2004). "Bolivia: La erosión del pacto democrático". In: *Revista Fuerzas Armadas y Sociedad 18:1 – 2.* 3 – 22.

Ames, Barry/Pérez-Liñan, Aníbal/Seligson, Mitchell A. (2004). "Elites, Institutions and the Mass Public: A New Look at Bolivian Democracy". *USAID Bolivia Study.* Pittsburgh: Department of Political Science University of Pittsburgh.

Arrueta, José Antonio (2008). Interview, Cochabamba. May 20, 2008.

Arze, Carlos, Kruse, Tom (2004). "The Consequences of Neoliberal Reform". In: *NACLA Report on the Americas 38:3.* 23 – 28.

Astuhuamán, César W./Daggett, Richard/Julio César Tello Rojas (2006). *Arqueólogo. Unabiografía.* 13 – 48. URL: http://sisbib.unmsm.edu.pe/bibvirtualdata/libros/historia/paracas_1/01_astuhuamán.pdf [accessed on Mar. 27, 2010].

Balarín de Mujica, Claudia (2008). "Los indígenas y el Estado: reflexiones en torno a los Acuerdos de San Andrés y el Informe Final de la Comisión de la Verdad y Reconciliación". In: Balarín Benavides, Claudia ed.: *Voces de la tierra: reflexiones sobre movimientos políticos indígenas en Bolivia, Ecuador, México y Perú.* Lima: UNMSM.

Buitrago, Miguel A. (2010). "Bolivien hat gewählt: Absolute Macht für Präsident Morales?". In: *GIGA Focus 4.* 1 – 8.

Central Intelligence Agency (CIA) (2010). *World Factbook 2010.* URL: https://www.cia.gov/ [accessed on Mar. 25, 2010].

Condo, Freddy (2008). Interview, La Paz. May 27, 2008.

Crabtree, John (2005). *Patterns of Protest: Politics and Social Movements in Bolivia.* London: Latin America Bureau.

Dangl, Benjamin (2007). *The Price of Fire: Resource Wars and Social Movements in Bolivia.* Edinburgh, West Virginia: AK Press.

De Ferrari, Ignazio (2008). Etnia, clase y movimientos indígenas en el Perú. In: *Perupolitico.com.* URL: http://www.perupolitico.com/?p=590. [accessed on Apr. 15 2010].

Economic Commission for Latin America and the Caribbean (2007). *Statistical Yearbook.* URL: http://www.eclac.org/. [accessed on Mar. 25, 2010].

Eguren, Fernando (2006). "Reforma agraria y desarrollo rural en el Perú". In: Eguren, Fernando ed.: *Reforma agraria y desarrollo rural en la región andina, Lima: Centro Peruano de Estudios Sociales.* http://www.cepes.org.pe/cendoc/

eventos/Libro-Foro-Reforma-Agraria-2007/01 %20–eguren-peru.pdf [accessed on Mar. 13,2010].

Escárzaga, Fabiola (2005):"Avances en estudios comparativos: la comunidad indígena en las estrategias insurgentes en México, Perú y Bolivia". In: Escárzaga, Fabiola; Gutiérrez, Raquel ed.: *Movimiento indígena en América Latina: resistencia y proyecto alternativo.* México. D.F.: Gobierno Distrito Federal.

Espinoza, Ovidio (2008). Interview, Cochabamba, May 20, 2008.

Goedeking, Ulrich (2003). *Politische Eliten und demokratische Entwicklung in Bolivien1985 - 1996.* Münster: Lit Verlag.

Gordon, Gretchen (2006). "The United States, Bolivia and the Political Economy of Coca". In: *Multinational Monitor January/ February.* 15 - 20.

Graubner, Cornelius(2007). Drugs and Conflict. How the Mutual Impact of Illicit Drug Economies and Violent Conflict Influences Sustainable Development, Peace and Stability. *The Development-Oriented Drug Control Programme (DDC),* Eschborn: Deutsche Gesellschaft für Technische Zusammenarbeit.

Guerrero, Andrés (1997)."Población indígenas, ciudadanía y representación". In: *Nueva Sociedad N° 150.* Julio-Agosto. 98 - 105.

Guillerot, Julie (2003)."Hacia la reparación integral de las víctimas del conflicto". In: *Informe sobre la situacion de los DESC 2002 - 2003 en el Perú: "Dos años de Democracia ... y ¿los DESC?".* Lima: APRODEH, CEDAL.

Hylton, Forrest; Thompson, Sinclair (2004). "The Roots of Rebellion. Insurgent Bolivia". In: *NACLA Report on the Americas 38:3.* 15 - 19.

International Crisis Group (2006). "Bolivia's Rocky Road to Reforms". In: *International Crisis Group Latin America Report.* No. 18. July 3. Bogotá/ Brussels.

International Crisis Group (2007). "Bolivia's Reforms: The Danger of New Conflicts". In: International Crisis Group Policy Briefing. Latin America Briefing. No. 13. Jan. 8, 2007. Bogotá/ Brussels.

International Crisis Group (2008). "Bolivia: Rescuing the New Constitution and Democratic Stability". In: *International Crisis Group Policy Briefing. Latin America Briefing.* No. 18. June 19. Bogotá/ Brussels.

Jost, Stefan (2006). "Bolivien nach dem politischen Erdrutsch". In: *GIGA Focus Lateinamerika.* No. 2. 1 - 15.

Landa, Ladislao (2006)."Los espejos opacos del movimiento indígena peruano". In: Toche M., Eduardo ed.: *Perú Hoy: Los Nuevos Rostros de la escena nacional.* Lima: Desco. 117 - 140.

Matos Mar, José; Mejía, J. M. (1980). *La reformaagraria en elPerú.* Lima: Instituto de Estudios Peruanos.

McNeish, John-Andrew (2006). "Stones on the Road: The Politics of Participation and the Generation of Crisis in Bolivia". In: *Bulletin of Latin American Research 25:2.* 220 - 240.

Mosley, Paul (2007). The 'Political Poverty Trap': Bolivia 1999 - 2007. Working Paper Series. London: World Economy & Finance Research Programme.

Nueva Crónica (2009). "Se abre un Nuevo ciclo estatal". In: *Nueva Crónica 2009:*52.3.

Pajuelo Teves, Ramón (2005)."Política, etnicidad y organizaciones indígenas:

lecciones de la experiencia peruana". In: León T., Jorge ed.: *Participación política, democracia y movimientos indígenas en los Andes.* La Paz: IFEA.

Pajuelo Teves, Ramón (2006). *Participación política indígena en la sierra peruana: una aproximación desde las dinámicas nacionales y locales.* Lima: Fundación Konrad Adenauer: IEP. 2006.

Perreault, Thomas (2006). "From the Guerra del Agua to the Guerra del Gas: Resource Governance and Popular Protest in Bolivia". In: *Antipode 38:1.* 150–172.

Quijano, Aníbal (2006). El "Movimiento Indígena" y las cuestiones pendientes en América Latina. URL: http://sisbib.unmsm.edu.pe/BibVirtualData/publicaciones/san_marcos/n24_2006/a01.pdf. [accessed on Mar. 12, 2010].

Reátegui, Felix (2008). *Hatun Willakuy, Versión abreviada del Informe Final de la Comisión de la Verdad y Reconciliación. 2th ed.* Lima: Comisión de Entrega de Comisión de la Verdad y Reconciliación.

Reátegui, Felix (2009). *Colección cuadernos para la memoria histórica: etnicidad y exclusión durante el proceso de violencia. Selección de textos del Informe Final de la Comisión de la Verdad y Reconciliación.* Lima: Idehpucp.

Rochlin, James (2007). "Latin America's Left Turn and the New Strategic Landscape: the Case of Bolivia". In: *Third World Quarterly 28:7.* 1327–1342.

Romero, Simon (Dec. 6, 2009). "Morales Headed for Re-election in Bolivia". New York Times. URL: http://www.nytimes.com/2009/12/07/world/americas/07bolivia.html?_r=2&scp=6&sq=bolivia&st=cse. [accessed on Mar. 25, 2010].

Romero, Simon/Schipani, Andres (Dec. 5, 2009). "In Bolivia, a Force for Change Endures". New York Times. URL: http://www.nytimes.com/2009/12/06/world/americas/06bolivia.html?fta=y. [Mar. 25, 2010].

Sánchez León, Pajuelo (Sept. 2001). "Todos tenemos derecho a ser peruanos, interview with Rodrigo Montoya Rojas". In: *Quehacer N° 132 "La guerra de los mundos".* Lima. URL: http://w3.desco.org.pe/publicaciones/QH/QH/qh132rm.htm. [accessed on Mar. 12, 2010].

Salman, Ton (2007). "Bolivia and the Paradoxes of Democratic Consolidation". In: *Latin America Perspectives 34:6.* 111–130.

Salmón, Elizabeth (2007)."El largo camino de la lucha contra la pobreza y su esperanzador encuentro con los derechos humanos". In: *SUR, Revista Internacional de Derechos Humanos, N° 7. URL:* http://www.surjournal.org/esp/conteudos/pdf/7/salmon.pdf. [accessed on Mar. 17, 2010].

Toledo, Hugo (2007). "Coca Substitution and Free Trade in Bolivia: The Pending Crisis". In: *Review of Development Economics 11:1.* 63–77.

Final Report. Peruvian Truth and Reconciliation Commission (2003)

Urioste, Juan Cristobal (May 25, 2010). Interview. La Paz.

Vellinga, Menno L. (1998). "Alternative Development and Supply Side Control in the Drug Industry: the Bolivian Experience". In: *Revista Europea de Estudios Latinoamericanos y del Caribe 64.* 7–26.

Webber, Jeffery R. (2005). "Left-Indigenous Struggles in Bolivia: Searching for Revolutionary Democracy". In: *Monthly Review 57:4.* 34–48.

Wolff, Jonas (2004). *Demokratisierung als Risiko der Demokratie? Die Krise der Politik in Bolivien und Ecuador und die Rolle der indigenen Bewegungen. HSFK Report 6.* Frankfurt am Main: Hessische Stiftung Friedens- und Konfliktforschung.

World Bank Atlas (2010). *URL:* http://web.worldbank.org/WBSITE/EXTERNAL/DATASTATISTICS/0,,contentMDK:20420458~menuPK:64133156~pagePK:64133150~piPK:64133175~theSitePK:239419,00.html [accessed on Mar. 25, 2010].

Yashar, Deborah J. (206)."Indigenous Politics in the Andes: Changing Patterns of Recognition, Reform, and Representation". In: Bejarano Sandoval/Ana María ed.: *The crisis of democratic representation in the Andes.* Stanford, CA: Stanford UP.

Zilla, Claudia (2006). *Externe Demokratieförderung in Bolivien. Die Politik Deutschlands und der Europäischen Union.* Berlin: Stiftung Wissenschaft und Politik.

Elizabeth Lira/Brian Loveman

The Politics of Reconciliation

Discourses, Sacrament, and Pragmatism in Chileand Post-Cold WarLatin America

Introduction[1]

National reconciliation has been a recurrent issue in Chile since the civil war that became a war for independence against Spain (1810 – 1818). It reappeared as a prominent theme of political discourse after 1978, with the amnesty decree by the military dictatorship that conferred broad impunity for violations of human rights in the name of national unity and "reconciliation."[2] It is also an issue that, since the 1978 change of government in Ecuador, arises in much of Latin America in the context of political transitions from military dictatorships and authoritarian regimes to elected governments or at termination of internal insurgencies.

The call for political reconciliation nearly always appears in the form of an invitation to put aside differences and "forget" past conflicts in the name of the common good and the "national family" which should be reunited in the name of patriotism and loyalty to the nation-state. The appeal to reconciliation is presented as a unifying discourse that subordinates all differences to a predominant rationale: the achievement of social peace and national "unity." Yet, reconciliation does not have the same meaning for everyone. The differing meanings attached to the idea of reconciliation presuppose various political, social, and personal considerations that are, at times, contradictory or fundamentally antagonistic. Thus the call for "reconciliation," and defining its significance, becomes itself a part of the political struggle to redefine political and social life in the wake of transitions from the military and anticommunist regimes of the Cold War era, to a new global and regional political reality from the late 1980s into the 21st century.

1 Elizabeth Lira is the director of the Center of Ethics of the Jesuit University Alberto Hurtado. Santiago. Chile, Brian Loveman is Professor of Political Science, Emeritus. San Diego State University. Research for this article was supported by the Ford Foundation, Andean Region and Southern Cone (Santiago, Chile). This article summarizes and expands on the introduction of Loveman, Brian, and Lira, Elizabeth (2000). *Las suaves cenizas del olvido. La vía chilena de reconciliación política 1814 – 1932.* 2nd ed. Santiago: LOM Editores.

2 Decree Law 2.191, 1978. For full text of this decree see Brian Loveman and Elizabeth Lira, (1999). *Leyes de reconciliación en Chile: Amnistías, indultos y reparaciones 1819 – 1999.* Santiago: DIBAM. 207 – 208.

Political reconciliation is typically sought through political accords, legislation, including amnesties and pardons, and various administrative measures. It also requires diverse psychosocial, ethical, and symbolic initiatives that derive from the particular characteristics of conflicts in each country. The experience of political transitions in Central and South America indicates that the major obstacles to defining and implementing reconciliation as policy can be traced to the persistence of problems that led to the conflict in the first place as well as to the consequences of violence and political repression. In this sense, political reconciliation is both a generic dilemma after political conflicts and also an idiosyncratic dilemma, subject to the particular circumstances embedded in local culture and history. For this reason, political reconciliation in Chile cannot be entirely similar to the "same" process in Guatemala, Peru, Brazil, Argentina – or Colombia, where a more-than-half century conflict continues in 2011 even as a "truth commission" seeks to emulate some of the procedures of such commissions in Latin America and elsewhere.

The origins of violent political and social conflict nearly always stem from the existence of conflicting visions of the common good, of the legitimate political regime, of ethnic and religious differences, and of antagonistic social utopias. The existence of groups willing to define political opponents or social "others" as enemies to be eradicated, rather than as compatriots who share responsibility for the nation's future, is a decisive factor in producing a climate of polarization, prolonged, systematic violence and an outcome that produce fractures in society. But this disposition to demonize adversaries originates in very real normative, moral, ideological, or even religious antagonisms which, at the margin, define adversaries as "enemies" of the Fatherland, God, or some imagined utopia – making their extirpation (or conversion) not only just, but necessary.

Understandably, then, as political transitions begin there exist different views on the meaning of, and the requisites for, reconciliation. Latent conflictiveness resulting from opposing historical ideologies and from the politics that gave rise to the conflict and rupture is likely to persist as well. Resistance to the idea of reconciliation is, likewise, an extension of the previous conflict, reaffirming the lost cause or the victory, as the case may be. Victims of political violence and their family members often reject amnesty laws as morally and politically unacceptable as the price of reconciliation. For the victors, legal "forgetting," that is amnesty, or at least pardons, is a necessary and fair condition for bringing an end to the conflict, which in their judgment, was produced by those they consider to be the enemy, although sometimes they argue that there is nothing at all "to forgive and forget." (After all, the violence was done to "save" the Fatherland from its enemies, or the Church from apostasy, or, simply, to save "our way of life"). In this last case, proposals for reconciliation and forgiveness lack meaning; even amnesty laws tend to be resisted as unnecessary, since either no crime was committed or the crimes committed were crimes "against humanity", making any amnesty unthinkable.

In these circumstances, underlying questions regarding political reconciliation commonly include: Reconciliation with what? Reconciliation with whom? Reconciliation for what? And, above all, what is meant by reconciliation? How might reconciliation differ from resignation and impunity?

In the following pages, we consider the different meanings of "reconciliation" implicit in the political reconciliation proposals discussed in Latin America, and more particularly in Chile, in the 1990s. These different significations led to recurrent political debate and, ultimately, to a dynamic stalemate on "turning the page" on the past.[3] These diverse models of reconciliation derive from cultural, religious, family, social and historical traditions; once they are identified and made explicit they appear "obvious", though the political actors in the 1990s and into the 21st century were not consciously aware of their influence.[4] They presently play, as they did in the past, an important political role, precisely because the various models have points in common as well as incompatible aspects. Those who advocate reconciliation or those who oppose it, nearly always identify simultaneously with several different models, which arise (spontaneously and almost "naturally") in the course of proposing policies and counter-policies for reconciliation.

Reconciliation: Notions and Concepts

Dictionaries define reconciliation, conciliation, and to conciliate as related terms. Reconciliation is defined as bringing back of friendly relations; to become friends again after quarreling (the former enemies), rapprochement (cf. *Roget's International Thesaurus* 1992: 372). Reconciliation is also defined as a process that allows forgetting past grievances between political parties and hostile nations and reestablishing collaborative relations. Reconciliation is also the given name to the sacrament of confession in the Catholic Church

3 In other publications we have analyzed the politics of reconciliation in Chile during this period; in the present article we limit ourselves to consideration of the implications of the differing, sometimes antagonistic or even entirely incompatible, definitions of political reconciliation implicit in the post-1990 period. See, for example, Loveman, Brian, and Lira, Elizabeth (2002). *El espejismo de la reconciliación política.* Santiago: LOM/DIBAM.; (2005). *Políticas de reparación: Chile 1990 – 2004.* Santiago: LOM/DIBAM.

4 The authors interviewed all members of the National Truth and Reconciliation Commission, known as Rettig Commission (Comisión Nacional de Verdad y Reconciliación) and directors of the Corporation of Reparation and Reconciliation. None of them expressed any awareness of the historical patterns of political conflict and reconciliation in Chile, described in our research. In contrast once made aware of the study's findings all of them recognized the "Chileaness" of their own behavior.

(cf. Paul 1982: 1627). To reconcile is to reincorporate a believer who had been separated from the Church (cf. Real Academia Española 1992: 1742).

Reconciliation is a synonym of a consensus, accommodation of people, unanimity, reunification, confluence of minds (cf. *Roget's International Thesaurus* 1992: 602). Depending on the context, reconciliation is a synonym of conformity, adaptation and flexibility, to be in agreement (cf. ibid.: 656). To reconcile can be understood as a process which implies finding agreement between two ideas, situations that seem to be in opposition, to bring back friendly relations between, make friendly again.

To conciliate implies making another less angry or more friendly, especially by being pleasant or making some concessions (cf. *Oxford Advanced Learner's Dictionary* 1993: 241; *Longman Dictionary of Contemporary English* 1995: 281). To conciliate also means to bring people who are disagreeing into agreement (people who are divided by opinions and interests). To conciliate precedes to reconcile. If there were no conciliation at the beginning, there would be no "re-conciliation." But language-in-use does not always make these logical distinctions. Conciliatory is associated with forgiving (unresentful, tolerant) unbelligerent, (peace-loving, nonviolent) pacificatory (placative). It is also used to refer to somebody who patches things up, such as a friendship or quarrel, to smoothing it over, weaving a peace between (cf. *Roget's International Thesaurus*. 1992: 372–373).

Personal Reconciliation

When relations between a couple, members of a family or friends enter into conflict that risks breaking the bond itself, a permanent rupture may occur or there may begin a process of reconciliation in search of the reestablishment of these bonds. The appeal for reconciliation is founded on the previous unity and a shared history.

The possibilities for reconciliation depend generally on the following factors: (1) the type of pre-existing bond and its duration; (2) the way in which the parties have experienced the conflict; (3) the ways the conflict has been expressed; (4) the personal and social meanings attributed to the conflict and the emotions associated with these meanings; (5) the level of "working through" of the crisis by the parties with each other and with third persons (cf. Willi 1978: 298); (6) the abilities of the parties to reframe the conflict and imagine modes of reconciliation; (7) the conscious commitment to overcome the conflict and agree upon concrete steps to reach reciprocally acceptable agreements; (8) the capacity of both parties to accept the concrete conditions required for reestablishing conviviality.

Conflicts and their various possible outcomes, including reconciliation, at the individual level, tend to be defined and framed by discourses that channel, discharge, or exacerbate emotions associated with them. The communication style foreshadows the possible outcomes. Intense, threatening and violent discourse both provokes and exacerbates conflict, potentially leading to rupture. Difficulties in reconciliation are therefore associated with the persistence and rigidity of the discourse and emotions of the protagonists, as these tend to condense and maintain intact the conflict. All these emotions are generally associated with the perceived threat of loss of the bond.

The conflict tends to intensify because mutual expectations and demands are perceived as unyielding and associated with identity, self-respect, values, and dignity. This manner of perceiving and expressing the conflict creates obstacles to positive communication. When this occurs, rupture seems the inevitable outcome. Often the conflict is expressed through physical violence. In other cases, the aggression is psychological: threats, humiliation, insults, demeaning remarks, hostility.

When it is possible to acknowledge and address the existence of the conflict and crisis, despite opposing versions as to the origins and contents, it may be possible to develop a common base from which to identify the points in agreement and those in disagreement. The strategy of denying the conflict (avoid it, minimize it, attributes it to the imagination of one of the parties) hinders the possibility of reconciliation.

The possibilities for resolving the conflict may be impeded by: (1) the difficulty in reaching a consensus regarding the nature of the former association; (2) the difficulty in obtaining a shared perception regarding the conflict and its expressions over time; (3) the impossibility of acknowledging and accepting differences concerning present feelings and perceptions; (4) the nearly always reciprocal tendency to discount the validity of motivations, feelings and perceptions of the other party, as if in this way it were possible to annul the existence of the conflict itself; (5) the tendency to avoid confronting the conflict and rupture out of anxiety and fear of causing a permanent rupture; (6) ambivalent feelings related to the hope and also skepticism as to the possibility for change; (7) difficulty in acknowledging and expressing the expectations reconciliation could bring; (8) external pressure and influences in favor of rupture or reconciliation upon one or both sides in the conflict.

In most cases reconciliation between individuals is limited. They attempt to reach at least partial agreements, which ensure the continuation of the bond, avoiding reopening old wounds and suppressing most everything associated with the conflict and rupture. Reconciliation of this kind does not carry full agreement or complete satisfaction.

Reconciliation unleashes a permanent human dilemma: the contradictions between desires and reality. The limited ranges of possibilities shape the concrete reality of reconciliation. On the other hand, desires are expressed in the dream of returning to a state of preexisting and imaginary harmony, analogous to paradise lost. These desires tend to be present in the resistance to accepting concrete conditions imposed by the reality with all its achievements, limitations and frustrations.

This reconciliation model has certain recognizable structural aspects which correspond to shared human experience. The discourses associated with this model simultaneously stimulate needs, emotions, values, desires, expectations, and processes which were first learned in childhood. Requisite to this model of private reconciliation are: acknowledgment of the conflict and its origin; signs of repentance for mutual offenses; reciprocal forgiveness; a tacit or explicit agreement not to reopen old wounds; the daily forgetting that allows living together, even though it is not intended to erase the memory.

Private reconciliation is always embedded in particular social and cultural norms, even when the parties do not share, or do not share entirely, the hegemonic norms of the societies in which they live. In most of Latin America, the United States, and Western Europe, these norms include explicit or implicit reference to a Biblical and theological tradition found in the Old and New Testaments – whether or not the protagonists are "believers."

Reconciliation in the Judeo-Christian and Catholic Traditions

The Jewish vision of a reconciled world community begins with the recognition that enmity exists among human beings when they alienate themselves from one another and from God (cf. Wells 1997: 3). The utopia of a reconciled world is expressed metaphorically by Isaiah, who writes:

And he shall not judge after the sight of his eyes, neither reprove after the hearing of his ears: but with righteousness shall he judge the poor, and reprove with equity for the meek of the earth; and he shall smite the earth with the rod of his mouth, and with the breath of his lips shall he slay the wicked. And righteousness shall be the girdle of his loins, and faithfulness the girdle of his reins. The wolf also shall dwell with the lamb, and the leopard shall lie down with the kid; and the calf and the young lion and the fatling together; and a little child shall lead them. And the cow and the bear shall feed; Their young ones shall lie down together; and the lion shall eat straw like the ox. And the sucking child shall play near the hole of the asp, and the weaned child shall put his hand on the basilisk's den. They shall not hurt nor destroy on all my Holy Mountain; For the earth shall be full of the knowledge of the Lord, as the waters cover the sea.[3]

In the Holy Scriptures some of the elements of private reconciliation have been formalized into social and religious rituals, which refer to the ruptures of individuals with their community. These ritualizations of forgiveness and reconciliation have become psychological and cultural models that form part of individual customs and religious and political practice.

3 Isaiah 11, 3–9. *The Holy Scriptures* (1956). According to the Masoretic Text. Philadelphia, The Jewish Publication Society of America. 5717. 492 s.

In this Biblical tradition, the history of conflicts and ruptures has been largely identified with the concept of sin. Reconciliation is a social relation that responds to the possibility of overcoming a conflict between persons, between persons and the community, and between persons and God. The stories of Esau and Jacob, of Joseph and his brothers, and of Isaac and Ishmael indicate how enmity was produced from acts of injustice, which are eventually resolved by joint reconciliation of these injustices; by the will to leave the past behind; and by the desire to live in mutual respect in the future. The stories show that in order for this to take place reconciliation requires processes of symbolization, religious ceremonies, liturgies and sacraments which acknowledge what occurred between individuals and the community. These rituals require spelling out the motives for the reconciliation; identifying implicit ethical values; and continuing with the necessary process to produce a rapprochement between those who are distanced.

The Holy Scriptures, as in contemporary Judeo-Christian tradition, indicate the importance of acknowledging the origin of the conflict, bearing responsibility for the actions and their consequences. In other words, acknowledging that a wrong, a sin, or an offense was committed, while emphasizing the psychological and moral need to ask for forgiveness, not only of the person who was offended but also of God and the community and to offer reparations, either by way of material compensation or in a symbolic act intended to restore the bond. Ultimately, the process requires pledging before God and the community that the transgression or sin shall not be repeated and making the commitment not to repeat it. Forgiveness from God allows reintegration in the community as the gesture that affirms the reconciliation.

Actions intended to repair the damage inflicted on another, while conscious of the fact that the wrong can never be completely set aright, is a gesture that expresses the intention and the concrete evidence of the will to restore the bond. The Old Testament describes the procedures of sacrifices for atonement:

> And the LORD spoke to Moses, saying: If anyone sin, and commit a trespass against the LORD, and deal falsely with his neighbour in a matter of deposit, or of pledge, or of robbery or have oppressed his neighbour; or have found that which was lost, and deal falsely therein, and swear to a lie; in any of all these that a man doeth, sinning therein; then it shall be, if he hath sinned, and is guilty, that he shall restore that which he took by robbery, or the thing which he hath gotten by oppression, or the deposit which was deposited with him, or the lost thing which he found, or anything about he hath sworn falsely, he shall even restore it in full, and shall add the fifth part more thereto; unto him whom it appertaineth shall he gives it, in the day of his being-guilty. And he shall bring his forfeit unto the LORD, a ram without blemish out of the flock, according to thy valuation, for a guilt-offering of the priest. And the priest shall make

atonement for him before the LORD, and he shall be forgiven, concerning whatsoever he doeth so as to be guilty thereby.[4]

The subjective processes detailed in this notion of expiation and reparation have endured in various essential aspects. Variations or departures from the original model are related to cultural notions of sin, punishment, and forgiveness prevalent in each era. In the Biblical context, reconciliation means the reestablishment of relations between two enemies. The factors that provoked the enmity must be overcome in order to reach this state. This occurs through expiation and reparation.

In contemporary Judaism the notion of reconciliation also involves belonging to the community and the relation with God:

I am not indifferent to human misery because I am composed of the same material as the victims and victimizers ... To help our fellow being to repair injustice that signifies extreme inequity is what our tradition calls Tzedakah, one of the three forms a person has to influence the judgment of Yom Kippur. Teshuvah (atonement, repentance), the return to ethical conduct, is the possibility for improving our interpersonal relations ... it is a change of attitude toward life, reached through introspection, looking within ourselves to discover that which distanced us from the person we can strive to be ... Tefilah is sincere prayer, spiritual elevation in our communication with God.[5]

To make Teshuvah there must first exist an internal feeling of regret for having committed a sin.

Teshuvah originates in remorse for transgressions committed and an irrevocable decision not to repeat them. The emotional state is an initial, preparatory step (cf. Nisson Wolpin 1993: 6). Teshuvah implies a profound inner search, candid acceptance that an error was made, verbal expression of the sin, and recognition of the road to follow. This is Viddui or confession (cf. Nosson Scherman 1993: 21–22). Atonement consists of two elements: remorse for the past and resolve not to sin in the future. Forgiveness requires sincere repentance (cf. Nosson Scherman 1989: 11–12).

In the Catholic Church reconciliation appears in Saint Paul's letters which describe: the religious dimension that identifies God as author of reconciliation: Reconciliation as the work of God is definitive and unconditional; the human response to the divine call to reconciliation that presents a dual plane: the religious (acceptance of reconciliation) and ethical (acting as one reconciled); the cosmic dimension, because in Christ, human history has been reconciled with God and the destructive force of sin has been overpowered by divine grace (cf. Mifsud 1987: 37–39).

4 Leviticus 5, 14–26. *The Holy Scriptures* (1956). According to the Masoretic Text. Philadelphia: The Jewish Publication Society of America: 5717. 122 s.

5 *IOM KIPUR: Reflexiones-Teshuvah, Tefila, Tzedaka.* (IOM KIPUR: Reflections- Teshuvah, Tefila, Tzedaka) Comunidad Israelita de Santiago. Manuscript. 1992.

Jesus insists on conversion of the heart, indicating that if one has quarreled with a brother – understood in the generic sense as another human being – one must reconcile with him before making an offering to God:

Therefore if thou bring thy gift to the altar and there remember that thy brothers' hath ought against thee; leave there thy gift before the altar, and go thy way; first be reconciled to thy brother, and then come and offer the gift. (Matt.5, 23 – 24).[6]

Another dimension of this version of reconciliation is love of enemies and prayer for those who persecute us:

Ye have heard that it hath been said, *Thou shalt love thy neighbour and hate thine enemy.* But I say unto you, Love your enemies, bless them that curse you, do good to them that hate you and pray for them which despitefully use you, and persecute you; That ye may be the children of your Father which is in heaven: for he maketh the sun rise on the evil and on the good and sendeth rain on the just and on the unjust. (Matt. 5, 44 – 45).[7]

Forgiveness is the fundamental condition of reconciliation (2 Cor. 5, 18 – 21): "You shall have no other debt with anyone other than mutual love" (Rm. 13, 8) (cf. *Catecismo* 1992: 180.567.618).

The sacrament of repentance, known also as reconciliation, consecrates a personal and ecclesial conversion process of repentance and reparation. Confession or admission of sin is an essential element of the sacrament. Repentance, also called contrition, is needed for this sacrament to take place (cf. *Catecismo* 1992: 328 – 334). Repentance in this case is defined as an intense regret and abhorrence of the sin that was committed, with the resolve not to sin again. (The Council of Trent, DS 1676). Catholic Catechism indicates that the sacrament must be preceded by the following: examination of the conscience, pain of sin, the intention to change, confession and reparation. The two principal requirements are the repentance for the sins committed and reparation for the damage caused (cf. *Catecismo Católico.* 1960: 171). Reparation means to repair the pain and damage caused another with restitution of that which was destroyed, expiation for one's actions. The offended party must be left satisfied, in other words, in repentance the spirit that moves the sinner is visible.

The emphasis on sin, on the presence of evil, and on reconciliation have been indicated in different ways throughout the history of the Catholic Church. However, in a catechism developed for adults (1969) the issues of sin and reconciliations are presented in the context of a process that occurs in community and in society as a whole, comprising both believers and nonbelievers. Reconciliation occurs not only in the individual conscience or in

6 *Catecismo de la Iglesia católica.* (Official version. Property of the Holy See. España (1992). Asociación de Editores del Catecismo. 180.

7 *Catecismo* 1992, 567.

the interior of the Catholic Church. This perception of society and humanity clearly emerges in the definition of the Church as God's tillers: "For we are laborers together with God" (1 Co. 3, 9). In this orchard grows the ancient olive tree whose holy roots were the patriarchs, and where reconciliation between Jews and gentiles took place and shall take place in the future (Rm. 11, 13–26) (cf. *Nuevo Catecismo* 1969).

In the papal document *Reconciliatio et Penitentia,* Pope John Paul II insisted on the mutual relationship between reconciliation and conversion because liberation from sin is a prerequisite for full reconciliation. Translated to secular language, this means recognizing the fundamental principle of the social teachings of the Church that confirms and proposes once again (1) the universal dictums of reason and the conscience of nations, supported in great measure by (2) the hope for a peaceful solution in social conflicts, and, definitively, (3) universal reconciliation (N°26) (cf. Tony Mifsud 1987: 39–40). In this sense, the word reconciliation carries its own theological horizon which cannot be discounted as a simple forgetfulness of discrepancies; "reconciliation leads to a prophetic reality of human coexistence" (ibid.: 40). The Old Testament already notes the contradiction generated by concrete transgressions and God's commandment: *Therefore you shall not oppress one another* (Lev. 25, 17). This commandment includes the notion of human beings as brothers created in the image of God, thus providing the subjective and social foundation for reconciliation.

The Model of Reconciliation of the Sanctum Officium of the Inquisition

Although it was a major institution of the Catholic Church for centuries, the Inquisition's use of the term "reconciliation" varied significantly from both Biblical and more modern usages. The reconciliation model of the Inquisition was both political and religious. In this model reconciliation refers to a judicial sentence issued after an *inquisition.*

The Spanish Inquisition was more extensive than all the other European Inquisitions in the 16th century. It was created in the second half of the XV century, and in the XVI century brought to the American continent, with Tribunals located in Mexico and Lima.[8] In Chile, it was established in 1572, and abolished in 1811 by a decision of the National Congress as part of the process of decolonization that ended with Chilean independence in 1818.

8 The crimes against faith are: heresy, witchcraft, apostasy, sacrilege, blasphemy and others. See Gajardo San Cristóbal, Lucia (1946). *Estudio sobre el tribunal del Santo Oficio de la Inquisición.* Santiago: Colección de Estudios y Documentos para la historia del Derecho Chileno. 13, 15 and 17.

Trials by the Inquisition could be initiated either by a formal accusation or by a denunciation: "Denunciation could result either in a conventional trial with a charge or in a completely new procedure, an Inquisition . . . the initiative. . . in the case of inquisitions . . . came from the judge himself. He heard not only the denunciation but also the accused's statement, and he accused, tried, and sentenced him. The powers of the inquisitor were unlimited and unprecedented, a departure from both secular and canon law. The accused had to conduct his own defense and prove his innocence, which was frequently difficult since the verdict on his "guilt" lay in the hands of one person, the accuser and inquisitor … the main role of the inquisitor was to extract a confession from the accused, with all the necessary means to do this at his disposal" (Miroslav, Hroch and Skýbová, Anna 1988: 16 – 17). When a person was denounced and accused of heresy or merely suspected of heresy, the inquisitors gave the order for arrest and all the assets of the accused were confiscated when the arrest was made. A clerk made a full inventory of the goods confiscated and the bailiff took as much money from the confiscated assets as was necessary to transport the accused, provide him with clothing and food and with his plank bed in prison. All the assets were taken for the Inquisition treasury.

Although the inquisition was ostensibly an investigation to determine guilt or innocence of the accused, the procedures appeared only *to look for corroboration of guilt*. After the arrest, no one was allowed any contact with the accused, and he was allowed to have nothing with him, no money, no paper or writing instruments, no gold or silver, and he had to spend the intervening period in solitary confinement. The interrogations employed various forms of torture, which were meticulously recorded, noting not only the procedure used but its effectiveness in obtaining a confession.

The accused could be sentenced to life imprisonment, which meant complete isolation in a cell on a regimen of bread and water. But if he gave signs of sincere repentance, he could be sentenced to publicly wear a large yellow cross on his clothing as a sign of his shame, the so-called "sambenito," either for a specific period of time or for the remainder of his life. Those who had made a full confession could be pardoned but were stripped of all their assets. If the confession came under torture and indicated repentance, the detainee could become *reconciled* with the Church. Yet, he lost all rights as citizen. This was the sentence of reconciliation. *The Inquisitor's Manual* establishes the following:

In general the repentant heretic should be sentenced to life imprisonment; however, there are exceptions to the rule and its rigor may be mitigated with those who reconcile themselves with the Church before they are accused or denounced; with those who confess their crime once prisoners, revealing their accomplices in heresy, and those who at a later date confess, before having been notified of witnesses' statements, since in the latter two cases it has greater value and conforms to law, the heretic shall be sentenced to perpetual confinement, pardoning him afterwards, and that is the practice of the Inquisition of Rome (Anot. lib.3, escolio 142).[9]

Chilean historian José Toribio Medina researched the Inquisition (cf. 1956: 129); in the archives of the Spanish Inquisition he discovered the document titled "Chronicle for the Supreme Council of the Holy Office of the Inquisition on the case of the doctor (*bachiller*) Francisco Maldonado de Silva ... tried (*relaxado*) and burned alive in the Auto de la Fe celebrated by this Holy Office on 23 January of 1639." *(La Relación para el Consejo Supremo della Santa y General Inquisición de la causa del bachiller Francisco Maldonado de Silva [...] relaxado y quemado vivo en el Auto de la Fee que celebró este Santo Oficio en 23 de Hen° de 1639 años)* This individual was the most noted Jew of the colonial era and martyr of his faith (cf. Böhm 1984: 3–6; Aguinis 1993).

Francisco's father, the doctor Diego Nuñez de Silva, was arrested in San Miguel de Tucumán, Argentina and accused of being a "Judaizer".[10] He was taken to the city of Lima for trial. Subjected to torture, he finally gave "signs of pain and repentance" and also asked "to be allowed to reconcile and to abjure for his errors, and swearing to live and die in the holy catholic faith, was convicted, consistent with reconciliation, in Public *Auto de Fee,* with confiscation of assets (which no longer existed), imprisoned for six years, and fulfillment of certain acts of spiritual penitence" (Böhm 1984: 11).[11]

Francisco Maldonado de Silva was arrested in the city of Concepción, Chile and brought to Lima. Accused by the Holy Office, during his first interrogation, he stated: "I am a Jew, sir, and profess the Law of Moses, under which I live and shall die, and if I must swear, I shall swear by the living God who created the heavens and the earth and who is God of Israel." (ibid: 85). After numerous theological discussions during the 13 years he was imprisoned, he was finally burned alive. The elder De Silva was sentenced to "reconciliation." His son, who consistently affirmed his religious faith and never denied it, even under torture, was burned at the stake.

Francisco Maldonado de Silva describes his perceptions of these procedures and their political and existential meaning in the first letter he clandestinely sent from prison addressed to *The Synagogue of Fellow Jews who are in Rome.* Originally written in Latin, the letter states as follows:

In truth, since the day I was taken, I promised God to die fighting for his truth with all my strength and power with arguments against enemies of his Law, and uphold them until the day I am bound to the altar of fire that will soon be prepared for me, (so I have been told) so that God may receive me as sacrifice for our sins and cease his

9 Benjamin, Vicuña Mackenna (1868). "Estracto del Manual de Inquisidores para uso de las Inquisiciones de España i Portugal, Capítulo XII, De la cárcel perpétua". In: *Francisco Moyen o lo que fue la Inquisición en América.* Valparaiso: Imprenta del Mercurio. 129.

10 Judaizer was the term used to characterize persons who practiced and promoted the Jewish religion.

11 "Audiencia, Lima 11 de Julio de 1601"

wrath which has been so inflamed in these kingdoms under Philip, King of Spain ... for him who openly confesses to be a Jew and that there is no other true God other than the God of Israel, is cast to the flames and from him is taken all property, and if he happens to have children there is no compassion for them; on the contrary, they are subjected to perpetual shame. If they convert to Christianity, all assets are expropriated, they are forever taunted in shame, by obliging them either for a short or long period of time to wear over their garments the cape known as the Sambenito; however, the stigma of their shame is stamped in their blood and in that of their children in generations to come, and neither they nor their children may conduct public duties in the Christian states.[12]

What is the meaning of reconciliation in this context? Reconciliation was the process of being readmitted to the community – the Catholic Church – after having experienced the rigors of justice. Reconciliation was considered a gesture of mercy from the law. The accused inevitably had to "choose" his own destruction, for his own good and for the good of his loved ones. Either he renounced his beliefs and loyalties or he chose prolonged torment and certain death. Reconciliation for the Holy Office, then, meant betraying one's self and loyalties, including family and friends, in order to end the torment or to preserve one's life.

Under the Inquisition's version of reconciliation, the reconciled person confesses to having sinned, suffers the penal and social consequences, then pledges in the future to accept the official truth and the institutional order. The reconciled person renounces his error, his false faith (Judaism, pagan or indigenous idolatries, Islam, witchcraft, treason to the king) and is accepted back into the community of believers under certain conditions: renouncing the error, public expiation of sin, becoming a constant and dissuasive example of the personal, social, and moral cost of committing the error. The inquisitor is perceived as acting fairly, fulfilling his duty to God and to the community and even with the reconciled victim, having saved him from sin and eternal damnation.

The public punishment and the miserable life that affected even the children of the persecuted are evidence of the totalistic political vision of the Inquisition. In this context, social and political relations were seen through the prism of transgression and religious betrayal. Anyone might fall suspect. Identification and persecution of the heretic was "for his own good" and for the good of his family, as well as for the political good of society identified with the salvation of the soul. At the same time, continued and systematic vigilance was necessary in order to identify transgressors and to persecute them, by separating them from society and preventing their ideas and practices from spreading and contaminating others, even their own family. The underlying justificatory discourse for these practices was the notion of the threat of

12 Ibid.: 311 s.

contagion, similar to what appeared in political speeches of the 19th and 20th centuries in Chile, regarding ideas that merited persecution, transforming persons who propagated them into "germs," "gangrene," "virus," or "cancer"– to be extirpated or surgically removed.

The procedures unleashed by secret police under regimes of state terrorism in the 20th century and the moral and political rationale for their actions under the guise of the doctrine of national security, present evident analogies with the proceedings of the Holy Office. These include the notion that a suspect is always guilty, the use of torture to extract confessions, prove guilt, and to achieve the subordination of the accused individuals. Death might come under torture without a legal sentence from any tribunal. The moral, physical, and psychological effects on the victims and the terror instilled in society, and lastly, the moral justification – the notion of a higher good – justified all these procedures.

Unlike reconciliation between individuals, groups, communities and nations after a conflict based on clashing interests, ideologies and political systems, the reconciliation sentenced by the Inquisition demanded that the person uphold the official truth, the true religion, and the authority generated and exercised in the name of God and the King. Political and religious orthodoxy were inseparable; offense against the King was an offense against God. The Inquisition fostered a form of ideological and political conversion, under the guise of a religious conversion. In the Inquisition's version of reconciliation, to be reconciled and the state of reconciliation had profoundly different meanings. This model is present in the proposals for reconciliation that conceive the community or national identity in a religious or fundamentalist ideological form that is, either openly or implicitly, homogenous and intolerant. The possibility of readmission as part of society depends on the unconditional acceptance of the dominant social order, not only in political terms but also in psychological, ideological, and religious terms.

Human Rights and a Theology of "Genuine" Reconciliation

Some 127 years after the abolition of the Inquisition in Chile, a unanimous vote from the United Nations General Assembly approved the Universal Declaration on Human Rights (Dec. 10, 1948). In Latin America the issue of human rights is interwoven with demands for freedom, justice and solidarity. Peruvian theologian Gustavo Gutiérrez proposed distinguishing between human rights in general and the rights of the poor with the following argument:

> […] this is a criticism of a liberal focus that assumes a state of equality that in fact does not exist in our society […] Only from the standpoint of the poor in Latin

American society [...] is it possible to understand the true meaning and biblical demand of the defense of human rights.[13]

Gutiérrez adds:

The Latin American Church could fall in the trap of facile and naive acceptance of "protected democracy." In other words, a formal recovery of certain freedoms and individual rights, but which leaves the profound societal and economic inequalities intact.[14]

These dilemmas were intensified with the development of a theological perspective on the issue of reconciliation as generated in the transitions from military regimes to elected governments, in Latin America (cf. Aldunate 1997: vii). The Chilean situation, in particular, led a number of theologians to reflect specifically on the issue of reconciliation. Four of these theologians whose thoughts had particularly broad dissemination and relevance were Joseph Comblin, Robert Schreiter CPPS, Tony Mifsud SJ and José Aldunate SJ.[15]

Joseph Comblin asks: What is the meaning of reconciliation for Latin America? What are the demands for a genuine reconciliation in Latin America (cf. 1987: 10)? First, he suggests that we differentiate the theological concept of reconciliation and reconciliations proposed by political platforms which do not draw upon theological influences. According to Comblin, the *political* call for national reconciliation signals and also conceals the desire and the plan to restore social peace without addressing the problems underlying the political violence and dictatorships of the recent past. In other words, reconciliation of

13 Gutiérrez, a Peruvian priest, published his widely-read *Teología de la liberación. Perspectivas.* (Lima: CEP) in 1971.

14 The texts of Gustavo Gutiérrez are cited in Aldunate SJ, Jose; Boff, Leonardo et al. (1989). *Derechos Humanos. Derechos de los Pobres.* Santiago: Rehue. 161 s.

15 José Comblin, a Belgian-born priest (1923) and doctor of theology, lived in Brasil and Chile between 1958 and the beginning of the 21st century. He offered classes in the Instituto de Teología de Recife until 1972, when a decree by the Brazilian military government impeded his further work in Brazil. He moved to Chile until 1981, when the military junta banned his reentry into the country after a trip abroad. He subsequently returned to Brazil; Robert J. Schreiter is a priest and member of the Province of Cincinatti of the Missionaries of the Precious Blood. He served as a professor of theology of the Catholic Theological Union in Chicago, Illinois;. Tony Mifsud S.J. is a doctor in Moral Theology. He was born in Malta. He arrived in Chile in the 1970s and lived there during most of the miltary dictatorship (1973–90). Mifsud directed ILADES and was the first director of the Center of Ethics at the Jesuit University Alberto Hurtado in Santiago de Chile. He is currently working in Brazil as advisor of the "Conferencia de Provinciales Jesuitas de America Latina". José Aldunate S.J. was born in Chile in 1917. He is Doctor of Theology (Universidad Gregoriana, Rome), and served for more than thirty years as professor of Moral Theology at the Universidad Católica de Chile. Associated with P. Alberto Hurtado in the creation of Acción Sindical Chilena and with the Jesuit review, *Mensaje*, Aldunate was Master of Novices and the Superior Provincial of the Company of Jesus. He also was a founding member of the Sebastian Acevedo Movement against Torture (Movimiento contra la Tortura Sebastián Acevedo). After 1973 he committed himself to working class and human rights organizations. He is living in Santiago and he is still participating in some Human Rights activities.

this type would have the exploited and oppressed give up their demands and resign themselves to the situation in which they live. Under the guise of reconciliation, a conservative ideology is promoted, which makes patently clear that conflict is incompatible with the Christian faith. According to Comblin, this view is known as theological reductionism, and consists of applying the Biblical notion of reconciliation to a specific political plan and a clearly defined ideology (cf. ibid.: 40). Most victims and oppressed people interpret the call for reconciliation with transition from military regimes to elected civilian governments in this sense, which leads them to mistrust it, considering that such a proposal exacerbates the original abuse (cf. ibid.: 62–63).

From theological foundations of reconciliation, Comblin stresses the importance of acknowledging guilt by the victimizers, the commitment to make restitution for the damage done or destruction, true remorse, and the need to ask for forgiveness. He also contends that reconciliation must be linked to liberation, linking concrete conditions of human life to evangelization as a humanizing plan. For Comblin, any specific reconciliation plan must be preceded by the need for reconciliation in the structure of society itself (cf. ibid.: 69). Thus Comblin's notion of "genuine" reconciliation returns to certain tenets of "liberation theology" – the bête noire of conservative theologians and U.S. policymakers during the Cold War era.

Robert Schreiter's interest in the reconciliation process began when someone asked him in Chile in 1986: "How do you seek reconciliation with someone who does not think he has done anything wrong" (cf. 1992: 2)? The question stemmed from the Chilean armed forces' insistence on their salvational mission and the legitimacy of using extreme measures such as disappearances and torture against the Marxist and antipatriotic "enemies." Schreiter suggests that reconciliation emerges as a challenge when experiencing extreme situations and the central question is:

> how people move from a situation of violence and suffering to something new and different. Our first impulse may be to envision the move from violence and suffering as a step back to the way things might have been prior to the cataclysmic events that have wracked our societies and our lives. But a little reflection teaches us that the experience of violence and suffering is burned into memory and has changed us irrevocably. *We are not the same people we were, and so any return is not a return; it is coming to a new place.*[16]

Schreiter indicates the issue of reconciliation emerges in South Africa, Latin America and other places in the world that experienced prolonged periods of political repression. The political transitions following removal of the repressive regimes could not elude the weight of the past on the present, *a burden compounded by memories of violence, betrayal, and oppression. The*

16 Schreiter 1992: 11.

lifting of that burden comes about through reconciliation (1992: 1). He adds that it is not only a matter of healing memories and receiving forgiveness, *it is also about changing the structures in society that provoked, promoted, and sustained violence.* He indicates that the challenge is how to come to terms with violence and suffering . . . *the redemption from both violence and suffering that lie at the heart of the reconciliation process* (ibid.: 17).

Thus Schreiter emphasizes the need for social and political reform, not merely negotiating an end to conflict between unequal adversaries. Reconciliation is not the same as conflict mediation, a process whose goal is to lessen conflict or to get the parties to accept and live with the conflictual situation.

> Reconciliation [then] becomes a process of bargaining in which both sides are expected to concede some of their interests in order to reach an end to conflict. The process acknowledges that both sides have legitimate interests, but that both sets of interests cannot be met in a finite world [...]. A balancing process must be undertaken that will require both sides to give something up, but not to give up so much that the conflict flares up again [...].[17]

From a Biblical understanding, reconciliation is not a skill to be mastered, but rather, something discovered: "To see reconciliation as a form of technical rationality [...] is to reduce reconciliation to the form it takes in one kind of culture. [...] but when the conflict has implied violence perpetrated upon individuals, families and whole societies that causes such great suffering [...] suffering is essentially an erosion of meaning. The nucleus of our humanity is restored to us in reestablishing the ability to trust [...] and recover and reconstruct memory [...] and then to put the question of how to suffer and how to regain our humanity" (ibid.: 36–39).

Schreiter goes even further than Comblin, requiring for genuine reconciliation not only social and political reform but also forgiveness by the victims of oppression and repentance of the victimizers. He argues that in the Christian understanding of reconciliation,

> we discover and experience God's forgiveness of our trespasses, and it prompt us to repentance. In the reconciliation processes then, because the victims have been brought by God's reconciling grace to forgive the tormentor, the tormentor is prompted to repent of evil doing, and to engage in rebuilding his or her own humanity [...] In the reconciliation process as understood from such a perspective, the process is initiated by the victim, not the oppressor [...] the proper subject of reconciliation is the victim, not the oppressor. And that can only be understood if we realize that the object of reconciliation is not the violent deed done, but the humanity of the deed's perpetrator [...] For there to be reconciliation, the victims must forgive; the perpetrators cannot forgive themselves.[18]

17 Ibid.: 25.
18 Ibid.: 45 s.

Tony Mifsud S. J. directly considers the case of the Chilean military regime. He points out that concern for reconciliation is revealed in declarations of the Episcopal Conference and the Permanent Committee of the Chilean Episcopate, which presumably would indicate a conscious application of theological thought to the importance of this issue for Chile (cf. 1987: 41). According to these declarations, the national situation was perceived in terms of violence, division, lacks of respect for human rights, lacks of participation and freedom. Episcopal authorities decried obstacles to reconciliation: violence, the lack of information, restrictions on freedom of expression, lack of respect for individual rights, lack of solidarity in business, the closed attitude of the governing class, the prolonged suffering of so many Chileans, the lack of political participation, the military nature of the regime, police brutality, political terrorism of various stripes, doubts as to the efficacy of the judicial system (cited by Mifsud 1987: 41 – 42).[19] Mifsud remarks that the word reconciliation is ambiguous, despite the specific meanings given to it in Church statements. Reconciliation is related to and takes on greater meaning in a situation perceived to be conflictive and without solution.

> However, this does not mean that reconciliation is achieved by forgetting the past or ignoring the conflict, or, worse, ignoring the origins of the conflict [...]. Reconciliation cannot be taken to mean renouncing aspirations against oppression in order to maintain "a social order" built on the foundation of exploitation and injustice. The only valid route to peace for reconciliation is one that includes a search for truth, the desire for repentance, and the concrete gesture of reparation. The conflict can only be overcome by eliminating the source of the conflict: only in this way can there be justice for victims and the oppressors be humanized. Reconciliation is conflictive because it is unyielding [...] Reconciliation does not look for conflict, but rather confronts it when needed in order to forge a road toward genuine social peace by eliminating that which fosters lies, oppression and hatred.[20]

This broader definition of reconciliation proposed by Misfud is clearly expressed in the invitation to political reconciliation made by the Chilean Catholic Church in the 1980s. The Chilean Church returned to elements of the Social Doctrine inspired by *Rerum Novarum* but also harkened to the themes of liberation theology of the 1970s, despite the declining legitimacy of liberation theology in the 1990s. Thus, within the Church itself, the concept of reconciliation continued to have ambiguous, even contradictory, usages.

José Aldunate SJ. more explicitly links human rights issues to social justice as part of the reconciliation process. He indicated that there were some successful advances in the Chilean political process of reconciliation but "the important task of reconciliation still remains largely unfulfilled". He added:

19 See *Mas allá de la protesta y la violencia* (June 24, 1983) and *¡Felices los constructores de la paz!* (Mt 5, 9) July 13, 1986. Cited by Mifsud 1987: 41 s.

20 Ibid.

"but it calls for a metanoia (conversion) through adherence to democracy and service to common good. Reconciliation needs to move forward among groups of people who are still imbued with ideologies. *They must learn to acknowledge the human dignity of those they have injured, make restitution, offer forgiveness, and accept that no one is deserving of hate or ought to be excluded from fraternal coexistence" (Aldunate 1997: 65).*

As seen in the texts cited, these theologians of reconciliation emphasize the ethical and transformative dimension of the reconciliation process. They associate reconciliation with an ongoing political project to create a more just society; reparation, along with truth, contrition, and forgiveness is an essential piece of any "genuine" political reconciliation. Reconciliation is viewed as a social utopia similar to the notion of the City of God. It is also a utopia which requires *conversion* of the members of the society and of the groups that are responsible for the common good. Conversion is both a spiritual and psychological process, based on the notion of a historico-mythical original conciliation of the human community, a wistful quest for paradise lost. This formulation transforms reconciliation into a revolutionary personal and political proposal, the antithesis of the Inquisitor's subordination of subjects to the official truth and also a rejection of reconciliation as pacted pacification and governability, that is, the version so popular in the Western Hemisphere in the 1990s.

The Politics of Reconciliation Post-Dictatorship

In contrast to the utopian requisites of the theology of reconciliation, the politics of reconciliation throughout Latin America from the 1980s into the 20th century was founded on the basis of subjective, ethical, cultural and political *agreements.* The contexts for reconciliation varied, but in post-dictatorship Latin America there has been no underlying consensus on the meaning of reconciliation itself – or on the gamut of public policies required to achieve a minimally acceptable restoration of "social peace". Indeed, the varying moral, ethical and political meanings given to reconciliation became an integral – and unyielding – part of everyday politics, with debates over punishment of past crimes, degrees of impunity, and proposals for reparation a part of the usual struggle, in periodic elections or renewed political violence, for control of national governments.

Understanding and making explicit the overlapping and sometimes contradictory notions of reconciliation did not (and does not) solve the basic dilemmas impeding *political* reconciliation in the region. Indeed, making these contradictions explicit suggests that the dilemmas cannot be reconciled within the parameters framed by these antagonistic paradigms, so long as groups within each society hold to different models of, and significations of reconciliation. Reconciliation as practiced by the Inquisition (submission by the victims and acceptance of the hegemony of the oppressors) would be inconceivable in the political transitions of the 1980s and 1990s, just as reconciliation as a conversion of the heart (by the supporters of the ex-military regimes or their adversaries) was even less politically conceivable. Governability and "democracy," the fashionable buzz words among regional elites and U.S. policymakers, seemed limited in their referents to "successful" elections and macro-economic stability. But renewed challenges in the hemisphere to liberal democracy and to capitalist-consumer societies, along with the shift from anti-communism to the global war on terror as the framework for regional politics, made such invocations ring hollow. In short, manipulation of the varied meanings and significations of the seemingly benign term "reconciliation" emerged as a central component of the discursive struggle to define the post-dictatorial and post-Cold War era in Latin America.

And just as there would be no "end to history" with termination of the Cold War, there could be no facile "turning of the page" throughout the hemisphere in the name of national reconciliation.[21] Ultimately, the meaning of political (or "genuine") reconciliation and its policy implications was a discursive conflict within the ongoing struggle to shape and govern Latin America in the last decades of the 20th century and the first decade of the 21st-century. In 2011 no end to history, nor to this fundamental struggle to define the future – by controlling interpretations and uses of the past – seemed likely.

References

Aguinis, Marcos (1993). *La gesta del marrano.* Barcelona, Buenos Aires: Planeta.

Aldunate, José S. J. (1997)."The Christian Ministry of Reconciliation in Chile". In: Baum and Wells ed.: *The Reconciliation of Peoples' Challenges to the Churches.* New York: Orbis Book. vii, 65.

Benjamín, Vicuña Mackenna (1868). "Estracto del Manual de Inquisidores para uso de las Inquisiciones de España i Portugal, Capítulo XII, De la cárcel perpétua". In: *Francisco Moyen, o lo que fue la Inquisición en América.* Valparaíso: Imprenta del Mercurio. 129.

Böhm, Gunther (1984). "Período Colonial. El bachiller Francisco Maldonado de Silva 1592 – 1639". In: *Historia de los judíos en Chile.* Vol. 1. Santiago: Editorial Andrés Bello. 3 – 6.

Catecismo de la Iglesia católica (1992). Property of the Holy España. Asociación de Editores del Catecismo. Official version. 180, 567, 618.

Catecismo Católico (1960). Barcelona: Editorial Herder. 171.

21 On the euphoric celebrations of the victory of liberal democracy at the end oft he Cold War see Fukuyama 1992.

Comblin, Joseph (1987). *Reconciliación y Liberación.* Santiago: CESOC. Ediciones Chile América. 10, 60, 62 – 63, 69.

Chapmann, Robert L., (1992). *Roget's International Thesaurus.* 5th ed. 372 – 373, 602, 656.

Fukuyama, Francis (1992). *The End of History and the Last Man.* New York: Free Press.

Gutiérrez (1971). *Teología de la liberación. Perspectivas.* Lima: CEP (cited in Aldunate, José S. J. Jose; Boff, Leonardo et al (1989). *Derechos Humanos. Derechos de los Pobres.* Santiago: Rehue. 161 – 162.

Hroch, Miroslav/Skýbová, Anna (1988). *Ecclesia Militans: The Inquisition.* (translated from the German by Janet Fraser). New York: Dorset Press. 16 – 17.

Comunidad Israelita de Santiago. (1992). *IOM KIPUR Reflexiones-Teshuvah,Tefila, Tzedaka.* Manuscript.

Longman Dictionary of Contemporary English (1995). Longman Group Ltda. England. 281.

Lira, Elizabeth and Loveman, Brian, (2005). *Políticas de reparación: Chile 1990 – 2004.* Santiago: LOM/DIBAM.

Loveman, Brian/Lira, Elizabeth (2002). *El espejismo de la reconciliación política.* Santiago: LOM/DIBAM.

Loveman, Brian/Lira, Elizabeth (2000). *Las suaves cenizas del olvido. La vía chilena de reconciliación política 1814 – 1932.* 2nd ed. Santiago: LOM Editores.

Loveman, Brian and Lira, Elizabeth (1999). *Leyes de reconciliación en Chile: Amnistías, indultos y reparaciones 1819 – 1999.* Santiago: DIBAM. 207 – 208.

Medina, José Toribio (1868/1956). *Historia del Tribunal del Santo Oficio de la Inquisición de Lima.* Santiago: 129.

Mifsud, Tony (1987).“El rostro ético de la reconciliación”. In: *Persona y Sociedad.* Revista de ILADES. AZo 1 N° 1. Santiago. 37 – 42.

Nisson Wolpin, Rabino (1993). “Anatomía de la Teshuvá”. In *El Kolel.* (XI N° 35 ELUL. 5753. Santiago. 5 – 6.

Nosson Scherman, Rabino (1993). “Reflexiones: Iom Kipur, pureza y confesión”. In: *El Kolel.* (XI N° 35 ELUL. 5753. Santiago. 21 – 22.

Nosson Scherman, Rabino (1989). “IOM KIPUR: Un día de perdón y pureza”. In: *El Kolel.* (VIII N°. 21 TISHREI. 5750. Santiago. 11 – 12.

Nuevo Catecismo para adultos (1969). Full version of Dutch Catechism. Barcelona: Editorial Herder.

Oxford Advanced Learner's Dictionary (1993). New York: OUP. 241.

Paul, Robert (1982). *Le petit Robert. Dictionnaire de la Langue Française.* Paris. 1627.

Real Academia Española (1992). *Diccionario de la lengua española.* Tomo II. Madrid. 1742.

Schreiter, Robert J., (1992). *C.P.P.S., Reconciliation, Mission and Ministry in a Changing Social Order.* The Boston Theological Institute Series. Vol. 3. Maryknoll, N.Y.: Orbis. 1 – 2, 11, 17, 25, 36 – 39.

The Holy Scriptures (1956). According to the Masoretic Text. Philadelphia: The Jewish Publication Society of America. 5717: 122 – 123, 492 – 493.

Wells, Harold (1997). “Theology for Reconciliation”. In: Baum, Gregory and Wells, Harold ed.: *The Reconciliation of Peoples: Challenge to the Churches.* Maryknoll New York: Orbis . 3.

Willi, Jürg (1978). *La pareja humana: relación y conflicto.* Colección Estudios de Sexología Ediciones. Madrid: Morata S.A. 298.

Hugo Rojas[1]

The Recognition of Victims of Human Rights Violations in Chile

An Analysis of the Complaints of the Chilean Labor Unions Presented to the International Labor Organization during Pinochet's Dictatorship

> ... more important than punishment –and even than reparation– it is yet the voice of justice that publically establishes the responsibilities of every actor, and designates the corresponding place for both the aggressor as well as the victim in a relation of fair distance
>
> Paul Ricœur[2]

1. Introduction

As we all know, during the dictatorship of General Augusto Pinochet the rights of the workers and trade union leaders were violated. This article revisits the subject, exclusively focusing on two aspects: (1) how the Chilean legal system was modified and used by the authorities to avoid that the workers could effectively defend their human rights (*infra* II), and (2) why denouncing human rights violations in international organizations is not only a convenient legal strategy, but also a historical record and evidence that could contribute to obtain reparations once democracy is restored, as it happened in the Chilean case (*infra* III). At the end, I offer some final reflections and remarks that might be useful for other societies in transition (*infra* IV).

This paper is a revised version of my lecture about "The Complaints at International Organizations as Evidence of Human Rights' Violations: The complaints of the Chilean trade union/workers presented at the International

1 The author would like to acknowledge the contributions made by Martín de la Ravanal, Jorge Donoso, Susan Flämig, María Angélica Garrido, David Gippner, Pedro Irureta, Martin Leiner, Elizabeth Lira, Monika Merrbach, Karen Tapia, and the organizers of the Summer School "Societies in Transition: Latin America Between Conflict and Reconciliation", Friedrich-Schiller-Universität Jena.

2 *Ricœur*, Paul (2008): *La memoria, la historia, el olvido.* Fondo de Cultura Económica. 2. Vol. in Spanish, Mexico, F.D. 606.

Labor Organization and Freedom of Association Committee (1973 – 1990)", presented at the Summer School *Societies in Transition. Latin America Between Conflict and Reconciliation* (Friedrich-Schiller-Universität Jena, Aug. 2009), complemented with information mentioned in the book *Freedom of Association and Human Rights,* which Elizabeth Lira and I edited in 2009.[3]

2. The Use and Abuse of the Legal System on Violations of Workers' Human Rights between 1973 and 1990

The Armed Forces overthrew President Salvador Allende in a military coup d'état in Sep. 1973. Since then, an authoritarian government was established in Chile, which strongly repressed people with left and center-left political thoughts, including the trade union movement and its leaders. The dictatorship remained until Mar. 11, 1990, when democrats returned to power after a complicated transition to democracy, following the referendum on Oct. 5, 1988, and by winning the presidential elections in Dec. 1989, when President Patricio Aylwin was elected with 54 % of the suffrages.

Between Sep. 1973, and Mar. 1990, the "legal system" *–latu sensu–* was controlled by the Armed Forces and the authorities of the Executive Power. If we carefully revisit the evolution of the legal system within this period, it is interesting to observe how a *de facto* situation gradually became *de iure,* obviously with the complicity of the main legal actors who were related to the dictatorship.

In those seventeen years, the Military Junta exercised the attributions of creating, modifying and derogating the laws of the Republic. In 1973, the Armed Forces dissolved the National Congress, which only restarted to have sessions by 1990. Also, for over a decade, the functioning of political parties was suspended and it was only until 1987 when they were able to legally establish. Intellectuals and supporters of the High Command of the dictatorship took seven years in drafting a new Constitution that was approved in 1980 in a referendum of dubious legitimacy, setting the basis of a new political and economic system in Chile that, significantly, still remains in place, although it has experienced important modifications between 1989 and 2005.

Since the Government controlled and determined the nominations of the judges in the country, it is obvious that the majority of judges of the Courts of Appeals and Supreme Court were supporters of Pinochet's Government. As it is mentioned in the National Commission on Truth and Reconciliation Report (1991), "the Judicial Power did not react strongly enough against the human

3 *Lira*, Elizabeth, *Rojas*, Hugo ed. (2009). *Libertad Sindical y Derechos Humanos: Análisis de los informes del Comité de Libertad Sindical de la OIT, 1973 – 1990.* Lom Ediciones. International Labor Organization. Alberto Hurtado University, Santiago.

rights' violations" and neither exerted an effective job on the protection of people's essential rights when these were threatened, disturbed or infringed by the authorities or by individuals, in complicity or tolerance of those" (1991: 95). The former was corroborated by the National Commission on Political Imprisonment and Torture (Apr. 2003), which stated that "the Supreme Court not only gave in the field for the discretional action of the new authorities and their agents but also ignored the abuses perpetrated against the people, by leaving them totally defenseless when facing such governmental arbitrariness... Strictly speaking, the highest tribunal offered the country its decisive support to the military government" (*Report of the National Commission* 2004: 171). In fact, during the dictatorship the judges did not apply any sanctions against those who violated people's human rights, in spite of being aware of the facts, for instance, through the statements included in the *habeas corpus* petitions presented to the highest courts. As Brian Loveman mentions, of about 2,500 *habeas corpus* petitions presented by human rights organizations between September of 1973 and October of 1975, the courts approved only one, not to mention that the Government responded to the court by issuing a detention order against that person whom the court intended to rescue (cf. 2001: 264).[4]

The situation at universities was also complicated, including the situation of the Law Schools.[5] Since the presidents of the universities were assigned by the Military Junta, many opposing scholars were expelled and an important number of intellectuals had to go into exile, without mentioning those who were disappeared or executed. In the words of Carlos Huneeus:

> The Junta decreed the intervention of senior officers of the three branches of the Armed Forces, both in active service as well as retired and assigned delegate-presidents into colleges. These officers received full authority to modify the internal structures inside the institutions, especially through the dismissal of professors and administrative staff and disciplinary measures that could be taken against students. The goal was the political neutralization of the student movement. (*Huneeus* 2000: 116)

When the authorities that exert power concentrate the executive and legislative functions without any counterbalance and have influence on the

4 The National Commission on Torture and Political Imprisonment notes: "Only in Santiago, between 1973 and 1989, *Comité Pro Paz* and *Vicaría de la Solidaridad* presented 9,000 *habeas corpus* petitions... which [the courts] rarely accepted. For example, between 1985 and 1989, the courts of Santiago accepted only 28 of 2,357 petitions presented by *Vicaría de la Solidaridad*" (173).

5 In the 70s, the legal community was small in terms of the size of the population, affecting the access of justice. For example, in 1975 only 3,000 students studied law in Chile (at the University of Chile, the Catholic University of Chile, the Catholic University of Valparaíso, the University of Concepción and the University of Chile in Valparaíso). Now that number can be easily multiplied by ten, in regard to the number of students and law schools.

nomination of judges, control the media and what is taught at colleges, there is no question that the legal system can be revised and modified according to the values and discernment that the political authority considers appropriate for a particular society, because there is no room for dissent, public debate and confrontation of ideas. Thus, the military government was fabricating and articulating a labyrinth of laws, attempting to elude and hide its lack of legitimacy.

Between 1973 and 1990, Pinochet's government approved a whole set of rules that in general restricted workers' rights and labor unions. These norms were used as an instrument for social repression, imposing a punishing vigilance towards those workers who opposed to the military government. In fact, the authorities took measures in order to restrict the activities of labor unions and many of these measures were imposed by force, without any chance to have a *due process* in courts. Right after the coup d'état, the Junta decreed a constitutional regime of exception throughout the county, such as the state of siege or emergency, thereby affecting the constitutional guarantees of citizens (cf. *Loveman* 2001: 263).

On Sep. 17, 1973, the Junta dismissed the legal personnel of the historically most important labor union *Central Única de Trabajadores* (CUTCH) (Decree Law N° 12). Moreover, the Decree Law N° 32 from Sep. 21, 1973 established that the dismissed workers could only complain before special courts, formed by a labor judge, a representative of the Armed Forces and the *Carabineros* (Police) and a Labor Examiner.[6] It also stated that workers could be dismissed if their actions were aimed against the production process or the national reconstruction, and strikes were forbidden.

It is true that many of the rules approved within the early years of the military dictatorship were afterwards modified, but still the regulation of working relations and labor unions suffered deep modifications during that time, having a strong and negative effect on workers' rights. Not only the labor law was modified, but the legal system was changed in such a way that human rights lost efficacy, including the rights to life, freedom of reunion and association, freedom of expression, personal security and physical integrity. For example, in 1978 the Junta approved the Amnesty Decree Law, forbidding the indictment of almost all human rights violations since 1973 (cf. *Hayner* 2008: 66), many of which were performed by a new secret police agency, *Dirección de Inteligencia Nacional* or DINA (created by Decree Law N° 521, in 1974), an entity that was subsequently replaced by the *Central Nacional de Informaciones* or CNI.

A very polemic situation for the efficacy of freedom of association was the impossibility to carry out collective bargaining between 1973 and 1979, a

6 In 1981, civil judges got jurisdiction to solve labor conflicts. Labor courts were reopened only in 1986.

situation that was only amended once the *Plan Laboral* (Labor Plan)[7] was approved. The Labor Union's meetings were limited to be merely informative (cf. *Brown* 1983: 29), affecting, during the entire period, the right to hold peaceful meetings. Moreover, labor organizations and unions were dissolved. I agree with Edmundo Fuenzalida when he argues that labor and social security legislations were dismantled and that the rights achieved by the workers and trade unions in the decades before were cancelled (cf. 2003: 195).

The intervention of authorities was so strong that the messages received by the trade unions leaders in that time were clear: if any trade union had the intention to function, it was preferable that the union leaders were in accordance with Pinochet's government.

These and many other restrictions to freedom allowed the authorities to violate workers' human rights with total impunity, affecting also the normal functioning of trade unions. There is no doubt that between 1973 and 1990 the legal system was used and abused by the military government against the Chilean workers.

3. Workers Complaints before the ILO: Legal Strategy, Evidence and Reparation

In the context of the above mentioned adverse scenario, the use of concrete legal mechanisms to register part of the truth and/or provoke reactions by the military government must be evaluated as valuable historical material to be considered within the complicated process of national reconciliation, but also as a solid contribution to the promotion, defense, and protection of human rights, including the possibility to achieve reparations for victims of abuse.

Precisely that has happened with the complaints presented by several labor unions before the Freedom of Association Committee of the International Labor Organization (ILO).[8] The complaints on detentions, exonerations, tortures, forced entries, disappearances, homicides, and other serious human rights violations obligated the *de facto* regime to respond before the ILO with

7 The transformation of the employment, labor and pensions laws during the dictatorship is known as *Plan Laboral*, and it should be understood as a key element in the project of transforming the social-economic model towards the establishment of Neoliberalism in Chilean society.

8 Since its establishment 55 years ago, the Freedom of Association Committee (FAC) has dealt with more than 2,500 complaints of infringement of freedom of association submitted to it either by governments or by organizations of employers or workers. For more information about the proceedings, decisions and principles of the FAC, see *ILO: Freedom of Association – Digest of decisions and principles of the Freedom of Association Committee of the Governing Body of the ILO.* Available at http://www.ilo.org/wcmsp5/groups/public/—ed_norm/—normes/documents/publication/wcms_090632.pdf.

official statements about such complaints. As it is possible to imagine, the authorities denied many of the denounced events at the time.

The formulation of complaints before the ILO can be understood as a legal mechanism used by trade union leaders, with several aims: (1°) to put an end to human rights violations against Chilean workers, (2°) to prevent further repressive actions of the state, (3°) to denounce before the international community the abuses of human rights by the military government.[9] Such accusations also can be useful afterwards, as (4°) a source of historical record of the perpetrated abuses and (5°) as a direct evidence to prove human rights violations, in order to obtain a reparation from the state.

The Freedom of Association Committee, after analyzing either the received claims or the answers of the Government, formulated concrete recommendations to be intended to put an end to the abuses perpetrated against trade unions leaders and Chilean workers.[10] In that sense, the recommendations of the ILO also serve as an invaluable back up of the workers requests in order to see their human and labor rights recognized. The content of these complaints and recommendations deserves to be acknowledged in public, because it is an important contribution to the (fragile) historical memory of Chile, and also because of the creativity of those using international law which, opposed to domestic law, offered them better possibilities to claim their individual and collective rights.

These accusations, formulated since 1973 until the return of democracy in 1990, contributed to an international awareness of the magnitude of the repression in the country, showing the failure of the judicial system and legal actions. The responses given by the Government also provide information of the situation of thousands of workers, even when the Government denied the facts or (hypothetically) adopted certain measures.

The records regarding labor law and violations of workers' individual freedom were provided by labor union leaders to a small group of people in charge of their formulation, most of them lawyers who worked for the Catholic Church at the Vicarage of Pastoral Laborers (*Vicaría de la Pastoral Obrera*) – and before it for the Vicarage of Solidarity (*Vicaría de la Solidaridad*) – or for more specialized entities, such as the *Corporación de Investigación y Asesoría Sindical* (CIASI) and others.

It is possible to classify the claims before the ILO into two larger groups: (1°) on one side, claims referring to the violation of civil liberties, as it happened when the regime performed illegal detentions, arrests, freedom deprivations, banishment, exile, tortures, murders and the loss of citizenship,

9 See the complaints presented to the Inter American Commission of Human Rights, the Commission of Human Rights of the United Nations Organization, Amnesty International, the World Council of Churches, the Jurist International Organization, and other institutions, which provoked an international reaction against Pinochet's dictatorship.

10 All the cases are available in ILOLEX, database of the International Labor Organization: http://www.ilo.org/ilolex/english/caseframeE.htm.

and (2°) on the other side, claims that refer to the violation of collective labor rights and freedom of association, which included the prohibition of affiliation of workers and organizations, the dissolution of trade unions, the prohibition of strike and collective bargaining, among others. Indeed, the exercise of freedom of association requires the recognition of civil liberties.

Figure 1: Classification of claims before the ILO (Chile, 1973–1990)
Source: Own representation.

Dimension	*Type of Complaint*
Civil Liberties	1. Unjustified detention of workers and trade union leaders and, in some cases, their subsequent disappearance.
	2. Detentions and interrogations of workers and trade union leaders, including their imprisonment in concentration and torture camps.
	3. Relegation and exile of workers and trade union leaders.
	4. Execution of workers and trade union leaders.
	5. Denial of permits to leave the country, e. g., to trade union leaders refugees in embassies.
	6. Deprivation of Chilean citizenship.
Freedom of Association	1. Limitation and suppression of affiliation, reunion, organization, petition and strike rights.
	2. Dismissal of workers because of their union affiliation or participation in strikes. Destitution of trade union leaders who belong to a political party declared illegal, through administrative ways.
	3. Prohibition of collective bargaining.
	4. Limitations to the finances of trade unions.
	5. Denial to the attainment of legal capacity.
	6. Cancellation of legal personality and confiscation of goods.
	7. No authorization for the celebration of May 1st.
	8. Assault of trade union facilities.
	9. Government intervention into some trade union organizations.

All the claims stated by the labor unions before the ILO, in the period between September 11, 1973 and March 10, 1990, were grouped by the ILO into 35 cases,[11] and the Freedom of Association Committee (FAC) of the ILO gave account of these cases in 123 reports.

It is not possible here to explain every situation acknowledged by the FAC of the ILO, but as an example that demonstrates the legal and strategic meaning and relevance of the mechanism of presenting solid and founded complaints at the international level, I will focus particularly in the main aspects of the *Case 765*, which is about the unjustified detentions of workers and trade union leaders and, in some cases, their subsequent disappearance. The accusation made by the trade unions, the response of the Chilean Government, and the recommendations made by the ILO will be described in the following paragraphs.

In Sep. 17, 1973, the World Trade Union Federation (*Federación Sindical Mundial*, FSM), referred to the detention of several trade union leaders of the *Central Única de Trabajadores* (CUTCH)[12]: Luis Figueroa Mazuela (President of the CUTCH), Ernesto Vogel Ramírez (Vice President of the CUTCH and President of the Industrial Railway Federation), Rolando Calderón, Eduardo Rojas, Octavio González, Luis Guzmán, Fidelma Allende, Manuel Dinamarca, Mario Navarro, Aldo Ramaciotti, Tucapel Jiménez Alfaro (leader of the National Association of Government Workers (ANEF) and first provisional executive Vice President of the National Workers Central Office (*Central Nacional de Trabajadores*, created in Dec. 1973), Jorge Godoy, Juan Ponce, Gilberto García Aravena and leaders of the secretariat of the Permanent Congress for Freedom of Association (*Congreso Permanente de la Unidad Sindical*): Jorge Espinoza, Benedicto Cerqueira de Silva, and Roberto Prieto (Uruguayan trade union leader, Vice President of the International Alimentary, Tobacco, Hotels and Similes Industries Labor Unions).[13]

Case 765 referred to Lina Benítez, known as Lina Kleovan, a trade union leader of the CUTCH, who was sentenced to death by the Chilean authorities. It

11 Cases 765, 823, 1028, 1046, 1051, 1094, 1095, 1096, 1109, 1117, 1126, 1136, 1137, 1144, 1152, 1156, 1162, 1170, 1183, 1184, 1186, 1191, 1194, 1200, 1205, 1205, 1212, 1229, 1272, 1276, 1278, 1280, 1285, 1297 and 1309 (Chile).

12 The Latin American Association of Workers (*Central Latinoamericana de Trabajadores*, CLAT) reported to the ILO, on Sep. 13, 1973, and Oct. 13, 1973, that the government was violating all the rights of the workers and their associations, organizing a brutal repression against them and also against the Latin American trade union leaders that were in Chile at that time. *See* Report No. 142 (1974). Vol. LVII, S. Chile. Case 765 (Sept. 17, 1973). Final Report. Chile: 227. As it is mentioned in that report, several trade unions claimed that a large number of trade union leaders had been detained or were under surveillance by the military authorities.

13 Report No. 139 (1974). Vol. LVII, S. Case 765 (Sept. 17, 1973). Provisional Report. Chile: 557 and 560. "In his communication of Oct. 4, 1973, the FSM declares that the President of the CUTCH, Mr. Luis Figueroa, is being wanted by the authorities" and promised money to any person who provided information that helped to capture him. See Report No. 142 (1974). Vol. LVII, S. Chile. Case 765 (Sept. 17, 1973). Final Report. Chile.

also mentions the execution of David Miranda, Secretary of the Chilean Miners Federation, who was shot to death on Oct. 19, 1973, Iván Gordillo, leader of the CUTCH in Antofagasta, Héctor Rojo, Samuel Yañez, Armando Jiménez, Guillermo Álvarez, trade union leaders of the longshoremen in San Antonio, Isidoro Carrillo, Bernabé Cabrera, Vladimir Araneda, coal workers in Lota, Luis Valdivia and Luis Mamani, trade union leaders in Calama, Ricardo García, worker and director of Cobre-Sal mine and other five trade union leaders, Héctor Martínez, rural leader, Manuel Donoso, teacher and leader. It also mentions the detention and demise of leaders of the National Union of Chemistry and Pharmacy Laboratories and Simile Subjects Workers (SUTRAL) and the Union of the Plastic Industry Workers (cf. Report No. 142 (1974). Vol. LVII, S. Chile. Case 765 (Sept. 17, 1973). Final Report. Chile: 244/45/50 and 267).

The Government responded to the ILO by saying that the trade union leaders were neither arrested nor persecuted and the fundamental rights of human beings were never violated (cf. Report No. 139 (1974). Vol. LVII, S. Case 765 (Sept. 17, 1973). Provisional Report. Chile: 564). It was argued that some people had the title of trade union leaders but they were actually *extremists* who performed violent actions: "sabotage, illegal possession of weapons, armed resistance to the forces of order and illegal traffic in the black market with products that, in most of the cases, came from the same companies where they worked" (ibid.). Considering this, those people should appear before a court, like other common criminals. The Government stated that some of those people were judged by the courts of justice, in accordance with the procedures and legal dispositions existing in Chile for many years, while others took refuge in foreign countries embassies. For the Government, these actions were equal to the recognition of their participation in felonies. It also said that Chile was in a situation of *internal war* and therefore had to decree certain temporary and exceptional legal restrictions, "even though they will be over once the civil peace is restored by the disarming of the *guerrilla* forces" and the restoration of free elections and democracy (ibid.).

Within an appendix to its report, the Government referred to some people hypothetically arrested (cf. ibid.: 565). It sustained that Luis Figueroa Mazuela, Fidelma Allende and Benedicto Cerqueira de Silva were refugees at embassies and Rolando Calderón was arrested and processed in Dawson Island (cf. ibid.). With respect to the rest of the list and the allegations of detention and/or disappearances, the Government denied the facts by expressing that "every other person mentioned in the claim of the FSM was not under arrest" (ibid.).

In the same way, the Government added that allegations about the detention of people were not proven by the accusers, insisted that no trade union leaders were persecuted whatsoever, and that the situation of people under arrest corresponded to the process of due justice and to regular proceedings before the courts (cf. Report No. 142 (1974). Vol. LVII, S. Chile. Case 765 (Sept. 17,

1973). Final Report. Chile: 236). Finally, the Government pointed out that "human rights have been respected at all times" (ibid.).

The Government sent to the ILO two new official statements, dated Feb. 8 and 11, 1974. In the second, it responded to several allegations formulated by the denouncers and attached documents as a proof of its position. For instance, it referred to the situation of Ernesto Vogel and Aldo Ramaciotti who were not arrested or interrogated by the new authorities (cf. ibid.: 253). With respect to the well-known national trade union leader Tucapel Jiménez, the Government reported that he declared he was not bothered either in his residence or in his job. Moreover, according to the Government, Gilberto García declared that he was not arrested either interrogated on his tasks at the CUTCH. Ernesto Vogel, Vice President of the CUTCH and President of the Chilean Industrial Railway Federation, continued to work and exercise his official duties, and Tucapel Jiménez was the leader of the *Central Nacional de Trabajadores* (CNT), founded in Dec. 1973. Jorge Godoy, former Secretary of Labor, was a refugee at the Swedish Embassy; Rolando Calderón – wounded by a gunshot inside the facilities of the Swedish Embassy and treated at the Military Hospital –, was not in Dawson Island, but he was a refugee at the Cuban Embassy (which, indeed, was under the direction of the Swedish Embassy). Eduardo Rojas was a refugee at the Finnish Embassy. Luis Guzmán Robinson was a refugee at the Argentinian Embassy and then moved to that country. Fidelma Allende was a refugee at the Finnish Embassy. Roberto Prieto, a Uruguayan, was a refugee at the Swedish Embassy and then expelled to that country. Benedicto Cerqueira de Silva, a Brazilian, was a refugee at the Panamanian Embassy and then traveled to that country. Lina Benítez (Lina Kleovan) was arrested for apparent felonies and afterwards was released. According to the Government, Manuel Dinamarca was not arrested. Juan Ponce was not arrested and traveled to Moscow on June 28, 1973. Luis Figueroa was a refugee at the Swedish Embassy. Finally, Patricio González Verdugo was free (cf. ibid.).

In regard to claims about homicides of union leaders and workers, the Government did not take any responsibility on those actions and provided very little information. For example, it reported that some of the demises were the result of clashes between the armed forces and dangerous extremists, militants of the *Movimiento de Izquierda Revolucionario* (MIR, Leftist Revolutionary Movement) and the Communist Party (PC). No trade union leaders participated in the confrontations (cf. Report No. 159 (1976), Vol. LIX. B. 3. Case 823 (Aug. 12, 1973). Provisional Report. Chile: 67), and press clippings were attached to corroborate the provided explanations. It also explained that some of the demises that took place during the period of military government were caused by demonstrators who left people seriously wounded, and they were not trade union leaders but common criminals. The Government also reported situations in which non-identified people would have performed kidnappings on the streets, in order to weaken the Government and to make the normalization of the country difficult; all this would be an international organized campaign. In other cases, the Government expressed to be deeply concerned and also disapproved the actions with energy, just as it happened after the demise of leader Tucapel Jiménez, head of the Chilean trade union movement.

The Government declares that a prospect around the case has arisen, which pointed to the possibility that Tucapel Jiménez would have been "executed" as part of an international conspiracy aimed at putting the Government in trouble (Report No. 217 (1982). Vol. LXV. B. 2. Case 1117 (March 1, 1982). Provisional Report. Chile: 490).

The Freedom of Association Committee understood that the seriousness of the political and social situation in Chile after September 11, 1973, affected the entire trade union movement. Without criticizing the state of siege within the early years right after the military coup, it examined the repercussions of this new political-legal status on labor law. The FAC performed an important task by receiving the annunciation of workers' detentions, requesting information from the Government on the conditions of these people, obtaining records about the actions that motivated such measures and by pointing out the rights and guarantees that should protect these workers during their detentions. In the *Case 765,* the FAC consciously took note of the provided information in respect to some of the workers and leaders who seemed to be arrested and others whose situation was unknown.

In this way, the FAC was able to find out information about the situation of several labor union leaders through the reports worded by the Government. These reports pointed out that some people were free, while others had left the country, some had been arrested according to the state of siege, others were prosecuted at military courts, and some were prosecuted for felonies under the Penal Code (Report No. 159 (1976). Vol. LIX, 1976, B, 3. Case 765 (Sept. 17, 1973). Evolutionary Report. Chile: 55).

The FAC expressed its concern in the *Case 765* about the execution (by shooting) and demise of several militants of political parties and trade union leaders and asked the Government for information on those actions. In some cases, however, the insistence of the FAC before the government, in order to investigate the demises of leaders and to have all the attained information at its disposal, was denied based on legal restrictions during the indictment stage of the investigation conducted by criminal judges. As a part of its recommendations, it also pointed out that the level of violence was a serious obstacle for the normality of the trade unions' lives. Besides requesting information, the FAC tried to advocate a restraint of the violence against trade union leaders: "... the cases of murder and other violent actions that involved trade union leaders are serious enough to demand that the authorities take severe measures in order to restore a normal situation" (Report No. 254 (1988). Vol. LXXI. B. 1. Case 1309 (Oct. 3, 1984). Provisional Report. Chile: 340).

As we can see in this example, the existing records at the ILO are a valuable historical document. They are part of the traces that today allow us to restore a past that for many years remained hidden or silent. If we revise the records of every other case known by the ILO about Chile, we can see that the Chilean Government indeed responded, by officially acknowledging information that has proven to be of great help for more than 800 victims and their relatives.

The strategy of legal resistance by presenting complaints before the FAC of the ILO, alerted the international community. The extended exchange of reports and recommendations of the FAC and its permanent insistence in respect to freedom of association and human rights of the workers helped the trade union movement to stick to their rights and actively participate in the complex process of restoration of democracy in the 80s.[14]

Many years later, in 2004, those documents were useful as an argument to verify the illegal detentions and torture actions perpetrated against more than 800 workers, mainly trade union leaders, whose cases were acknowledged by the National Commission on Torture and Political Imprisonment. I had the honor of assisting its work by coordinating the tasks of searching for evidence, with the help of sixteen law students of Alberto Hurtado University, who voluntarily reviewed, classified and organized documents provided by the Commission during several weeks.[15]

The ILO reports were a valuable supply for the Commission and were useful as a direct evidence to prove human rights violations against specific persons. Law 19.980, approved in 2004, allowed the victims of torture and political

14 One should take into account that the first non-permitted public demonstration against the dictatorship was organized by the workers in the Craftmen Square (*Plaza de los Artesanos*), located near the Mapocho river, on Dec. 2, 1982. The workers involved in it were attacked by police officers and agents from the CNI. Four people were injured and 37 were arrested. The major First Public Demonstration against Pinochet was on May 11, 1983, and it was organized by the workers and trade union leaders. Two people died. In Santiago alone, 350 people were arrested and in the following days 500 more persons. Thousands of students did not go to school that day, and there were demonstrations all over the country. On June 14, 1983, the second National Demonstration took place, which was also strongly repressed by authorities. These demonstrations forced Pinochet and his ministers or secretaries to negotiate. In that way, it was possible to restart political activity and the legal existence of political parties was finally allowed, leaving aside the ones that were connected to Marxism. New leaderships appeared, because the two biggest leaders of the time were killed: former President Eduardo Frei, who ruled between 1964 and 1970, died from poisoning during a hospital procedure on Jan. 22, 1982, and Tucapel Jiménez died on Feb. 25, 1982. The new front row leaders of the 80s were also arrested: Ricardo Lagos, who then became President of Chile between 2000 and 2006, Gabriel Valdés, president of the Senate between 1990 and 1994, union leaders Rodolfo Seguel, Manuel Bustos, and Arturo Martínez, today the president of the National Union Association of Chile (CUT), among others. The repression continued until Mar. 11, 1990, when President Patricio Aylwin took charge as President of the country.

15 I would like to acknowledge the volunteer work of law students Ignacio Alarcón, Carolina Álvarez, Pedro Bello, Carlos Campos, Boris Hau, Luis González, Sergio Lillo, Mónica Osbén, Juan Cristóbal Palma, Cristián Peñaloza, Álvaro Rivera, Aníbal Robles, Rocío Salgado, Sebastián Salazar, Natalia Sánchez, and Francisca Terminel. Some of them were hired afterwards by the Commission to help in the process of reviewing testimonies.

imprisonment to have access to reparation measures provided by the Chilean state.

4. Final Comments

The workers claims before the ILO, the answers of the Chilean government and the recommendations of the ILO against the Chilean government, are a valuable testimony for the defense of workers' human rights. It is necessary to recognize (1°) the spirit of those who dared to speak up and bring forward the claims presented to the ILO against the Chilean government and (2°) the substantial contribution of the ILO, for more than ninety years, towards the standing of workers' human rights, especially in instances when these are violated by authoritarian governments as it happened in Chile between 1973 and 1990. In fact, the documents give a closer look into human rights violations thousands of workers and trade union leaders suffered in that long and dark night of the Chilean history.

During the last years, I had the chance to interview many people who, due to several reasons, feel discriminated, ignored or denied in Chile. Although truth, justice, and reparation were mentioned in this kind of conversations as essential values, I am convinced that the struggle and the attainment of "recognition" is a key element when studying the concept of peoples' dignity and that we have not reflected upon it sufficiently. The suffering of a person who is not recognized or who receives only insincere recognition is tied to the frustration of not feeling integrated into a society in which we wish to belong. For many years in Chile human rights violations were denied and an important percentage of the population preferred to turn the page and not to talk about such a relevant matter. The denial of such an evident reality prolonged the time of sorrow.

It is true that from 1990 to the present, symbolic acts and important signs towards the victims have taken place (cf. *Lira and Loveman* 2005), but real reconciliation will occur when they feel recognized and valued by every other sector of society. As long as this does not occur, Chilean society will live with an open wound. I agree with Pablo Salvat when he states that the aspiration to reunion and reconciliation cannot take place if actions are being denied and particular responsibility for what happened is not assumed (*Salvat* 2005: 14). Therefore, reparation and recognition of the dignity of the victims are key elements in the reconciliation process.

More important than the beatings or the physical tortures, the deepest pain is connected to the dignity of the victims as human beings. Many want to have justice but also want to be asked for forgiveness. President Aylwin asked for forgiveness on behalf of the Chilean state in 1991. The Chief Commander of the Army, Juan Emilio Cheyre said "Never Again" in 2004. Those speeches were very relevant but not sufficient for some of the victims. For example, Pinochet never recognized anything and this has caused a deep grief in the victims' hearts.

Reconciliation in Chile will not be possible as long as the victims do not recover their dignity. This is not a matter of money. We are not arguing over the question if the pension is high enough, if the scholarships for studying are good enough, or if health programs have improved the quality of the victims' lives; the point rather is that many of the victims still feel excluded and not being considered adequately, as if they were second-class citizens. After so many years, the victims want to be recognized by the rest of society and they want to recover their dignity, that is, the essence of their lives. As long as it does not happen, reconciliation in Chile remains a mere utopia.

References

Brown, C. G. (1983). 10 años de atropellos a los derechos humanos en Chile: Report of the Americas Watch Committee. Mexico: F.D. 29.

Fuenzalida, Edmundo (2003). "Derecho y Cultura Jurídica en Chile (1974 – 1999)". In: Fix-Fierro, Héctor, Friedman, Lawrence M., Pérez Perdomo, Rogelio ed.: *Culturas Jurídicas Latinas de Europa y América en Tiempos de Globalización.* Universidad Nacional Autónoma de México. Serie Doctrina Jurídica. 39. Mexico: F.D. Available at http://www.bibliojuridica.org/libros/3/1078/6.pdf [accessed on May 2010]. 195.

Hayner, Priscilla (2008). Verdades innombrables: Fondo de Cultura Económica. Mexico: F.D. 66.

Huneeus, Carlos (2000). *El Régimen de Pinochet.* Editorial Sudamericana. Santiago. 116.

ILO: Freedom of Association – Digest of decisions and principles of the Freedom of Association Committee of the Governing Body of the ILO. Available at http://www.ilo.org/wcmsp5/groups/public/—ed_norm/—normes/documents/publication/wcms_090632.pdf. [accessed on May 2010].

Lira, Elizabeth, Rojas, Hugo ed. (2009). Libertad Sindical y Derechos Humanos: Análisis de los informes del Comité de Libertad Sindical de la OIT, 1973 – 1990. Lom Ediciones. Internacional Labor Organization. Santiago: Alberto Hurtado University.

Lira, Elizabeth, Loveman, Brian (2005). Políticas de Reparación. Chile 1990 – 2004. Lom Ediciones. Santiago.

Loveman, Brian (2001). Chile: The Legacy of Hispanic Capitalism. 3th ed. New York: OUP. 263 – 264.

Report of the National Commission on Truth and Reconciliation (1991). Santiago. Available at http://www.ddhh.gov.cl/ddhh_rettig.html [accessed on May 2010].

Report of the National Commission on Torture and Political Imprisonment (2004). Santiago. Available at http://www.comisionvalech.gov.cl/InformeValech.html [accessed on May 2010].

Ricœur, Paul (2008): La memoria, la historia, el olvido. Fondo de Cultura Económica. 2th Vol. in Spanish. Mexico: F.D. 606.
Salvat, Pablo (2005): "Derechos humanos: caminos pendientes". In: Lira, Elizabeth and Morales, Germán ed.: Derechos humanos y reparación: una discusión pendiente. Lom Ediciones. Santiago: Alberto Hurtado University. 14.

ILO Cases and Reports[16]

Case 765 (Sep. 17, 1973). Chile.
Case 823 (Aug. 12, 1975). Chile.
Case 1117 (Mar. 1, 1982). Chile
Case 1309 (Oct. 3, 1984). Chile
Report No. 142 (1974). Vol. LVII, S. Chile. Case 765 (Sept. 17, 1973). Final Report. Chile.
Report No. 139 (1974). Vol. LVII, S. Case 765 (Sept. 17, 1973). Provisional Report. Chile.
Report No. 159 (1976). Vol. LIX, 1976, B. 3. Case 765 (Sept. 17, 1973). Evolutionary Report. Chile.
Report No. 159 (1976), Vol. LIX. B. 3. Case 823 (Aug. 12, 1975). Provisional Report. Chile.
Report No. 217 (1982). Vol. LXV. B. 2. Case 1117 (March 1, 1982). Provisional Report. Chile.
Report No. 254 (1988). Vol. LXXI. B. 1. Case 1309 (Oct. 3, 1984). Provisional Report. Chile.

16 See ILOLEX Database of the International Labor Organization, Geneva. URL http://www.ilo.org/ilolex/english/caseframeE.htm [accessed on May 2010]

Katharina Freudenberg

Ecumenical Human Rights Movement during the Military Dictatorship in Argentina

During the 20th century the Argentinean government experienced six military coups (cf. Quiroga 2004: 33 – 55).[1] The last one occurred in 1976. The following military dictatorship (1976 – 83) differed immensely from the earlier ones in the high level of violence and human rights violations. In this situation members of Christian Churches felt urged to help in defending the rights of their fellow men. To be able to fulfil this difficult and dangerous task effectively different Christian Churches founded the "Ecumenical Human Rights Movement".[2]

The purpose of this case study is to outline some of the main aspects of the commitment of the MEDH during the dictatorship, in order to illuminate one form of committed Christian engagement against human rights violation. It will become clear that there is a strong connection between the theological key aspects (prophetic call, social responsibility) and the concrete working practice of the MEDH members (prophetical sermons as well as juristic, pastoral and social tasks).

In order to be able to understand their specific engagement, it is helpful to start off with (1) a rough outline of the historical context, which includes (1.1) the political situation in Argentina before 1976, (1.2) the military coup and (1.3) the dictatorships' oppression methods. In this context (2) the foundation process and working fields of the "MEDH" becomes clearer. In order to provide a deeper understanding of the attitudes towards human rights issues inside of the MEDH-churches, (3) the United Church IERP will be portrayed more in detail. At the end (4) some final reflections are going to give a few examples indicating further considerations, together with a short summery of this case study.

Because the activities of organisations like the MEDH were partly monitored by the military government, it was a high risk to have written documentation. Therefore only a few written sources can be used for this study. Consequently a lot of the following information is derived from interviews with members of the MEDH and the IERP following the "Oral-history-me-

1 Precisely in 1930, 1943, 1955, 1963 and 1976.

2 Its original Spanish term is "Movimiento Ecuménico por los Derechos Humanos" (MEDH), which will be used in this article as well.

thod".[3] It is a historical method used for the research of contemporary topics. The interviews for this case study were accomplished in autumn 2009.[4]

1. Historical Context

1.1 The Political Situation

Looking at the training program of the Argentinean military during the 1960s and 1970s, it is striking to see that the higher officers went to training centres in the United States, such as the National War College. Against the background of the Cold War the concept of this military formation was ideologically polarized. The guideline was called "Doctrine of National Security" (cf. García 1995: 85 – 106). It described a strategic shift from one mainly concentrating on the defence of their own country or the assault on a hostile nation, to one focusing on the enemy within the borders of their own country. The Cuban Revolution served them as daunting example par excellence. In order to eliminate at all cost the "Communist Subversives", opponents were declared state enemies (cf. ibid.: 38). To be able to identify this loosely defined enemy they introduced the concept "lucha contrainsurgente",[5] which legitimised cruel oppression methods and the development of a broad intelligence service (cf. ibid.: 85 – 93). Furthermore it was not only the military officers from Argentina that underwent the training program described, but also officers from other South American countries (cf. Quiroga 2004: 33 f.; Marchak 1999: 71 f.).[6] For this reason the national secret services of those countries cooperated and exchanged information under the headword "Operation Condor" (cf. Eichner 2009; Stella 2006).

In the case of Argentina, the military coup in Mar. 1976 was not received with major disturbances (cf. Andiñach and Bruno 2001: 19 f.). Several different reasons can be found for this in the history of the country:

A) As was mentioned earlier democratic governments in Argentina have been overthrown by the military often before. Therefore the population was already used to this pattern of a sudden change in regnancy.

B) The Peronean government (1973 – 76) was lead by the former president's

3 For detailed information see Niethammer, Gedächtnis; Ritchie, Oral History; Howarth, Oral History; Thompson, Oral History; Wierling, Oral history, 81 – 151; Grele, Methodologische Probleme, 195 – 220.

4 For the transliteration of the interviews see: Freudenberg, Menschenrechtsarbeit MEDH, Annex, 1 – 59.

5 The term means the "combat against insurgents".

6 Among them were quite a few of the South American dictators of the 1960s and 1970s: Hugo Banzer (Bolivia), Augusto Pinochet (Chile), Ernesto Geisel (Brazil), Alfredo Stroessner (Paraguay), Jorge Videla (Argentina).

wife, Isabel Martinéz de Peron, after her husband had died in 1974.[7] The political leadership got out of hand due to internal fights between the different factions within Peronism.

C) This governance disorder provoked a stronger operation of those paramilitary groups, which came into existence at the beginning of the 1970s. Just to name a few, there was the Marxist-Leninist ERP (Ejército Revolucionario Popular) and the Montoneros as the guerrilla movement of the extreme left-winged Peronists. In reaction to the rising levels of violence the government authorized the military to act against these groups. Many of the authorised military actions were lead by the secret paramilitary group AAA (Alianza Anticommunista Argentina), which emerged out of the extreme right-winged Peronists. Due to the very brutal fights between those groups the population soon felt seriously threatened (cf. Marchak 1999: 93 – 127; García 1995: 49 – 65).

D) Additionally the economic situation became very fragile. Already in 1975 Argentina suffered a massive inflation, which rose up to 600 % in the beginning of 1976.

As the result of the political instability, the brutal attacks of the paramilitary groups, and the difficult economic situation, many Argentineans hoped for a quick change.

1.2 The Military Coup

This change came about on Mar. 24, 1976. Military groups arrested the President and formed a military junta.[8] It consisted of the commanders of the air force Orlando Ramón Agosti, the navy Emilio Eduardo Massera and the army Jorge Videla, who was declared president. Very quickly they started to rearrange the Argentinean government. All political activities were suspended, the parliament and the local governments were dissolved, the judiciary was put under the rule of the military junta, and the constitution was superordinated by new legal decrees (cf. Crespo 2007: 165 – 170). All these changes were legitimised by the headword “Process of National Reorganisation”. This program was proclaimed to reconstruct the state, reintegrate essential values, develop the economy and eradicate all kinds of communist subversion (cf. Quiroga 2004: 74 f.; Marchak 1999: 146 f.; García 1995: 208 – 210).[9] This strategy was orientated on the already mentioned “Doctrine of National

7 Peronism describes an Argentinean political movement named by its founder and leadership figure Juan Perón, who became president for the first time in 1946 and for the second time in 1973. It is difficult to integrate Peronism into traditional political classifications, as one has to consider manifold developments and different factions within Peronism. One keyword of its original ideology was “A third way”. It refers to an economical approach that is neither socialist nor capitalist but integrates elements of both.

8 For chronological details see Troncoso, Proceso.

9 The junta also proclaimed to defend the “Christian Civilization”.

Security", which legitimised rough methods to eliminate the subversive enemy in order to sustain inner peace and protect morality.

1.3 Methods of Oppression

As a consequence of a ruined economy and a devastating defeat in the Malvines/Falklands war, the military dictatorship broke down in 1983.[10] The new democratic government headed by the president Raúl Alfonsin appointed a "National Commission on the Disappearances of Persons".[11] Its task was to investigate one of the main oppression methods used by the dictatorship, which is called the "disappearance" of people. Shortly outlined, that means the kidnapping of a person and the transference to a secret detention centre without any information available for the relatives – not even about the whereabouts of the kidnapped person, the reason for the kidnapping or the identity of the kidnappers.

By the synopsis of the statements, which were given by survivors and relatives of the "disappeared"[12] this report describes recurrent procedural methods of the military and similarities in the profiles of the victims. It showed that a high percentage of the "disappeared" were aged between 16 and 35 and socially engaged, ranging from teenagers hoping for a socialist revolution, trade unionists fighting for higher salaries, journalists unsympathetic to the junta or nuns and priests evangelising in shanty towns. 21 % were students and 10.7 % professionals, among them artists and writers (cf. Invernizzi and Gociol 2003: 49–403; CONADEP 1987: 155–80). A profile of a typical "communist subversive" didn't exist. Instead it seems clear that the military junta wanted to eliminate not only the potential political and social critical opposition, but also the intellectual elite.

The report of the CONADEP describes the pattern in "making disappear" people. According to it the kidnapping often happened at home or at the working place of the person. He or she was brought to a secret detention centre, at times also called concentration camp. To identify potential accomplices, torture methods were used. Many victims spoke of regular physical or psychological torture (cf. CONADEP 1987: 21–46). The "total disappearance" included the death of the kidnapped person. But as the relatives never received any answers from the military, these killed people stayed in the status of being

10 Four military juntas ruled the country during the dictatorship headed by: Jorge Videla (1976–1981), Roberto Viola (1981), Leopoldo Galtieri (1981–1982) and Reynaldo Bignone (1982–1983). For more details about the whole period see Quiroga, Proceso, 57–345. Information about the Malvines/ Falklands war gives García, Autonmía militar, 225–256.

11 The original term, that will also be used in this text, is "CONADEP" (Comisión Nacional sobre la Desaparición de Personas).

12 The Spanish term is "Desaparecidos", which is also used in other South American countries for describing the same phenomenon.

"disappeared". There is a difference in opinion as to the number of victims. The CONADEP states 8960 (cf. ibid.: 17),[13] whereas many human rights organisations speak of 30.000 "disappeared" people.

As mentioned before the propaganda of the military junta was strictly against everyone who could be connected to "communism". As we have seen that included all kinds of political critics and socially engaged people, who were therefore in danger of being wrongly defamed as "communists". This misleading identification also brought human rights activities in the dangerous position of counting as mainly political. Therefore they were put into the risk of being controlled or even persecuted. What made the whole situation even more difficult was the fact that the government denied throughout their rule that they gave the order to let people "disappear".

2. Foundation and Working Fields of the MEDH

The MEDH was founded as a consequence of experiencing the "disappearing" of people, which had already started at the end of 1975 (cf. Blatezky 2006: 80 f.). This was such an unknown and threatening phenomenon that the relatives of the "disappeared" looked out for help in all direction, including towards the church. To answer that need pastors, priests and laymen of different Christian denominations gathered in Feb. 1976 to lay the foundations for an ecumenical human rights movement (cf. Blatezky 2006: 84 – 89; Ponsati 2004: 18; MEDH 2002: 16). On Mar. 23, 1976, the night before the military coup, the first general assembly of the MEDH gathered (cf. MEDH 2002: 17). From the early days on there was a strong connection to the World Council of Churches, which supported the MEDH including financially (cf. Freudenberg 2010: 30).[14] In 1978 the churches supporting the MEDH – the Methodist Church (IEMA), the Reformed Church (IRA), the United Church (IERP), the Church of the Nazarene and a few Catholic dioceses – joined the MEDH officially.[15]

With regard to content the MEDH was oriented towards a theology of liberation, which has a political outlook (cf. Ponsati 2004: 75). That means that the perspective of faith and the interpretation of biblical texts are focused on the concrete present situation especially of those at the edge of society. The foundation document of the MEDH points out two main themes: the social

13 The commission's report also states 600 cases of kidnapping during the months before the military coup.

14 The MEDH received financial support also from other organisations such as Bread for the World and different European Churches.

15 An overview of the different positions within Protestant Churches towards the dictatorship in Argentina is given by Añdinach/ Bruno, Iglesias Evangélicas, 22 – 28. For a detailed portrait of the reactions within the Catholic Church see Mignone, Dictadura.

critic of the Old Testament prophets like Amos and the discipleship concerned with social responsibility (cf. MEDH 2002: 16 – 21.). It is made very clear, that all people in need – coming from whatever religious, political or ideological background – were welcome. This position is grounded on the godlike creation of all people, which gives them dignity and leads in the consequence to concrete human rights (cf. Freudenberg 2010: 17; MEDH 2004; 2002: 17).

The MEDH's fields of work covered three areas: pastoral, social and juristic tasks.

The pastoral work was lead mainly by the pastors and laity of the churches cooperating in the MEDH. They wrote public declarations and theological documents (cf. Freudenberg 2010: 31 f.; MEDH 2002). One group published a regular journal called "Informed", which consisted of articles on current questions or actions concerning human rights, but also related biblical reflections. As publications were examined by the military, they were forced to avoid delicate themes. The churches of the MEDH also invited relatives of "disappeared" people to intercession services (cf. Freudenberg 2010: 32 f.). The sermons linked biblical texts to current themes. For example, the situation of the prophet Isaiah marked by injustice and fear was compared to the last decades and the nowadays situation in Argentina. Referring to Isaiah 9, 1 – 7 the sermon also opened the perspective of hope for the promised light illuminating darkness (cf. MEDH 2002: 33). After the services the relatives of the "disappeared" had the chance to get into contact with one another and also to receive pastoral care from pastors, priests or nuns. As well as the official services, relatives of "disappeared" also had the opportunity of pastoral accompaniment (cf. Freudenberg 2010: 34 f.).

The legal and social work was operated by lawyers and social workers, who were employed by the MEDH.

The main task of the lawyers was to help the relatives of "disappeared" to file a "Habeas-Corpus-Petition" to the government, in order to get information about the whereabouts of the "disappeared" (cf. ibid.: 35). The main difficulty was that the military dictatorship had the executive power and the rule of the judiciary. Consequently there was no independent level of jurisdiction, to which one could appeal. Therefore all those thousands of petitions were answered negatively, at times with threadbare arguments (cf. Freudenberg 2010: 13 f.; Marchak 1999: 128 – 145). Nevertheless the amount of petitions put a certain pressure on the government. The MEDH saved all of the copies of those documents in secret archives. Nowadays they serve as evidences in court cases (cf. Freudenberg 2010: 3, 13). Another part of the lawyers work had to do with the legal complications following the disappearance of a relative. For example if it was the father of a family and he was the holder of the bank account, it was very difficult for any other family member to get access to it. Or when he has bought the car or the house, it was nearly impossible for the relatives to sell it (cf. ibid.: 36). The lawyers tried to find – if there was – a way out of those juristic obstacles.

Families could be in a very fragile financial situation if a family member disappeared especially if they were the principle earner or even, in some cases, both parents (cf. ibid.: 10). Therefore one part of the social work consisted of supplying food or school material. The social workers also offered mentoring to the children, whose parents had both "disappeared". To aid the development of these children, psychologists introduced different creative and playful activities for them (cf. ibid.: 37 f.). These projects took place in facilities of churches supporting the MEDH. Their members also got involved into special programs such as "If all Children"(cf. MEDH 2002: 124),[16] which took place at Christmas in 1982. It was aimed for those children, whose parents had been transferred to an official jail. Often they were far away and it was too expensive to get there. For that reason this program invited people to finance a ticket for one child to be able to see their parents at Christmas.

The synopsis of the fields of work described shows the practical implementation of the theological grounding: The prophetic task is visible in the publications of the "Informedh", in the social critical sermons of the intercession services, but also in the legal language of the "Habeas-Corpus-Petitions" by pointing out human rights violations. The call for social responsibility as a part of following Christ gets substantiate in the different financial, psychological and social support for the family and children of the "disappeared".

3. Portrait of One Member Church of the MEDH: The United Church IERP (Iglesia Evangélica del Río de la Plata)

Within the churches supporting the MEDH there is a wide range of different opinions regarding the human rights topics in general and the work of the MEDH in particular.

To get a closer view into the inner church discussions the following chapter portraits one example, the IERP. As this is not an internationally known church, the description starts off with a short review of its history:

The foundation of this church goes back to the beginning of the 19th century. After Argentina won independence from the Spanish rule in 1816, it promoted immigration from Europe. Also non-catholic trading partners, farmers, scientists, artists and many other people were welcomed (cf. Zorzin 2009: 29; Blatezky 1997: 4). Therefore German speaking Protestants from Germany, Switzerland and the Volga-region in Russia also followed this call. Although during the following decades mainly merchants and politically interested upper class members immigrated, the people arriving in the second half of the

16 The Spanish title was: "Si todos los niños".

19th or at the beginning of the 20th century were rather poor craftsmen hoping to find work.

In 1843 tradesmen founded the first German congregation in Buenos Aires (cf. Zorzin 2009: 29; Luetge 1981: 217–219). Until the end of the 19th century 13 other "immigration churches" came into existence.[17] Economically there was a notable difference between the well-off town congregations and the poor churches in the countryside. Those churches continued each with its Lutheran, Reformed or United tradition depending on the background of its people. In 1899 they formed a United "German Protestant la Plata Synod" and got connected to the Prussian Church (cf. Haefner 2008: 52–67).[18] Over the decades there were tendencies to hold Spanish services and to get more independent from the German church. Finally in 1965 they became independent and founded the "Protestant Church at the La Plata River" (Iglesia Evangélica del Río de la Plata), shortly called IERP. In those years there was also a discussion on the training of the pastors. Beforehand a high percentage of pastors had been sent directly from Germany. Only the younger generations had received their training at the Lutheran faculty in Buenos Aires, but it was financially difficult to sustain that faculty. So in 1976 the Lutheran faculty joined into the ecumenical faculty. Together they shaped the new theological faculty called ISEDET (Instituto Superior Evangélico de Estudios Teológicos).

To find out about the IERP's attitudes towards human rights topics among (1) church congregations, (2) the pastors and (3) the church leadership only part of the information can be found in written sources, such as the monthly church magazine or protocols of church meetings.[19] As was mentioned earlier, it was dangerous to publish delicate information during the military dictatorship. Therefore another important source of information is derived from interviews with church members.

3.1 Church Congregations

To find out about the attitude towards human rights activities, there are two basic questions: A) which attitude did the church members hold towards the military government? B) Which information did they receive?

A) Generally speaking, most Argentineans were not shocked by the military coup, but accepted it because of their frequent experience with military rule or because of the chaotic political situation of the former government. This tendency can also be found in the interviews with church members of the

17 For information about the different forms of "Migration Protestantism" see Villalpando/ Lalive d'Epinay/ Epps, iglesias trasplante.

18 It was called "German Protestant La Plata Synod" (Deutsche Evangelische La Plata Synode, DELPS), because it included congregations in Paraguay and Uruguay besides those in Argentina. La Plata names the river which connects those three countries.

19 Significant examples can be found in: Freudenberg, Menschenrechtsarbeit, Annex, p. 60–89.

IERP. They show a rather politically-conservative profile, which can be seen in connection to the history as immigrant church (cf. Freudenberg 2010: 12–17, 40 f.). However, although this was the typical situation, there are also a few notions of scepticism against political oppression among members of the IERP, especially in the later years of the military rule (cf. ibid.: 41).

B) As pointed out above the churches in the countryside differed from those in the towns. This holds true for the level of information as well, especially for critical information such as human rights topics. Although many people in Buenos Aires did not know about "disappeared" people during the first years of the dictatorship, it was even less so in the countryside (cf. ibid.: 41–43). Of course that cannot be generalized. There were informed and active laity in Buenos Aires as well as in different provinces, people who worked in human rights organisations or had an open ear to what happened around them. And there is also evidence of church members who suffered personally from the "disappearance" of a relative, and so the congregation had to deal with that situation. But the group that handled this topic in a critical way can be regarded as a minority (cf. ibid.: 43–45).

Another reason for the described situation within the IERP is that many congregations wanted to have a strict separation between the church and politics. Therefore the false identification of all kinds of human rights activities as political engagement, made it difficult to speak openly about these issues and to accept a critical position. Instead very often one could hear the opinion: "If the police came to take him, it must have been for a reason."(cf. ibid.: 44–47) Within cities, mainly in Buenos Aires, also economical interests of church members influenced their attitude towards such topics. As certain companies benefited from the economic conditions under the rule of the junta, they were not particularly keen on being critical (cf. ibid.: 43).

To summarize, it can be assumed that the majority of IERP church members did not get involved in human rights activity due to a positive or neutral attitude towards the military dictatorship, the wrong identification of human rights activities as mainly political issue, the lack of information or economic interests.

3.2 Pastors

The documentation of the pastoral conferences shows that there was a notable change in the general attitude on human rights work between 1976 and 1983. Whereas the protocol of a conference in 1978 records a complaint by the president for the missing support of the MEDH (cf. ibid.: 80), human rights protection seems to be an important task for a whole group of pastors in the pastoral conference in 1982 (cf. ibid.: 81). The same results can be found in the church monthly journal. Although it published a few articles concerning the general responsibility of the church for human rights at the beginning of the dictatorship (cf. ibid.: 60, 62–64), it was only in the later years that those articles got more concrete and also reported from time to time about the MEDH (cf. ibid.: 69, 72, 74 f.).

The interviews give a closer insight into different criteria which influenced the pastors' decision on the topic (cf. ibid.: 50–52). Those pastors, who had just finished their theological training at the theological faculty ISEDET in Buenos Aires were strongly influenced by the theology of liberation from theologians like José Míguez Bonino (cf. 1983; 1975). This theological perspective gave many of these young Argentinean pastors a sensitive perception of human right issues (cf. Freudenberg 2010: 23 f., 30, 33 f.). The older generation of pastors were mainly sent from Germany and still had their German passport, which gave them a certain protection in case they were in the situation of danger (cf. ibid.: 4–6). There were also quite a few examples of very engaged German pastors concerning human rights issues, some of them influenced by theologians like Karl Barth or Dietrich Bonhoeffer. One also has to consider those pastors who did not show publicly that they were defending human rights, but did it rather secretly. For example there was one pastor, who cared for relatives of "disappeared" and went regularly to visit prisoners during the whole period of the dictatorship without making it public (cf. ibid.: 49–52).

But this is not a complete picture. There are also interviews reporting of very anxious pastors, of those who did not want to take any risk or those who did not regard human rights issues as their responsibility (cf. ibid.: 32). In every case one has to look at their individual background.

Subsuming the written and oral records one can presume a very heterogeneous pastorate concerning the defence of human rights. But one can note the growing sensibility for those issues during the military rule.

3.3 Leadership of the Church

The most consistent evaluation can be found in the records about the church leadership. Almost all interviews reflect a positive view on its engagement regarding human rights issues (cf. ibid.: 52–54). One frequently mentioned factor is the high level of current information (cf. ibid.: 40). This advance of knowledge was due to the regular contacts abroad and the collaboration in different human rights organisation. It helped the leadership to get a broader picture on what happened in their country. Therefore they supported those pastors or laymen who got engaged in the defence of human rights, whether it was in their own congregations or outside (cf. ibid.: 43, 48, 51). From the early days on they supported the MEDH and became members of it. Apart from this generally very positive picture of the leadership there are also voices remembering discussions within the group due to a few members who were more critical about the support of the human rights defence (cf. ibid.: 53). But as it was possible to speak openly about those questions within the leadership group, solutions could be found (cf. ibid.: 41 f.).

4. Final Reflections

Pastor Everardo Stephan summarized his experience during the military dictatorship like this:

"It is difficult to find your way, there is this borderline. You can not go too far in one direction, neither can you go too far in the other direction." (cf. ibid.: 51)

These words reflect his situation as a pastor of a church, whose members did not all accept sermons with a social critical outlook. At the same time he opened the church for the relatives of German "disappeared", who knocked on his door in need of a place to meet. It was dangerous to do that, as other places where such groups met were attacked. So there was a great tension between his responsibility for his congregation and those people in danger. He neither wanted to put his church at any risk nor divide its people on this matter. But neither did he want to reject the responsibility that his outlook on Christian faith called him to in the face of threatened people outside the church doors–a borderline.

What were the possibilities for a pastor, a laymen or a Christian human rights organisation under the conditions of the Argentinean military rule to protect and help people under threat of death and their worried relatives?

Summarizing the written and oral reports one needs to consider the following aspects:

Basic condition for any action was the access to information. It was clear, that it was difficult to actually understand what was happening in the streets of Argentinean towns and sometimes even villages. A few things might have been seen by a critical observer, who did not believe the propaganda of the junta. But it was still difficult to explain what it meant that a person "disappeared". Will he or she eventually come back? What will they do with him? Where have they kept her? Who are those kidnappers? What is it all for? What does it mean in legal terms?

The situation was totally unknown. It was even difficult to find an appropriate term for it. Who is a "disappeared"?

Only those "disappeared" people, who could escape or where transferred into official prisons or even set free could answer those questions. But to get this information one needed quick and faithful connections. As became evident, the church leaders of the IERP and also of the other MEDH churches received up-to-date, delicate information. This information had to be handled discretely and cautiously. Those people working in the MEDH heard so many testimonies of the relatives of "disappeared" that a certain pattern in the proceedings of the military rule became clearer.

But all those engaged pastors and laymen did not know exactly about the risk of their actions. Some voices say that religious people enjoyed a certain level of personal protection (cf. ibid.: 30), but the number of "disappeared" priests and nuns speaks a different language (cf. CONADEP 1987: 181 – 186). Also within the MEDH people "disappeared" like the French nun Alice Domon. She was kidnapped in December 1977 with a group of others who gathered in a church to prepare the publishing of the first list of 4000 "disappeared" (cf. Freudenberg 2010: 12 f.). Also pastors of the IERP felt threatened. One pastor, called Armin Ihle, received a death threat due to his engagement in a refugee organisation (cf. ibid.: 29 f.). Others remember the permanent observation in their parish (cf. ibid.: 33).

At the same time other pastors and church members refused the confrontation with all human rights issues and went on with their normal lives and church activities (cf. ibid.: 11, 38 f.).

But all those people who constituted or supported the MEDH felt urged to face the situation as part of their identity as Christians. In line with critics of the Old Testament prophets they understood it as their task to denounce this threatening phenomenon of "disappearing" with theological and juristically words. At the same time they wanted to fulfil the social responsibility that Jesus asks his followers to remember. In response the MEDH set up extensive social programs and cared for the relatives of the "disappeared", often woman and children.

As we have seen there were many shades of opinion and responses amongst the pastors, leaders and laymen in the churches of the MEDH. In the end it was a personal decision for each pastor or layman on how to react and what to say.

References

Añdinach, Pablo/Bruno, Daniel (2001). *Iglesias Evangélicas y Derechos Humanos*[20] *en Argentina*

(1976 – 1983). Buenos Aires.

Blatezky, Arturo (1997). Deutschsprachige Einwandererkirchen in Südamerika: Bemerkungen zu ihrer Geschichte am Beispiel der La-Plata-Gemeinden. In: epd-Dokumentation (1/1997). Frankfurt am Main, 3 – 15.

Blatezky, Arturo (2006). Zwischen Völkermord und Befreiungshoffnung: Eine Chronologie der Menschenrechtsarbeit in der Evangelischen Kirche am La Plata. In: Gustav-Adolf-Werk ed.: Die evangelische Diaspora: Jahrbuch des Gustav-Adolf-Werks. Jg. 75. Leipzig. 64 – 95.

Bonino, José Míguez (1975). Doing Theology in a Revolutionary Situation. Minneapolis.

Bonino, José Míguez (1983). Towards a Christian Political Ethics. Minneapolis.

20 The underlined words show the short version of the title, which is used in the footnotes.

CONADEP (Comisión Nacional sobre la Desaparición de Personas) (1987). Nie wieder: Ein Bericht über Entführung, Folter und Mord durch die Militärdiktatur in Argentinien. Hamburger Institut für Sozialforschung ed. Weinheim/Basel.

Crespo, Victoria (2007). Legalidad y Dictadura. In: Lida, Clara/Crespo, Horacio/ Yankelevich, Pablo ed.: Argentina, 1976: Estudios en torno al golpe de Estrado. México D.F. 165 – 186.

Eichner, Klaus (2009). Operation Condor: Eine Internationale des Terror. Berlin.

Freudenberg, Katharina (2010). "Aspekte der Menschenrechtsarbeit der IERP (Iglesia Evangélica del Río del la Plata) während der argentinischen Militärdiktatur (1976 – 83) anhand des Engagements im MEDH (Movimiento Ecuménico por los Derechos Humanos)." Diplomarbeit. Friedrich-Schiller-Universität Jena.

García, Prudencio (1995). El drama de la autonomía militar: Argentina bajo las Juntas Militares. Madrid.

Grele, Ronald (1985) Ziellose Bewegung. Methodologische und theoretische Probleme der Oral History. In: Niethammer, Lutz ed.: Lebenserfahrung und kollektives Gedächtnis: Die Praxis der "Oral History". Frankfurt. 195 – 220.

Haefner, Claudia (2008). Heimischwerdung am La Plata. München.

Howarth, Ken (1999). Oral History. Stroud.

Invernizzi, Hernán/Gociol, Judith (2003). Un golpe a los libros: Represión en la cultura durante la última dictatura military. Buenos Aires [2].

MEDH (Movimiento Ecuménico por los Derechos Humanos) (2004). Convergencias. Buenos Aires.

MEDH (Movimiento Ecuménico por los Derechos Humanos) (2002). Documentos fundamentales y Declaraciones públicas del Movimiento Ecuménico por los Derechos Humanos. Buenos Aires.

Luetge, Wilhelm (1981). Deutsche in Argentinien. Buenos Aires.

Marchak, Patricia (1999). God's Assassins: State Terrorism in Argentina in the 1970s. Montreal.

Mignone, Emilio (1986). Iglesia y Dictadura: El papel de la iglesia a la luz de sus relaciónes con el régimen militar. Buenos Aires.

Niethammer, Lutz ed. (1985). Lebenserfahrung und kollektives Gedächtnis: Die Praxis der „Oral History". Frankfurt.

Ponsati, Miguel (2004). Praxis y Obediencia: Derechos Humanos y Teología en los Documentos y Declaraciones del Movimiento Ecuménico por los Derechos Humanos (1976 – 1984). Buenos Aires.

Quiroga, Hugo (2004). El tiempo del Proceso: Conflictos y coincidencias entre políticos y militares 1976 – 1983. Santa Fe.

Ritchie, Donald (1994). Doing Oral History. New York.

Stella, Calloni (2006). Operación Cóndor: Pacto criminal. La Habana.

Thompson, Paul (2000). The Voice of the Past: Oral History. New York [3].

Troncoso, Osacar (1984). El Proceso de la reorganización nacional 1. Cronologia y documentación. Buenos Aires.

Villalpando, Waldo Luis/Lalive d'Epinay, Christian/Epps, Dwain ed. (1970). Las iglesias del trasplante: Protestantismo de inmigración en la Argentina. Buenos Aires.

Wierling, Dorothee (2003). "Oral History". In: Aufriß der Historischen Wissenschaft, Neue Themen und Methoden der Geschichtswissenschaft. Vol. 7. Stuttgart. 81 – 151.

Zorzin, Alejandro (2009). Memorias, Visiones y Testimonio: 1899 Sínodo Evangélico Alemán – Iglesia Evangélica del Río de la Plata 1999. Buenos Aires

II. Comparative and Global Perspectives

Kanan Kitani

Invisible Christians: Brazilian Migrants in Japan

> This country is a swamp. In time you will come to see that for yourself. This country is a more terrible swamp than you can imagine. Whenever you plant a sapling in this swamp the roots begin to rot; the leaves grow yellow and wither. And we have planted the sapling of Christianity in this swamp.
>
> Shusaku Endo, *Silence* (1980: 147)

Introduction

History has proven that Christianity does not take root in Japan. Since its first introduction by St. Francis Xavier in 1549, Christianity remains a minority religion to the present day. From Xavier to Billy Graham, countless missionaries and evangelists have tried to christianize Japan. Despite their efforts, today's Christian population is still under 1 % (approximately 1.1 million) of the population.[1] In addition, church attendees are aging year by year, while only a few members of the younger generations ever attend church. Although Catholic, Orthodox, and Protestant churches together have over 9000 churches, the situation does not allow much room for optimism. In recent years, by contrast, there has been an increase of a new type of Christian: Brazilian immigrants. Their migration to Japan began about two decades ago, and today there are 312,582 Brazilians living in Japan, comprising the third largest ethnic group after the Chinese (655,377) and the Koreans (589,239).[2]

They also constitute the largest number of Portuguese speakers in Asia. Considering the geographical distance of Brazil compared to China and the Korean peninsula, the influx of Brazilians is a unique phenomenon, which has attracted both domestic and international researchers, especially those developing the study of the fields of sociology and education (cf. Kajita, Tanno and Higuchi 2005; Lesser 2003; Tsuda 2003; Roth 2002; Linger 2001). Although numerous studies have been conducted in these fields, hardly any

1 The Christian Yearbook 2010 lists the following numbers: Protestant churches: 641,352 (58,5 %); Roman-Catholic Church: 443,872 (40.5 %); Orthodox Churches: 10,380 (1 %).

2 Tsuda points out that Brazilians rank as the second-largest ethnic group, instead of Koreans, who are still registered as foreigners, although 80 % of them were born in Japan (cf. 2009: 230).

have been focused on the religious activities of these immigrants. Examining their religious activities is indispensable in order to understand their modes of living in Japan, as Brazilian migrants are experiencing a drastic change of environment, emigrating from a country where the population is almost 90 % Christian to a country where it is less than 1 %. In spite of the necessity for research, the reasons behind the lack of study in this field are as follows: firstly, religion in Japan is considered to be one of life's options, rather than an essential, which makes religion a relatively minor subject for examination. Secondly, the churches at which Brazilian immigrants gather are relatively invisible to Japanese society as a whole. Therefore, this paper examines the Christian churches at which Brazilian migrants gather, and also sheds some light on three aspects of their existence: 1) why Brazilian Christians are relatively invisible to Japanese society as a whole, 2) the function and role of Brazilian churches, 3) and the possible influences they have on Japanese society in the religious sphere.

Japanese Emigration to Brazil

Japan and Brazil are two distant countries, yet they have a special relationship. This bilateral relationship was established in Nov. 1895, with the signing of the Treaty of Amity, Commerce and Navigation. In 1908, a ship called *Kasato Maru* brought 781 Japanese emigrants to Brazil, which was the beginning of human interaction between Japanese and Brazilians, an interaction that has continued for over 100 years, up until the present day. The immigration of the Japanese was made possible by the economic conditions both in the sending country and the receiving country. Brazil was experiencing a labor shortage after abolishing slavery in 1888, and Japan was experiencing excess in the rural population due to industrialization, which caused the government seek ways to send excess workers out of the country as emigrants. Because in Japan only the eldest son was allowed to take over his parents' house, in most farming communities in Japan, younger brothers were required to make their own livings, independently of the family. Thus, impoverished farmers travelled to Brazil in the hope of making a fortune for themselves. Nowadays, Japan has developed into a major economic power, following the United States. It used to be, however, one of the most economically challenged nations. Other than Brazil, Japanese citizens also emigrated to Peru, Bolivia, and the United States, including Hawaii.

Japanese immigrants in Brazil mainly engaged in coffee plantations as peasants, or, more precisely, as slave substitutes. The treatment of immigrants was not always cordial, resulting in a significant number of runaway workers. Moreover, several years before World War II, the government under President Getúlio Dornelles Vargas began a process of forced assimilation of the immigrants, which involved the banning of Japanese newspapers, and the prohibition of teaching and speaking in Japanese in public spaces, leaving only

Portuguese as the language choice for Japanese descendants. Furthermore, as Japanese immigrants became isolated in Brazil during wartime due to the rupture of diplomatic relations between Japan and Brazil, they had no contact with Japan to become informed of their nation's defeat. This caused a rift in the Japanese community between two groups: those rejecting admission of the defeat of Japan and those who passively admitted the defeat of their nation.

Despite these circumstances, Japanese immigrants have overcome adversities, settling peacefully and achieving social prestige in Brazil over the last several decades. The "Japan Town" in São Paulo is the largest Japanese community in the world outside of Japan, and there are now 1.5 million people of Japanese descent living in Brazil (cf. Kinshichi 2009: 266 – 267).

The Influx of *Dekasseguis*

The flow of Japanese emigration to Brazil began to decline during the 1970s. In fact, the flow has now reversed, sending Brazilians to Japan. This reverse flow began about 20 years ago, when the economic boom in Japan coincided with the economic crisis in Brazil. Japan experienced rapid economic growth after the war, stabilizing its economic situation and increasing its presence in the international community. On the contrary, Brazil experienced economic and political instability, causing a major outflow of Brazilian citizens in the form of Brazilian diasporas around the world, including Japan. It is believed that about 1.4 million Brazilians emigrated abroad during this period (cf. Margolis 1994: 3 – 6). Brazilians who migrated to Japan are called *Dekassegui*, which originates from the Japanese term *Dekasegi*, meaning "go out and earn." What is interesting is that Japan and Brazil have been exchanging laborers bilaterally throughout their 100 years of mutual history. The *Dekassegui* trend was well underway in 1990, when the Japanese government revised the Immigration Control Law to authorize the legal entry of Japanese descendants and their spouses up to the third generation. About 310,000 Brazilians residing in Japan now are either the descendants or spouses of Japanese immigrants in Brazil (Figure 1). They were issued residential status visas without any limitations on their activities in Japan.[3]

In general, the Immigration Control Law does not allow unskilled foreign laborers to enter Japan. Therefore, the revision of the Immigration Control Law, which issued the special visa to Japanese descendants, is widely perceived as being a legal way to invite cheap laborers to alleviate the acute labor shortage in Japan caused by low birth-rate and rapid economic growth. However, there are apparently no legal documents supporting that perception

3 Some scholars tend to describe Brazilians in Japan simply as "Japanese Brazilians," but about one-fourth of them are non-Japanese Brazilians married to Japanese or Japanese Brazilians.

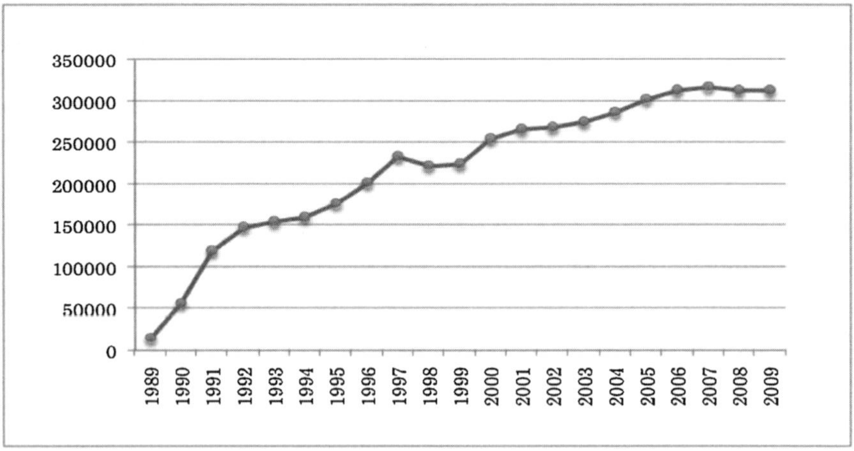

Source: Ministry of Justice (1990 – 2009)

(cf. Kajita, Tanno and Higuchi 2005: 113). Kajita argues that the revision was not intended to invite the newcomers as typified by the Brazilians, but rather was intended to issue legal status to the Korean and Chinese permanent residents called "old-comers," brought to Japan during wartime as forced laborers (cf. Kajita, Tanno and Higuchi 2005: 108 – 137). Therefore, the system for accepting the unexpected migrants from Brazil was not well established. Although unexpected, the influx of Brazilian migrants of Japanese descent was a perfectly predictable outcome, considering the economic differences between the two countries. After the Plaza Agreement in 1985, the exchange rate of the Japanese yen rose rapidly, and in 1990, the value of the yen against the U.S. dollars rose to twice its value of five years previously. At that time, Japan's GDP was 3.02 trillion, compared to Brazil's 462 billion, which made working in Japan attractive to Brazilians.[4]

The influx of Brazilian migrants was made possible by the assistance of recruiting agencies and brokers in conjunction with factories (cf. Roth 2002). Brazilians are primarily employed in the Japanese automotive and electronics factories, a trade considered below the local Japanese, but paying three to ten times more than the average Brazilian salary. Brazilians in Japan live mainly in certain prefectures: Aichi, Shizuoka, Mie, Gifu, and Gunma (Figure 2). Therefore, coping with the increasing Brazilian migrants is a regional issue, and measures are mainly left in the hands of local governments. Many Brazilians are subjected to over-work in hours of manual labor in the so-called three-K jobs (kitsui, kitanai, kiken, meaning hard, dirty and dangerous, respectively). Both the Japanese in Brazil and the Brazilians in Japan are pushed into severe conditions, but there is also a major difference between the two; that is, the

4 It is said that *Dekasseguis* bring about positive economic effects on Brazil for 20 billion yen (approximately 212 million US dollars) per year (cf. Kinshichi 2009: 267).

distance between their homelands. Japanese immigrants in Brazil had grave difficulties in obtaining information about their homeland, especially during wartime, when they decided to settle in Brazil and assimilation with the locals was the necessary choice for survival. In regards to the migration of Brazilians to Japan, on the contrary, much better conditions exist in terms of the connection to their homeland. They are blessed with the progress of information technology such as Internet, mobile phone networks and television, each of which enables migrants to easily communicate with their families and friends in the homeland. Consequently, leaving the homeland in modern times does not necessarily require integration into the host country. Linger and Tsuda, in particular, express that the Brazilian community in Japan is deterritorialized, forming transnational communities which allow Brazilian migrants to be connected with both the host society and the homeland society (cf. Tsuda 2003: 155; Linger 2001: 17). In addition, they are also maintaining their trans-border ethnic ties with Brazilian diasporas around the world. These strong ties contribute to the expansion of Brazilian based organized religion, such as the Universal Church of the Kingdom of God (cf. Reis 2006: 179). The mutual connection inherent to the trans-border ethnic ties of Brazilian diasporas are not limited to personal relationships or activities concerning their ethnic culture, but are also increasing their involvement even in the religious sphere.

Christianity in Brazil and Japan

Christianity has played an important role in Brazilian society. With approximately 150 million believers, Brazil is one of the most populous Christian nations in the world. According to the latest census in 2000 by Instituto Brasileiro de Geografia e Estatística (IBGE), 73.6 % of the population was Roman Catholic and 15.4 % was Protestant. Indeed, 90 % of the Brazilian population is Christian (Table 1). The number of actual churchgoers may not be this high, of course, but Christianity in Brazil is an everyday part of life. The same applies in terms of Brazilian migrants in Japan. Although most of them originally intended to work for only a short period of time in Japan, many gradually began to settle down and begin forming their own communities in Japan. Around 1993 – 1994, Brazilian migrants who had come to Japan on their own in 1990 began to bring their families over to Japan to live with them. As a result, during this period churches began to be founded in great number, along with schools, stores, and even discos (cf. Kajita, Tanno and Higuchi 2005: 219 – 232).

Table 1: Religious Population in Brazil

Denomination	Population	Percentage
Roman Catholic	124,980,132	73.6 %
Protestant	26,184,941	15.4 %
Non-religious	12,492,403	7.3 %
Spiritism	2,262,401	1.3 %
Others	3,414,337	2.1 %

Source: IBGE Census 2000

Until establishing their own churches, Brazilians had no choice but to attend services at Japanese churches. Japan, though, has only 1.1 million Christians, which is less than 1 % of the entire population. With such a small number of Christians compared to the 150 million Christians in Brazil, it was difficult to meet the Brazilians' expectations. The extremely small number of Christians is not a new phenomenon in Japan. It is called "the wall of 1 %" among Japanese Christians, as they have never been able to expand their ranks beyond this percentage. This does not mean that the Japanese are atheists, or are negative about Christianity. Rather, they take the stance of syncretism, instead of being attached to a particular religion. In most cases, Japanese people visit Shinto shrines during the New Year, celebrate Christmas extravagantly, marry in the Christian style and hold funerals according to Buddhist rites. Consequently, what Brazilian migrants can expect from Japanese churches in maintaining their religious practices is quite limited.

In spite of their small numbers, churches, especially those providing Portuguese services, play an important role for Brazilians, not only in terms of offering places to gather in prayer but also in terms of providing occasions for Brazilians to socialize with each other, exchange information, share memories of their homeland or simply speaking in Portuguese, helping them to feel at ease. Many Brazilians in Japan experience identity conflicts, leaving the white-collar jobs they held in their homeland for blue-collar manual labor and losing their social status as "Japanese-Brazilian" only to have it be replaced by a negative perception as a "complete foreigner" in Japan (Lesser 2003: 79–81). It does not require much imagination to recognize the hardships they face in Japanese society. For those ill adjusted to Japan, the churches where Brazilians can gather are havens of rest. Therefore, the church functions as a community of faith as well as ethnicity for the Brazilian migrants. The churches where Brazilians gather can be categorized into three types: the "grafting-type" churches, the "seedling-type churches," and the "sapling-type" churches. Churches of the "grafting-type" are the Japanese churches providing Portuguese services; churches of the "seedling-type" are the churches established by Brazilians residing in Japan; and the churches of the "sapling-type" are the imported churches from Brazil that have already been organized before coming to Japan. The characteristics of these three types are discussed in detail in the following sections.

Churches of the "Grafting-Type"

Catholic Church

Although the number of Catholics is declining in Brazil, they remain the largest Christian body in Brazil. That is considered to be similar in the Brazilian immigrant community in Japan. It is natural to assume that the first place where Brazilian immigrants would seek help would be the Catholic Church. According to statistics gathered in 2005, the number of foreign Catholics living in Japan is 529,452, for the first time outnumbering Japanese Catholics, who total 449,925. Especially in the four dioceses of Saitama, Yokohama, Nagoya and Kyoto, foreign Catholics outnumber Japanese Catholics (cf. Tani 2008: 25). In addition, in each of these dioceses, excluding Kyoto, most of the foreign Catholics are Brazilian (Table 2).

It is a pressing issue for the above-mentioned three dioceses how best to manage good relations with the rapid increase of Brazilian Catholics since 1990. The Bishop Daiji Tani of Saitama Diocese is the most dedicated person working on the issue, as the chairperson of the Catholic Commission of Japan for Migrants, Refugees and People on the Move. The book he published in 2008 is the only book related to the increase of foreign Catholics in Japan. In the Saitama Diocese (which has jurisdiction over four prefectures, Saitama, Tochigi, Gunma and Ibaragi) the Brazilian population totals 51,503 (Immigration Bureau, Ministry of Justice, 2008[5]). Applying the ratio of the Catholics in Brazil (73.6 %) to this population, there are 37,906 Brazilian Catholics in Saitama Diocese, which is larger than the total number of 20,746 Japanese Catholics (cf. Catholic Year Book 2010). Of course, this number is only calculated statistically, without counting the actual numbers of the congregations gathered in the churches. However, there are certainly visible changes in each church, with increasing numbers of foreign Catholics, especially Brazilians. In 14 churches out of the 59 in the Saitama Diocese, masses in Portuguese are offered from one to three times a month. Many churches offer services in other languages, including English, Indonesian, Korean, Spanish, Tagalog and Vietnamese. It is said that the churches are becoming revitalized by the new international members (cf. Tani 2008: 27–29). To respond to the

5 Ministry of Justice, Press Release Material (July 2009). URL: http://www.moj.go.jp/ nyuukoku-kanri/kouhou/press_090710-1_090710-1.html [accessed on May 30, 2010].

increasing pastoral needs from the members of various backgrounds, the Saitama Diocese also opened the Saitama Catholic International Center, in 1994.

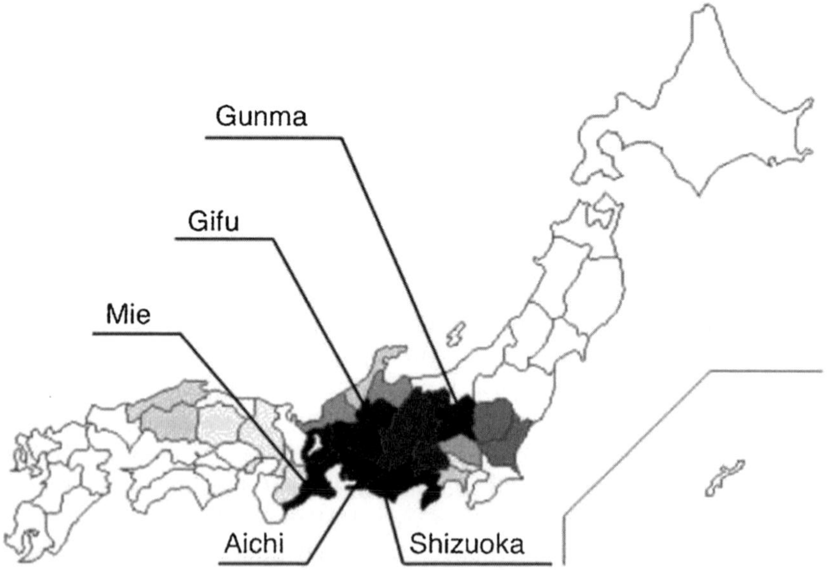

Figure 2: Density of Brazilian Residents in Japan
Source: Ministry of Justice 2008

Table 2: Brazilian Catholic Population in Saitama, Yokohama, and Nagoya Parishes

Parish	Prefectures	Brazilian Residents	Estimated Brazilian Catholics	Japanese Catholics
Saitama	Saitama, Tochigi, Gunma, Ibaragi	51,503	37,906	20,746
Yokohama	Kanagawa, Shizuoka, Nagano, Yamanashi	85,329	62,802	56,454
Nagoya	Aichi, Gifu, Ishikawa, Fukui, Toyama	108,065	79,535	25,953

Although Japanese churches are aging without much increase in the people filling the pews, inviting foreign members will rejuvenate the church. For example, at the Kusatsu Catholic Church in Shiga prefecture, there is a

Portuguese mass offered once each month. Upon visiting, the mass itself was alive, with three guitarists playing danceable hymns. During the "greeting of peace" in the Communion rite, Japanese congregants typically stay in their seats, simply nodding to each other. In contrast, participants in the Portuguese service actively walked around, greeting as many people as possible, hugging and shaking hands. Because Brazilian migrants are relatively young in their working age, their children are still small, and contribute to making the mass vibrant. The mass was filled with a lively humanness rather than with the beauty of liturgical form. Meanwhile, regardless of the liveliness of the Portuguese mass, there were very few Japanese attendees. According to the Brazilian attendees, they are not accustomed to seeing many Japanese congregants in their Portuguese service; in the same way that they seldom attend Japanese services. In most cases, it is a problem of the language difference. In other cases, which are more serious, it is the hidden barrier that both the Japanese and the Brazilians feel toward each other. Hearing the voices of Brazilians, it seemed that they are feeling isolation not only from the church, but also from Japanese society.

In fact, it is difficult for them to feel as though they are "official" members of the church. This is not due to their status in Japan as immigrants, but rather due to the system of church, not only that of the Catholic Church, but also that of most mainline Protestant churches. The term "Christian" in Japan only applies to a person who has been baptized and is registered in a particular church. The rest are degraded as "seekers" even if the person has attended church services for decades. The same applies to foreign Catholics residing in Japan. Although their presence has doubled the number of Catholics in Japan, they cannot contribute toward the "official" number of Catholics. According to the Catholic Bishop's Conference of Japan, the number of Catholics appearing in the statistics excludes the foreign Catholics, as they do not belong to any specific individual church. It is somewhat unreasonable to expect foreign nationals to register at a specific church, because becoming a member brings with it the responsibility of paying monthly offerings, something that is not so cheap for the foreign migrants (cf. Tani 2008: 45). Nothing comes for free in Japan, after all.

The Catholic Church in Japan is presently in the process of change, attempting to shift their way of thinking about the church from "Japanese church" to "church in Japan," which refers to a church not belonging to a single nationality but rather to a diverse group of people (Tani 2008: 33). To be able to respond to the needs of foreign national Catholics, the Catholic Church is inviting priests and nuns from various counties, and at the same time sending out Japanese priests and nuns abroad for language training and for learning the national character of various countries. Additionally, in a process of trial and error, they have initiated attempts at holding a multilingual mass in several parishes, to bring people of all ethnicities and nationalities together in one mass.

Protestant Church

Unlike the Catholics, the Protestants seem less excited about the influx of foreign Christians into the country. There are two types of "grafting-type" church: the type that takes the initiative in offering Portuguese services, and the type that merely provides a place for Brazilians to gather without providing the service itself. The Catholic Church is a good example of the former, while most Protestant churches are the latter. For example, the United Church of Christ in Japan, which is the largest Protestant united church, has not a single church out of 1725 local churches which would provide a service in Portuguese.[6] Because it is a mere collection of 35 different denominations, each denomination autonomously manages its own member churches. In the case of the United Church of Christ in Japan, therefore, it is difficult to create a coherent policy together as one church.

Two of the most engaging churches on this matter are the Assemblies of God and the Seventh-day Adventist Church in Japan. These churches have a large number of congregations in Brazil as well. The Assemblies of God is the largest Pentecostal church in Brazil, while the Seventh-day Adventist Church is the second largest of the mainline denominations. Several churches of the Assemblies of God in Japan offer Portuguese services, however, their activities are independent depending on the individual church. There are also many churches of the Brazilian Assembléia de Deus in Japan, which were formed by Brazilian migrants or missionaries from Brazil in recent years. While they are both affiliated with the World Pentecostal Assemblies of God Fellowship, they have little interaction with each other. By contrast, the Seventh-day Adventist Church in Japan has a coherent policy on supporting Brazilians. Not only do they provide Portuguese services in eight churches, they have also founded two Brazilian churches in Shizuoka prefecture. Brazilians appear as a number in the Christian Yearbook from these two churches, in contrast to most Brazilian Christians who are kept invisible to Japanese society, as they are not registered in any particular church. Additionally, the Seventh-day Adventist Church holds an annual summer camp designed to bring together all of the Latin Americans living in Japan.[7]

Besides the Protestant churches already mentioned above, there are a few denominational churches providing Portuguese services in their one or two local congregations. Mostly, as in the latter case of the two "grafting-type" churches, these churches are simply providing a place for Brazilians to gather. The case even exists that staff in the Japanese churches do not know basic

6 The Christian Yearbook 2010 lists one church as holding services in Portuguese, but this was proved to be a typo.

7 Seventh-Day Adventist Church, Mission Bureau for foreign residents in Japan (n.d.). URL: http://www.adventist.jp/cm/foreign/event/e080813.html [accessed on May 30, 2010].

information about their Brazilian gatherings. Brazilians who gather in these churches, of course, were not counted as "official" registered members. Apart from these churches, some non-denominational churches in areas where many Brazilians reside have Portuguese services inviting Brazilian missionaries through their own connections to Brazil.

To summarize, the characteristic of the "grafting-type" is that the stock (the Japanese church) and the scion (Brazilian Christians) are of two different natures, and their connected joint is visible. They offer both Japanese and Brazilian services in their churches, but the congregations are less flexible between those two services. The language difference is the critical issue for the "grafting-type" church. The Catholic Church is the only church of this type attempting to solve the language problem by holding multilingual masses to bring diverse people together in one mass. In terms of "grafting-type" churches, it can be said that the Catholic Church is the most stable stock on which to graft a new scion. For Brazilians, what churches can offer them is limited; conversely, what Brazilians can offer to the Japanese churches is far more meaningful. In agriculture, grafting is used as a method by which to repair damage to a stock by grafting a young shoot to the trunk of an older tree. In the same sense, grafting Brazilian Christians to the Japanese church desirably functions as a revitalization of the Japanese church, preventing it from withering. In Romans 11:11 – 24, the apostle Paul wrote in the passage "Engrafted Branches," that the Gentiles were like a wild olive shoot, engrafted onto Israel to make certain unfaithful Israelites (the branches broken off from the olive tree) envious. It might likewise work in a similar manner for the Japanese Christians. Nevertheless, the Brazilians in Japanese churches are still treated as guests, making them invisible from the outside of the church. The time when they finally become visible may be the time when the church will have regenerated into a new hybrid church, made up of a diverse group of people, or it may be the time when the church will have been taken over by foreign Christians. At the moment, the church of "grafting-type" is still taking on and developing its provisional form.

The Church of the "Seedling-Type"

It was mostly churches of the "grafting-type," which supported Brazilians in carrying on their religious activities in the beginning periods of their migration to Japan. Several years later, Brazilian immigrants began founding their own churches. The churches that have been founded by the Brazilian migrants in Japan can be defined as churches of the "seedling-type." In these churches, of course, members of other nationalities, such as Peruvians and Bolivians, participate as members of church, although most of the body of these churches consists of Brazilians holding Portuguese services. The "grafting-type" churches were searchable in Japanese through Internet records; at the least it was possible to find them on Christian Yearbook. In contrast, because the churches of "seedling-type" consist primarily of Brazilians, it is difficult to find records of these churches in Japanese, either through search engine or printed materials. For this reason, it is uncertain how many of these churches exist in Japan. There are about forty such churches exist in the Tokai region, which includes Shizuoka, Aichi, Mie, and the southern part of Gifu prefectures. These churches are mainly non-denominational singular churches with 30–200 members. Some of these churches can be found through search engines with Portuguese keywords such as "igreja + Japão." However, it is hard to imagine a lot of Japanese taking the time to search Brazilian churches on the web in Portuguese. Japanese people who are able to encounter these churches by chance are limited to the locals living in the nearby areas where such churches stand (cf. Graburn, Ertl and Tierney 2008: 121). These churches are almost underground churches, beyond comparison to the "grafting-type." Because it is impossible to cover all such churches in this section, the only churches discussed here as the exemplars of the "seedling-type" will be non-denominational church organizations that have branch churches. Typical churches fulfilling these conditions include Missão Apoio, Igreja Evangélica Betel, and Grace Community International Church (or Comunidade da Graça no Japão).

Claudir de Souza Machado at Nagoya, Aichi prefecture, founded Missão Apoio in 1993. It has since expanded to include 17 churches in Japan, and 31 churches in other countries, including Brazil. Igreja Evangélica Betel was founded in 1997, when a Brazilian gathering became independent from a local Japanese church. It has six churches around the Tokai region with the main church being at Suzuka, Mie prefecture (cf. Yamada 2008a: 188). Finally, Grace Community International Church was founded in 2000 by a couple who both studied theology in Brazilian. It has seven churches around the central part of Japan, with the main church at Anjo, Aichi prefecture.

The characteristics of these churches are that they are evangelical, with a contemporary worship style, services of 2 to 3 hours duration, multitalented pastors, and highly devout congregations. In most of such churches, several meetings are held in addition to the weekly Sunday service. The meetings held on weekdays start late, ranging from 8:30 p.m. to 10:30 p.m., reflecting the working hours of their congregations. The starting time of the Sunday service differs by church and regions. However, starting time does not seem particularly important, as the members of such churches frequently come and go freely during the 2 to 3 hours of service. This is quite different from the mainline churches of Japan. In most cases, they begin Sunday service around 10:00 a.m., setting the exact time with a radio-controlled watch, and very few members arrive late or leave during the service. As for the Brazilian churches of the "seedling-type," the time is more flexible. The service starts indeterminately, often 10 to 15 minutes late, with an opening prayer by a certain member, or with the band playing a worship song. There is also no printed formula by which the service is conducted, unlike the Catholics. At one church, for instance, the Portuguese version of "Happy Birthday to You" was sung during the service in order to celebrate the birthday of a church member. Instead of using printed materials, such churches generally use a projector to show the Lord's Prayer or the lyrics of the music. Without exception, they have worship bands consisting of more than one vocalist, a guitar, a bass, a keyboard and drums. The songs they sing are not the traditional hymns, of course. They use typical worship music, including songs by Hillsong. Before the pastor appears at the podium, about one hour of prayers, music and testimony by church members takes place. All of the warm-ups are done before the sermon begins, so as to deliver the message at the height of the service.

In the "seedling-type" churches, the pastors are expected to be multi-talented, in addition to their ability to deliver a powerful message. Without these pastors, the seeds of the church would not come into bud, now grown into major church organizations. Pastor Laelso da Silva Santos of Missão Apoio is the representative of the church in Japan, but also the president of the nonprofit organization Ação Mão Amiga, which supports people of all nationalities who are in need by giving away relief supplies. He was awarded the "Cavaleiro da Ordem do Rio Branco" by the Brazilian president Luiz Inácio Lula da Silva for the activities of Ação Mão Amiga. Pastor Hiroshi Hiramatsu of Igreja Evangélica Betel does most of the functions during his services, besides giving the sermon. He sings, plays the guitar, beats the drums and translates Portuguese into Japanese for Japanese members from time to time. In Igreja Evangélica Betel, they hold two services every Sunday, one in Portuguese and one in Japanese. Pastor Hiramatsu is the leading figure in each two-hour service. Pastor Koji Muto of Grace Community International Church also works as an administrative notary in the firm he owns. He is the CEO of the real-estate company as well. The followers of these pastors are also talented and devout. They absolutely have the sense of belonging to their church. During the service, they willingly serve as well; some of them openly offer prayers, some voluntarily do interpretations, and some play the instruments in the band.

What is significant about churches of the "seedling-type" is the inclusiveness created by the members. Even if they hold services in Portuguese, they also have some Peruvian, Bolivian, and Japanese members in the church. These churches also actively try to reach out to the Japanese by offering the services in Japanese or staffing interpreters during the Portuguese service. They clearly have the intention to convert the Japanese to Christianity, as they believe it as an assignment from God. In fact, Pastor Machado, the founder of Missão Apoio, describes that, although he came to Japan as *Dekassegui*, it was God's will, assigning him to "win some souls for

Jesus" in Japan.[8] Yamada suggests it as being a reversal of the *Dekasseguis* phenomenon, as newcomers in Japanese society are weak in social scale, yet consider themselves capable of "offering" God's grace to the people of the host society (cf. Yamada 2008b: 8). Moreover, Yamada also adds that this rhetoric helps Brazilian migrants who are living in the bottom of the society to embrace self-affirmation and to restore their dignity through outreach activities to the Japanese. That is to say, their hope to bring salvation to Japanese society is closely related to their own redemption. Therefore, from this perspective, it is important for them to engage in mission work to convert Japanese members of society, whose people are suffering from spiritual poverty, with 30,000 suicides per year. Their outreach activities are, in fact, having a positive effect on some Japanese citizens. A Japanese woman in her mid-50s, who is attending one of the churches of the "seedling-type," shared testimony saying:

> Before coming to the Brazilian church, I was completely alone. I had no family, no friends, no education, no skill, and no attraction. I did not exist in the society. In the factory I work, the Japanese co-workers always picked on me. One day, I visited Japanese church because I wanted to be relieved. Unfortunately, I understood nothing of what the pastor was talking about due to my lack of intelligence. The members of that church were cold to me. Because of this experience, I was originally skeptical about this Brazilian church. Soon after hearing the sermon saying that God loves even a failed person like me, I shed tears of joy. Since then, I am attending this church every week, and my life has changed completely. I had been rejected by the same Japanese in my whole life, and yet Brazilians warmly welcomed me in this church. Now I have a family and many friends.

The Church of the "Sapling-Type"

Concurrently with the formation of the Brazilian community, a church of a new type emerged after the "grafting-type" and the "seedling-type," and it can be defined as the church of the "sapling-type." This is a type of church imported from Brazil after it had already been established as a religious organization in Brazil. At present, the churches which can be categorized as this type are: the Universal Church of the Kingdom of God (Igreja Universal do Reino de Deus), Igreja Evangélica Avivamento da Fé, and some churches affiliated with the Assembléia de Deus. These churches have branches in several countries other than Japan and Brazil. What is different from the church of the "seedling-type" is that these churches send pastors to Japan with

8 Message from Pr. Claudir de Souza Machado, the founder of Missão Apoio (n.d.). URL: http://www.missaoapoio.com/modules/articles/article.php?id=2 [accessed on May 30, 2010].

sufficient funds to systematically plant the church as one of their saplings. From this point of view, the Universal Church of the Kingdom of God (UCKG) is the perfect example of this type of church.

The UCKG is a fast-growing neo-Pentecostal church founded by Pastor Edir Macedo in 1977. Since its foundation, the church has been attracting a great deal of attention and scrutiny concerning its controversial theology, numerous allegations surrounding money, political ties and use of media. The UCKG was made famous by two particularly inglorious events. One of the most well-known controversial incidents occurred in 1995, when one of the pastors of UCKG kicked an image of Our Lady of Aparecida, the patron saint of Brazil, during a show broadcasted by UCKG owned TV Record. The controversy grew to the extent of causing a "holy war" involving the Catholic Church and national TV Globo, drawing vast public attention (cf. Reis 2006: 172; Yamada 2004b: 69 – 70). The other case occurred in the United Kingdom in 2000, when two adoptive parents, who were members of the UCKG, murdered an eight-year-old girl, Victoria Climbie, through neglect and physical abuse. They took Victoria to one of the UCKG's temples in London four times in the last eight days of her life, because they believed that the girl was possessed by demons, in accordance with the UCKG's belief system (cf. Reis 2006: 178). The church's involvement in this incident was crucial enough to compromise its reputation.

Despite these controversial allegations, the church has continued to expand in 176 countries, while establishing 5000 temples in Brazil. It is said that its expansion is beginning to approach that of Assembléia de Deus, the most populous Pentecostal denomination in Brazil (cf. Reis 2006: 170). The UCKG began planting church in Japan around 1996. Currently, under its original Portuguese name, Igreja Universal do Reino de Deus (IURD), it has 2000 members with 14 temples, each opened every day. In the areas where they do not yet have temples, they strategically place their religious leaders to prepare the soil to setting up the church. According to its biweekly newsletter *Jornal do Brasil No.127* (Mar. 2010), they have 15 gatherings of such preliminary temples to support prospective converts. It seems that the Church is successfully expanding in Japan as well. The UCKG's methodology for success in numbers is highly influenced by that of the mega churches in the United States, especially in the use of multimedia and the setting of the location. At first, they often begin from house churches, then, by increasing, they rent a space in what used to be a commercial building in the suburb or exurb areas (cf. Thumma and Travis 2007: 10 – 12). In fact, the UCKG's churches stand in the suburbs or exurbs in most cases, along the national highways so that the Church's logo, which is a simple yet eye-catching combination of a red heart and a dove, appears prominently. These churches are also flexible in relocating to better places according to their growth. For example, a newly relocated church at Konan city, Shiga prefecture, has moved from the nearby city to rent a new, spacious, two-storied building. The new temple stands along Route 1, and it is only accessible by car, as it is a 30–minute walk from the station. Therefore, this church has little incentive for inviting a diverse group of people, serving instead as the ethnic church. Unlike its ordinary exterior, the interior was redecorated as the UCKG's uniform sanctuary, which has a large cross, a podium, and the line "Jesus Cristo é o Senhor (Jesus Christ is the Lord)" on the front wall, embossed in gold. Unlike churches of the "seedling-type," UCKG maintains the separation between Japanese and Brazilians. It does not seek coexistence together with different language speaking groups, but rather builds the church for each group separately. The churches of UCKG are homogenous communities where Brazilians can form close-knit communities of faith (cf. Yamada 2002: 87). The UCKG's temples commonly hold prayer meetings. There is a weekly cycle with particular daily themes, such as: Monday: financial problems, and Friday: liberation from evil spirits. These two themes explain the Church's theology well. Because it is one of the Pentecostal characteristics to emphasize the salvation in the present life, not only UCKG but also some other Pentecostal churches adopt this so-called "prosperity theology" (Steigenga and Cleary 2007: 221). As for the members of UCKG, they believe that God's grace comes in the form of financial success and spiritual health. The UCKG is famous for collecting tithes from its congregations, a practice which has been successful because of this very theology. The members of the Church manage to pay tithes out of their poor salaries, regarding the relationship between God and humans to be similar to a contract, in which the latter pays tithes (10 % of pre-tax income) in order to gain favor in God's eyes. Basically, "the more you give, the more you receive." Not to stop the flow of this "virtuous circle," the Church is willing to offer financial advice and prayer meetings, held every Monday. Another distinctive prayer meeting is the ritual of exorcism, held every Friday. It is a core element of the churches' teaching that physical and psychological illnesses are curable by casting out demons through intense prayer. The Church teaches that humans are not sinners, but are the victims of the actions of demons. However, their explanation of the exorcism varies depending on the target. For the Brazilians, the Church straightforwardly enumerates all kinds of symptoms that are curable by exorcism: constant headaches, insomnia, nervousness, visions of shadows, hearing voices, fainting, addictions, depression, undiagnosed illnesses, among other ailments.[9] For English speakers living in Japan, the Friday meeting is explained as "The Prayer for Deliverance – Strong prayers against all types of witchcraft, bad luck, curses, etc.[10]" For the Japanese, it is explained vaguely as "The Prayer for Freedom – Each one of us has worries. Some are resolvable, while the others, such as depression,

9 The Official Blog of UCKG in Japan, Weekly Schedule in Portuguese (n.d.). URL: http://agendasemanaleenderecos.blogspot.com/ [accessed on May 30, 2010].

10 UCKG Japan Official Website in English, Weekly Schedule (n.d.).URL: http://uckgjapan.org/english.htm [accessed on May 30, 2010].

hallucination or social withdrawal are only solved through God.[11]" There is no indication that this involves exorcism or witchcraft. This is because the Church has been actively shifting its modus operandi to ways more favorable to the Japanese.

The UCKG opened a temple exclusively for the Japanese in the center of Tokyo in 2005. Unlike the churches for Brazilians, this temple is located in the city and is in walking distance of two railway stations. This temple occupies an important place for the UCKG in terms of its intention to make Japan into the base of its Asian expansion (cf. Reis 2006: 179). Unfortunately, yet not surprisingly, it seems that the Church is having a hard time attracting Japanese to the temple in Tokyo. According to its Pastor, Yasuo Watanabe, who was in the street proselytizing at a station when interviewed, "Japanese are too skeptical to accept non-native organized religion. They show hesitation whenever they are told about it. We have taken many measures to invite Japanese to our temple, but we only have 20 to 30 members yet in the last five years to my regret." For over 460 years, the Japanese have been uninterested in Christianity. It is an impossible mission to convert large numbers of Japanese in as short a period as five or ten years.

According to Yamada (cf. 2004a: 87), the possibilities for the UCKG to expand in a particular country depend on fulfilling four conditions: 1) The low-income group is large; 2) Relatedness to spiritism; 3) Christian background; and 4) Religious pluralism or tolerance toward various religious rites. Given these conditions, Japan has not proved to be the ideal soil suited for planting the sapling of UCKG. Although the Church has grown rapidly in the last three decades in most continents by taking advantage of the Brazilian diasporas, including the Brazilian migrants in Japan, the Church is now confronted with its hardest mission. Shusaku Endo, in his novel *Silence*, portrays the apostate priest Cristóvão Ferreira, the Portuguese missionary who actually came to Japan in 1600s, as saying that Japan is a swamp, in which the sapling of Christianity is planted, but Christianity will not take root in Japan unless one plants something that has been adapted for growth even in a swamp. Although the UCKG has been flourishing among Brazilian migrants, it is difficult for the Japanese to accept, due to its non-native qualities that it has imported from Brazil as well as the simple fact that it is a *Christian* church.

11 UCKG Japan Official Website in Japanese, Weekly Schedule (n.d.).URL: http://uckgjapan.org/shukan.htm [accessed on May 30, 2010].

Conclusion

In early 2009, the Japanese government announced an offer of 300,000 yen (approximately 3,200 dollars) to each Latin American migrant who is of Japanese descent and in the condition of unemployment, to support their return home. Their spouse and other family members would receive 200,000 yen each. On the surface, the offer seems generous, if not for the fact that there was a strict condition that any person accepting the offer is not able to seek re-entry to Japan for the next three years using the same residential visa status as being of Japanese descent.[12] This is a political measure to send back manual laborers, especially those who were unable to find jobs during this time of economic recession, due to their lack of special skills and Japanese efficiency. Although there is no evidence that the crime rate of the foreign nationals in Japan increases in proportion to the rate of unemployment, the Japanese media has been attracted to stories of crimes committed by foreign offenders, often with exaggeration (cf. Tani 2008: 167 – 169). It is generally assumed that the increase of the immigrant population in such a small land as Japan may affect national security. In response to the public's rising chorus of concern, the government made the decision to send away unemployed Latin American migrants in return for money. In fact, many Brazilian migrants decided to fly back home with one-way tickets (cf. Nikkei Shimbun 2009).

The Brazilian churches are now unanimously experiencing the immense decline in the pews as well, losing one-third to one-half of their congregants compared to a year prior. Nonetheless, these ranks will soon be replenished, as Japan cannot resist the influx of immigrants. According to the United Nations report on "Replacement Migration" in 2000, Japan is estimated to require an intake of 381,000 immigrants per year between 2005 and 2050 to maintain its population, or else experience a sharp decline in national strength (cf. Research and Legislative Reference Bureau 2008: 9 – 11). The total fertility rate of Japan has continued to decline since 1989, to 1.37 in 2009, and the population is roughly estimated to drop from 120 million to 104.9 million in 2050. In this period of transition, the churches in Japan, as well as Japanese society as a whole, will be forced to accept that the future task will be to seek coexistence with diverse ethnic groups.

By looking at Brazilian immigrant churches in Japan, I have categorized these churches into three types: the "grafting-type," the "seedling-type," and the "sapling-type," and have showed that these churches are mostly invisible to Japanese society. However, they will gradually become visible with the increased Brazilian population in Japan and their presence in society. As one of

12 When it was first announced, the Japanese government set the period of limiting the re-entry as indistinct as "interim period," however, it was later changed into "three years" due to the public criticism.

the functions of the Brazilian church is to mediate Brazilian and Japanese society, the church is the prime place for Brazilians to seek help for both their spiritual and practical needs. Therefore, the churches for Brazilians function in two ways: as communities of ethnicity and of faith, and as the medium between the Brazilians and Japanese society. Brazilian churches in Japan are worthy of further study in order to comprehend the fact that the intake of Brazilian immigrants was not only a matter of obtaining the labor force, but also invites the possibility of the transformation of the religious dynamics in Japan. If Japan chooses to keep its doors open to the Brazilians, and if the churches were to grant official membership to Brazilians, the population of Christians in Japan will no longer be less than 1 %.

References

Christian Year Book 2010. Tokyo: Kirisuto Shimbunsha.

ENDO, Shusaku (1980). *Silence.* New York: Taplinger Publishing Company.

GRABURN, Nelson H. H./John ERTL/R. Kenji TIERNEY ed. (2008). *Multiculturalism in the New Japan: Crossing the Boundaries Within.* Oxford: Berghahn Books.

KAJITA, Takamichi, Kiyoto TANNO and Naoto HIGUCHI (2005). *Kao no Mienai Teijuka: Nikkei Braziljin to Kokka, Shijo, Imin Network.* Nagoya: University of Nagoya Press.

KINSHICHI, Norio (2009). *Burajirushi: História do Brasil.* Tokyo: Toyo Shoten.

LESSER, Jeffrey, ed. (2003). *Searching for Home Abroad: Japanese Brazilians and Transnationalism.* Durham and London: Duke University Press.

LINGER, Daniel (2001). *No One Home: Brazilian Selves Remade in Japan.* Stanford: Stanford UP.

MARGOLIS, Maxine L. (1994). *Little Brazil: an ethnography of Brazilian immigrants in New York City.* New Jersey: PUP.

REIS, Raul (2006). Media and Religion in Brazil: The rise of TV Record and UCKG and their attempts at globalization. In: *Brazilian Journalism Research. Vol. 2. No.2.* 167–182.

Research and Legislative Reference Bureau (2008). *The Problem of the Immigrant Policy and the Foreign Workers Policy In a Depopulation Society.* Tokyo: National Diet Library.

ROTH, Joshua Hotaka (2002). *Brokered Homeland: Japanese Brazilian Migrants in Japan.* Ithaca: Cornell UP.

STEIGENGA, Timothy/Edward CLEARY ed. (2007). *Conversion of a continent: contemporary religious change in Latin America.* New Jersey: Rutgers UP.

STOLL, David (1990). *Is Latin America Turning Protestant? The Politics of Evangelical Growth.* Berkeley: University of California Press.

The Catholic Bishops' Conference of Japan: Year Book 2010. Tokyo: The Catholic Bishops' Conference of Japan.

THUMMA, Scott/Dave TRAVIS, ed. (2007). *Beyond Megachurch Myths: What We Can Learn from America's Largest Churches.* San Francisco: John Wiley & Sons, Inc.

TSUDA, Takeyuki (2003). *Strangers in the Homeland: Japanese Brazilian Return Migration in Transnational Perspective.* New York: Columbia UP.

TSUDA, Takeyuki, ed. (2009). *Diasporic Homecomings: Ethnic Return Migration in Comparative Perspective.* Stanford: Stanford UP.

WATANABE, Norie (2010, February) Gekihen suru Dekasegi Jijo. *Nikkei Shimbun.* URL: www.nikkeyshimbun.com.br [accessed on Feb. 14, 2010].

YAMADA, Masanobu (2002). Brajiru ni okeru Seimeishugiteki Kyusaikan: Nikkei Shinshukyo to Pentekostarizumu. In: *Shukyo to Shakai.* Vol. 9, Additional Volume. 74 – 90.

YAMADA, Masanobu (2004a). Brajiru ni okeru Neo Pentekosutarizumu no Shinten. In: *Shukyo Kenkyu.* Vol. 342. 71 – 92.

YAMADA, Masanobu (2004b). Brajiru ni okeru Purotesutanto Kyokai no Shakaiteki Ninchi. In: *Ibero Amerika Kenkyu.* Vol. 26. No. 2. 63 – 78.

YAMADA, Masanobu (2008a). Anju no Chi toshite no Purotesutanto Kyokai: Mie-ken Beteru Fukuin Kyokai no Jirei. In: *Americasu Sekai ni okeru Ido to Grobarizasyon.* Tenri City: The publication department of Tenri University. 184 – 201.

YAMADA, Masanobu (2008b). *Dekasegi no Syukyo Katudo to Shakaika.* In: The handouts of the oral presentation at 67th convention of Japan Religious Society. 1 – 8.

Christo Thesnaar

A Pastoral Hermeneutical Approach to Reconciliation and Healing

A South African Perspective

1. Introduction

Human beings, communities and nations have been exposed to conflict for centuries. Some conflicts or disputes were limited to a single event caused by a specific incident, and managed not to resurface after the conflict was resolved. Others were deeply embedded and rooted in the history of the person, community or nation and kept on recurring through the ages. In terms of the latter, the divisions, conflicting presuppositions and contradictory world-views from the past continue to undermine the present. In this regard, Charles Villa-Vicencio remarked that ”these differences have the capability of destroying the future”.[1] The challenge that confronts theologians is how a responsible theology can contribute to dealing with existing differences in such a way that reconciliation and healing can actually occur within a nation.

The South African society chose to deal with its apartheid past in a very particular way. During the successful and rather peaceful period of transition it was mutually resolved by the opposing sides (mainly the Nationalist government and the African National Congress) to deal with the past by means of a Truth and Reconciliation Commission (TRC). It was evident that South Africans consciously chose to add ‘reconciliation’ to the term ‘truth commission’. The objective was not merely to deal with the truth but to actively work towards reconciling the sharply differing sections of society, thereby contributing to building a new nation. Although the commission tried it utmost to achieve the goal of reconciling our nation, it was soon evident that reconciliation posed a much greater challenge than could be met by means of one single process. The hurt of the past was simply too deep and severe for the TRC to deal with it in a constructive way within the short time the Commission existed.

After the TRC had completed its mandate and published its report, reconciliation has slowly slipped off the main agenda of the nation. It was almost exclusively left to non-governmental and faith-based organizations to actively try to lead the nation towards reconciliation. Organizations such as the Institute for the Healing of Memories, the Institute for Justice and

1 Charles Villa-Vicencio: Telling one another stories: towards a theology of reconciliation, in Many Cultures, One Nation, ed. by Charles Villa-Vicencio and Carl Niehaus, in 1995.

Reconciliation, churches and others continued to try their utmost to pursue the journey towards reconciliation in a constructive, though largely limited way.

Reconciliation is essentially about restoring relationships and thereby laying the foundation for redressing the injustices of the past. It is therefore clear that reconciliation is not just about accepting or, tolerating each other, providing space for everyone, hugging each other, receiving back what was taken away etc., much less trying to force people into unity. Rather, it is a deeply transformative process with a focus on healing for the individual, community or nation. According to Kraybill (1992:19), the hurts and needs are sometimes "emotional…or symbolic: to hear admission of error and apology. Other times they are political or material and require redress at this level." Where reparation, restitution and restoration form part of the process of reconciliation and healing, relationships can be restored. Therefore, reconciliation and healing is truly transformative when it will challenge everybody involved to start on the journey towards transformation and reconciliation and realize that no guarantees can be given in this endeavour. The central focus of this contribution is that reconciliation and healing is a deeply theological issue embedded in a pastoral hermeneutical process.

2. Towards a hermeneutical approach to reconciliation

The complexity is that there are many pastoral approaches theologians can use to deal with reconciliation and healing. In this article, I will only briefly deal with two opposite approaches to pastoral care. The first approach would be the kerygmatic approach. Louw (1998: 25) defines this approach as follows: "the central function of pastoral care lay in the kerygmatic components of proclamation and conversion. Pastoral care was then mainly viewed as the offer of redemption to sinners through the therapeutic process involved in forgiveness and the care of the soul." Louw (cf. 1998: 25) explains that the care of the soul must be understood in this regard as a kerygmatic pro-clamation of the Word in order to re-deem the sinner and convey forgiveness. Although this approach is practiced by many (e.g. E. Thurneysen, 1962 [Europe] and J. Adams, 1979 [USA]) it has essential shortcomings when applied to reconciliation and healing between individuals, communities, and nations in conflict. These shortcommings are:

- Reconciliation and healing could easily be reduced to an individual issue between God and the perpetrator;
- forgiveness could be limited to a personal confession before God with no obligation to the victim;

- reconciliation and forgiveness will take place and be settled in one single instant, thereby disregarding the importance of a process;
- reconciliation is easily detached from justice, reparation, restitution, forgiveness, and concrete actions that are essential for the reconciliation and healing process; and
- healing and reconciliation are reduced to the mere spiritual dimension of human existence.

The opposite of the kerygmatic approach is the individual client-centred approach. According to Louw (cf. 1998: 27), this approach to pastoral care insists that the dominant emphasis should not be on the Word, but on the person's need. In terms of pastoral care it is therefore not God's Word that brings about healing or reconciliation but rather the process of communication and counselling. In this regard, counselling involves the dynamics of human relations as these are expressed in communicative procedures (cf. ibid.). Although this approach is practiced by many (cf. Rogers 1951; Hiltner 1958), it has essential shortcomings when applied to reconciliation and healing between individuals, communities and nations in conflict. These shortcommings are:

- Reconciliation is narrowed down to a mere experiential affair on the level of emotional feeling and need;
- forgiveness will only entail a personal confession that is determined by the affective aspect of humans;
- reconciliation, forgiveness and healing are only possible if the inherent potential of victims and perpetrators is well enough developed so that they are able to accomplish their own personal reconciliation, forgiveness and healing;
- forgiveness and reconciliation will be considered sufficient if people believe that they experience self-assertion within the relations in which they function;
- victims do not need perpetrators (and vice versa) to experience reconciliation and healing, and
- healing and reconciliation are being reduced mainly to the personal dimension of human existence.

From the critical comments above it is clear that both the kerygmatic and the individual client-centred approach to healing and reconciliation are too limited and one-sided to deal with the current challenges within South Africa in a truly pastoral manner. Both of them are too concerned with trying to explain the reality of human existence in this world in terms of either their relation to God or to themselves. In this sense these two personal pastoral approaches are limited because both tend to focus exclusively on the cause of the problems humans are grappling with and then pressure themselves to present a *solution* how to reconcile people after the conflict. In this sense, they do not adequately take reconciliation and healing as process into consideration when providing the solution. They rather keep to their focus, trying to solve this conflict at all costs. It is exactly because of this pressure of finding solutions to conflicts that many critics will regard these approaches as too simplistic.

Within the complexities of the reconciliation and healing processes within South Africa, together with the complex socio-political and economic realities, this article argues that a paradigm shift is necessary within pastoral theology, in order to deal with reconciliation and healing in a constructive way. This shift implies to move away from the two personal pastoral approaches towards a hermeneutical approach within pastoral care.

For reconciliation and healing to take place within the complex South African context, it is essential that pastoral care should opt to make use of a hermeneutical approach. By using hermeneutics as a lens to address the challenges of reconciliation and healing within South Africa, it will inevitably be understood that reconciliation involves a process. As theologians we have to ensure that a theology of reconciliation and healing forms an integral part of the process of reconciliation and healing. This will have a decisive impact on how we implement a process of reconciliation and healing. A hermeneutical approach will, be more focused on the process of understanding within the specific contexts and, of course, it will be relational. This implies that it is more interested in the understanding and clarification of human problems than in trying to explain the problems or to provide quick fix solutions to the problems humans are grappling with. The hermeneutical paradigm wants to lead human beings to discover the meaning of the God-human relation within their life contexts. Therefore, the aim of committing ourselves to the hermeneutical approach in pastoral care would be to assist individuals, communities and nations on their journey towards reconciliation and healing in a constructive and responsible way. In order to achieve this goal, pastoral care will need to implement the hermeneutical approach and integrate the key components of the hermeneutical process within a theology of reconciliation and healing.

3. Key Components of a Hermeneutical Process

3.1 Wisdom Theology

For a hermeneutical approach to reconciliation to function in a concrete way, it needs to be grounded within a theological framework. The focus of this article is not to spell out a full theological framework but to focus specifically on a theology that is able to assist individuals, communities and nations on their journey towards reconciliation and healing. One of the key components in this regard would be wisdom theology. Wisdom theology, firstly, is about faith in action based on the promises of God and his faithfulness. Secondly, it reflects an ethic of unconditional love. Finally, it focuses on relationship on all levels, with justice and reconciliation as its goal (cf. Louw 1995: 50). Based on this understanding, wisdom theology provides pastoral care with a structure and direction to constructively contribute to the process of reconciliation and healing.

3.2 Eco-systemic Approach

The hermeneutical paradigm challenges pastoral care to move away from an individual approach with a focus on self-realisation and autonomy to a psycho-systemic approach with an emphasis on the network of commitments and structures within a social cultural context. Botman (cf. 1995: 10–11) refers to such an approach as a socio-theological constructionist approach in pastoral care with an emphasis on the healing of the group and community.

The hermeneutical paradigm further challenges pastoral care to move away from the importance of the data or the narrative to the importance of the processes that determine the content of the data or narrative. As stated earlier, pastoral care is also further challenged to move away from the so-called cause-effect thinking with its focus on finding solutions (by compiling separate parts together) to the principle of providing meaning. In this regard, Bosch (1991: 368) reminds us that "the emphasis throughout should therefore be on the wholeness and indivisibility of the paradigm, rather than on its separated ingredients."

Louw (1997: 396) argues that system theory is of particular importance to the pastoral encounter when he states: "systemic thinking means that the pastoral encounter does not only take note of the person and his/her psychic composition, but especially of the position held by a person within a relationship." The human being is always in interaction with others by means of a relational network. Davidson (Saayman and Kriel 1992: 35) emphasises this as follows: "Communal dimension of all human existence in Africa can hardly be over-emphasised. One can indeed say generally that in Africa 'the good of the individual is a function of the good of the community; the community thus represents the individual." The needs of the individual are always secondary to that of the group. The emphasis in the system-theoretical approach is on an inclusive process of relationships and interactions (cf. Augsberger 1986: 178).

The value of the systemic model for pastoral care is that the focus on the problem is less important than the focus on understanding the problems of human beings according to the position of the person within their network of relations. The systemic theoretical model, within a hermeneutical paradigm, brings forward an eco-hermeneutical perspective within pastoral care. According to Louw (1997: 397), pastoral care is willing "to take the risk of involvement with a system, not by explaining it or giving empathic advice from the outside, but by becoming part of the system and thus experiencing (and facilitating) the beauty of change. In doing so, it works towards wholeness as an eco-systemic reality and as a biblical goal" (Müller 1996: 13). Within this context, eco-systemic thinking should be seen as an attempt not only to understand problems within the context but also to understand the context itself.

3.3 Contextual Understanding

The hermeneutical paradigm empowers pastoral care to operate contextually. Thus, pastoral care has no choice but to take the cultural and societal context of South Africa seriously. Louw (1997: 393) challenges us not only to take the context seriously and to become community based but also to make sure that "pastoral care should become involved in the transformation and reconstruction of society."

Pastoral care therefore has the responsibility to facilitate the transformation, reconstruction and ultimately the healing of the whole society (individuals, groups, and communities). Within the African context, healing is the process of restoring harmony within the community, when someone breaks the moral rules of a community and thereby disturbs the cosmic ties between the person and the community. Healing is therefore a constructive process of restoring harmony in one's soul, body and cognition but also to live harmoniously with yourself, your neighbour's, your community and environment, including the physical, social, spiritual, natural and the supernatural. Berinyuu (cf. 1988: 7) explains this by comparing it to a cube. Each side of the cube has a colour, yet forms part of an integrated whole. If one of the sides should move and with it the colours, the colour harmony of the cube is distorted. For the cube to be whole again the colours need to be in the correct place.

For healing to take place within the African context, pastoral care will not only need to understand the African context but also interpret it within a process of healing. Although there are many characteristics that are important in the African context, for example wholeness, time, light and order, sickness, nature, life and life-force, the African pastoral scholar Emmanuel Larty (1991: 42) highlights the following to assist pastoral care to be contextual in Africa:

"1. Pastoral Counselling will begin where the people are taking seriously their own theological, sociological and psychological notions; recognizing that there are within these views a wealth of valuable insights which can enhance the process of counselling.
2. There will be scope for indirect modes of communication-proverbs, songs, stories, parables, poems and sayings – to be used to useful effect in the process of counselling.
3. There will be scope for a corporate (though therapeutic) approach which

emphasizes harmonious relationships and a sense of belonging.
4. Pastoral counselling will not omit a social-political or prophetic input aimed at effecting changing life-denying structures in society and seeking a community where all may live a human life."

If pastoral care does not succeed to take the context seriously as well as to facilitate harmony and healing, it will be estranged from the complexities of life and therefore not be able to contribute to the transformation and reconstruction of our societies.[2] If it does, it will contribute to lay the foundation for the process of reconciliation and healing. The way the process of reconciliation and healing will be structured in Africa will therefore be different than in Europe or South America.

3.4 Intercultural Communication

The hermeneutical paradigm further challenges pastoral care to be able to communicate interculturally within the context of South Africa, in order to play a constructive role in reconciliation and healing.

Through the ages, church traditions have formulated different models to deal with the relation between theology and the local cultural context (cf. Bosch 1991: 447–452). The Catholic Church proposed the integration-accommodation model to deal with this dynamic tension between theology and culture. This model focuses on the integration and accommodation of many of the traditional customs within the theology of Rome, as long as the basis of their theology is not affected. In this regard, Daneel (1989: 37) writes: "The Roman Catholic tradition of natural theology allows for a far-reaching accommodation or adaptation to the varied cultures of mankind." Their aim in integrating and accommodating the so-called 'good' indigenous customs was to try and bridge the gap between Christianity and the indigenous beliefs.

On the other hand, the Reformed tradition proposed the antithetical model to bridge the gap. The aim of this model was to denounce everything that is in conflict with Scripture. Their mission was to focus on justification by faith alone, along with the conviction that conversion to Christ implies a radical parting with the past. The implication of this approach was that they had a limited view of dialogue with other cultures. The general tendency was towards elimination and a measure of negation rather than confrontation and dialogue (cf. Daneel 1989: 42).

The independent African churches proposed a third option, namely the transformation model to address the tension in a constructive way. The aim of this model was to confront the Western approach in Africa. Their point of view was that the gospel could be used along with any traditional custom, and their

2 Jean Masamba ma Mpolo's (1991: 27) article confirms that the theological education model has no choice but to function in a contextual and action-reflection orientated way.

task was to transform the message of Christ into an African-friendly gospel. Daneel (1989: 42) explains this as follows: "Free from Western doctrinal structures and imported attitudes of negation or repudiation of their own world view and religious practices, they could incorporate or confront and transform these as they saw fit, whether through serious dialogue, symbolic ritual or dancing feet."

In distinction from the integration-accommodation, the antithetical and the transformation model, Bosch (cf. 1991: 453) proposes the inculturation model. This model empowers human beings to practice pastoral care in a constructive way within the intercultural context. He explains the basic elements of this model as follows:

a) It respects all the agents involved. "Neither the missionary, nor the hierarchy, nor the magisterium controls the process" (Bosch 1991: 453). This does not mean that the different agents do not play a role but that they do not approach specific situations with preconceived ideas.

b) The emphasis is placed on the local situation. "At this local level, inculturation comprises much more than culture in the traditional or anthropological sense of the term. It involves the entire context: social, economic, political, religious, educational, etc." (Bosch 1991: 443). He rightly underlines the importance of the total spectrum. It is in the holistic perspective that the system theoretical approach and pastoral care could function in a constructive way within an intercultural context.

c) Inculturation does not only focus on the local context; it also has a regional, macro-contextual and macro-cultural manifestation.

d) Inculturation follows the incarnation. This incarnational dimension, of the gospel being "en-fleshed", "em-bodied" in a people and its culture, of a "kind of ongoing incarnation" is very different from any other previous model. "In this paradigm, it is not so much a case of the church being expanded, but of the church being born anew in each new context and culture" (Bosch 1991: 454).

e) It is essential that the coordination between the gospel and culture is Christologically structured. This is not an attempt by the church to force Christ onto another culture but rather to give indigenous people's faith in Christ an opportunity to develop within their own culture and thoughts.

f) Inculturation is an all-including reality. According to this, it is not possible to only incorporate certain 'good' customs in the Christian faith. Everything that is part of a culture will need to be incorporated.

g) Inculturation also has a critical dimension. This dimension has the role to make sure that this approach does not become one-sided, as it emphasises that in the dialogue between culture and gospel it will help to find a balance between retaining the old culture and creating a new one.

According to Bosch (1991: 455), it is wise not to use the term "inculturated", the reason being that inculturation has to be a tentative and on-going process. The relationship between culture and gospel should always be a creative and dynamic process. Inculturation refers to the more comprehensive and continuous process associated with intercultural communication and contact, while 'inculturated' only refers to the contact with other cultures.

Pastoral theology will only be practiced responsibly if inculturation is implemented within an ecumenical paradigm. The challenge is whether a person is able to move from their own cultural context to that of another. Sometimes this is hampered due to immaturity, the lack of skills or fear that the person will lose his or her own culture. Pastoral care has the responsibility to assist the person in realising that when they practice inculturation it is not about losing your own culture. It is actually about becoming culture-aware. Therefore, it is valuable to know that ethnicity, culture, faith and race is an inherency that you need to care for and protect to be able to use it as a direction for your lifestyle. On the other hand, it is just as important to make sure that this does not create boundaries, barriers or blockages in communication and cooperation between people.

Interculturation empowers people to live on the boundaries between cultures and to have the ability to move with freedom between cultures. This is possible when people realise they need to dis-identify the self from old cultural identifications; when doing that, they will experience that it leads to the rediscovery of the self in at least three contexts: one's own culture, a second culture, and in that unique third culture that is continually being formed on the boundary between the two. The third-culture perspective enables the intercultural person to make communication easier, interpret cultural conflict and function with acceptable competence without any inappropriate or confusing switching of behaviour (cf. Augsburger 1986: 13).

Augsburger (cf. ibid.: 14) further argues that an intercultural person needs *interpathy* to be able to move between cultures. Interpathy is understood as the ability to enter the second culture in a cognitive and effective way. This develops interpathical respect, insight and appreciation which will enable a person to transcend him- or herself for a moment in a particular situation with regard to the shortcomings of your own culture. In Karaban's (cf. 1992: 267) opinion, intercultural pastoral care is not only about a method of pastoral care but also about the attitude in which it is practiced. Saayman (1992: 46) confirms this: "Even the best intentions ... can go astray if the necessary cultural sensitivity and analysis are lacking." Sensitivity, suppleness and maturity form an important part of interpathy and intercultural pastoral care. This underlines why a specific choice is made for a hermeneutical approach in pastoral care for reconciliation and healing.

For theologians, it is important to acknowledge the value of the process of contextuality and interculturation. It must, however, be emphasised that this process should not be detached from the process of theologising. Pastoral care has a priestly dimension which entails an outreach to all people and communities in love (cf. Louw 1997: 11). Christian care and compassion is focused on the world, is inclusive and wants to influence healing in individuals, communities and nations. Pastoral care, therefore, has no choice but to extend faith care to a broader context of life care. Pastoral care needs to constantly reach out to the need of people to ensure that it is true to its dynamic diaconical character (cf. Louw 1997: 20). In this regard, helping and caring will obtain a much wider contextual and social dimension where it demonstrates that it has a broader vision than merely focusing on the faith issues people are struggling with. This broader vision entails that it is essentially about finding meaning within the full spectrum of real life issues.

3.5 Metaphors, Symbols and Rituals

Against the backdrop of the hermeneutical approach and the key components thereof as described above, we also want to argue that a creative and practical way towards reconciliation and healing within the African context will have to include metaphors, symbols and rituals. The hermeneutical paradigm enables pastoral care to not only focus on the direct presence of God in life and creation but also on his indirect presence. Pastoral care thus has the task to focus on interpreting God and our human context. This is emphasized by Louw (cf. 1997: 4) when he states that such sensitivity will require pastoral care to allow more space for mysticism, metaphors, symbols and the sacramental dimensions of life, thus God 'in' creation. This is echoed by Kerecki (1997: 602) when he highlights that rituals have the ability to create meaning: "In the Christian context ritual deeds invite people of the worshipping assembly into the mystery of God who invites them to participate in that life of love and meaning." We could therefore acknowledge that the hermeneutical paradigm creates the space for the use of metaphors, symbols and rituals to assist pastoral care on the journey towards reconciliation and healing.

A **metaphor** is a creative way to use language to communicate meaning which cannot be expressed in a rational language. This is possible, because language can be written in an aesthetic, poetic and mystic way. Within pastoral care, the metaphor will have the task to connect the intention from God with human existence in this world or, rather, within the concrete life situation of humans. According to Louw (1997:60), a pastoral metaphor wants to communicate the connection between faith and our life in such a way that human beings will experience that God is present in their suffering. This happens when the experience is affirmed by the faith traditions, the reading of the Word and the celebrating of the sacraments.

A **symbol** fulfils a bridge function, via the representation of an image, between the reality of faith and human experience in the world. According to Louw (cf. 1997: 60), this bridge function wants to lead human beings to critical reflection, meditation and remembrance. A symbol has the ability to refer to another reality. The actions of human beings have specific images to which they can relate certain experiences. These experiences can then be linked to certain symbols. The parables in Scripture are well-known examples of how symbols are used. These parables succeed in using symbols from daily life to assist us in identifying with them. Both physical and psychological healing are symbols and signs of the kingdom of God (cf. Louw 1998: 55). The African scholar Berinyuu (cf. 1988: 96) affirms the importance of symbols and signs used to express relationships, because they derive from daily life situations and cultural contexts. Some examples of symbols in the religious context are the cross, the dove, meditation, cathedrals, the laying on of hands and anointment. It is true that some of these symbols have disappeared in churches and will need to be discovered again. It is also important to create new symbols that can assist human beings to find healing and reconciliation.

Karecki (1997: 601) describes **ritual** as "endemic to both individual and community life. It is the storehouse of a community's central values, or root metaphors of a community or culture." He continues to state that a ritual has a profound effect on identity formation and the ability to relate to the world in a meaningful way (cf. ibid.: 598). According to this, it is clear that the value and impact of a ritual should not be underestimated. It has the ability to challenge the actions of a whole community to evaluate its action in the presence of the broader community in relation to its basic religious identity.

The value of the ritual for those present is that everyone needs to participate in it. During the performance of the ritual nobody is allowed to be a spectator. The reason for this is because a ritual implies that a human being is involved with soul, body and spirit. Karecki (ibid.: 602) emphasises this when he explains: "Since ritual works on the trans-rational level, it generates wholeness because it engages the whole person and in that active engagement through myth and symbol, gesture and movement transformation occurs." When this is the case, a ritual has the power to open the participants to the meaning conveyed through the ritual actions, language and symbols (cf. ibid.: 601). It is therefore inevitable that a ritual has the ability to transform, affirm identity, bring meaning to the concrete situation of human beings and even to show them the way where no road exists.

Within the South African context, religious rituals form the key to assist and transform the South African community towards healing and reconciliation. To achieve this goal, pastoral care will need to contextualise the religious rituals. Karecki (ibid.: 603) quotes Luzbetak (cf. 1988) in this regard: "Contextualization must never overlook the fact that ritual, although imaginative and constantly aware of the need to keep pace with culture, is nevertheless by its very nature repetitive and traditional. Ritual is, after all, the memory of a faith community." In this sense, Holy Communion is a ritual that could be used at length within the South African reconciliation context. "This is one of the metaphors that can catch the vivid imagination of Africans in general and expresses a Christological truth which has parallels in the traditions of various communities in Africa. The place for sacrificial meals as part of a total package of healing is an important if not an indispensable one" (Berinyuu 1988: 119).

Although the ritual of Holy Communion may have different forms and names within different faith traditions the binding factor is that wine and bread are commonly used and that this takes place within communion, *koinonia.* Holy Communion refers to the meal of Christ. At this meal of Christ the broken relationship between human beings and Christ is being restored, time and again. This meal is about salvation and reconciliation. Accordingly, this ritual makes it possible for Christians from different cultural contexts to discover their faith, peace, forgiveness, reconciliation and healing in the mist of their pain and suffering. In terms of the above it is clear that symbols, metaphors and rituals can and should play a cardinal role in understanding and facilitating reconciliation and healing. It also emphasises that the hermeneutical paradigm leads to metaphorical theology. This will contribute immensely to the process of reconciliation and healing.

To summarise: The key components of reconciliation as indicated above need to form an integral part of pastoral theology in order to facilitate healing and reconciliation within the socio-political context in South Africa.

4. Elements of a Creative Way to Reconciliation and Healing

In conclusion, some practical elements of a creative way to reconciliation and healing are indicated. It must be emphasised once again that these elements should be grounded within the hermeneutical approach and embedded in the key components of the hermeneutical process. The challenge would be to construct such a way towards reconciliation and healing that it would enable people to journey on this road responsibly and constructively.

The Institute for the Healing of Memories[3] uses the following basic elements in their methodology to assist the reconciliation and healing process in a constructive way:

- There is no 'quick fix' or 'cheap' way to reconciliation, forgiveness and healing. It is always a process and a journey. For that reason, the Institute states clearly that a workshop is only the first step in the process of healing and reconciliation.
- Such workshops can take place anywhere where a safe space has been created for victims and offenders alike to engage on their journey.
- This journey is both an individual and a collective experience, exploring the effects of the apartheid years. The emphasis is on dealing with these issues at an emotional, psychological and spiritual level, rather than intellectually.

3 See URL: www.healingofmemories.co.za

- Participants should be allowed ample time to reflect on the past in order to try and find a way to deal with the memories that have a paralyzing or destructive effect on them. They need to identify and keep all that is life-giving; and to put all that is destructive behind them. The focus, therefore, is to find ways of preventing the negative part of their history from being repeated, and of breaking the cycle of victims and victimizers that we have lived with for so long. This journey is an attempt to assist victims to be victors, and to help all of us on the road to a new life.
- During a journey, time will be given for individual reflection, creative exercises (drawings and clay exercises), and opportunities to share their stories in small groups. There is also some reflection on common themes that come up in our journeys-such as anger, hope, hatred, joy, isolation, guilt, endurance- and a discovery of the depths of the common humanity we share.
- The first step of the journey has to be closed with a celebration or liturgy which is compiled by the group. It is put together by the participants by using various art forms, for instance mimes, poetry and songs. Metaphors, symbols and rituals play an important part in the stories of human beings and should form part of this celebration, for instance walking in a procession, washing of feet, burning what you want to leave behind, Bible readings, prayers, songs and dramas, and celebrating the Eucharist as a way to link the suffering of Christ to our suffering and his resurrection to filling us with a living hope.

It is evident from the above that the Institute for the Healing of Memories has managed to base its methodology on a hermeneutical pastoral approach to reconciliation and healing.

5. Conclusion

In South Africa today, the differences between races are just as wide as at the time of the 1994 elections. Even the role of the TRC could not pave the way sufficiently for a sustainable process of reconciliation and healing. The concern of many is that these differences have the capability of destroying the present democracy and the whole future of this country. This article tried to focus on dealing with reconciliation and healing in a responsible way, motivated by the conviction that a hermeneutical pastoral approach within theology can greatly contribute to the reconciliation and healing process in South Africa.

The emphasis in this attempt is to state clearly the aim of a hermeneutical pastoral approach, namely to actively transform and reconstruct the society we live in. To achieve this, the hermeneutical pastoral approach needs to focus on being contextual, eco-systemic and intercultural, making use of a wisdom theology that has the ability to set in motion a creative practical process of reconciliation and healing by implementing metaphors, symbols and rituals within this process.

References

Adams, J. E. (1979). More than Redemption, A Theology of Christian Counselling. Grand Rapids: Barker Books.

Augsburger, D. W. (1986). Pastoral counseling across cultures. Philadelphia: Westminister.

Berinyuu, A. A. (1988). Pastoral care to the sick in Africa. New York: Verlang Peter Lang.

Bosch, D. J. (1991). Transforming Missions. New York: Orbis Books.

Botman, H. R. (1995). Sosio-theological constructionist approach to pastoral care. Journal of Pastoral Ministry (7) (July).

Chubb, K./van Dijk, L. (2001). Between Anger And Hope. South African youth and the Truth and Reconciliation Commission. Johannesburg: Witwatersrand Press.

Daneel, M. L. (1989). The encounter between Christianity and traditional African culture: Accommodation or transformation?. Theologia Evangelica 22 (3). 36–51.

Karaban, R. A. (1992). Cross-Cultural Pastoral Counseling: Method or Hermeneutic? A Response. Pastoral Psychology 40 (4). 265–269.

Karecki, M. (1997). Religious ritual as a key to wholeness in mission. Missionalia 25 (4). 598–606.

Kayser, U. (1998). Creating the past-Improvising the present. Cape Town: Honours thesis. Centre for African Studies. UCT.

Kraybill, R. (1992). The cycle of reconciliation. Track Two. 19–20.

Krog, A. (1998). Country of My Skull. Cape Town: Random House.

Lartey, E. Y. (2003). In Living Color: An intercultural approach to pastoral care and counseling. London: Jessica Kingsley.

Louw, D. J. (1995). Wisdom as a New Paradigm for Practical Theology in a Post-Apartheid Society. Journal of Theology for Southern Africa. 90. 41–54.

Louw, D. J. (1997). Pastoraat as vertolking en ontmoeting. Wellington: Lux Verbi.

Louw, D. J. (1998). A pastoral hermeneutics of care and encounter. Wellington: Lux Verbi.

Ma Mpolo, J. M./Nwachuku, D. (1991). Pastoral Care and Counseling in Africa Today. New York: Peter Lang.

Müller, J. (1996). Om tot verhaal te kom. Pretoria: RGN.

Nouwen, H. (1990). The wounded healer. New York: Abide Press.

Peterson, R. M. (1996). The politics of grace and the Truth and Reconciliation Commission. In: Botman, H. R./Petersen, R. M. ed.: To Remember and Heal. Cape Town: Human & Rousseau: 57–64.

Saayman, W./Kriel, J. (1992). Aids. The leprosy of our time? Johannesburg: Orion.

Thesnaar, C. H. (1997). Crossing racial barriers: Story-telling as a method for healing in youth ministry. In: Kitching, D./Robbins, D. ed.: Youth Ministry: Basics and beyond. Wellington: Youth Specialties: 118–132.

Thesnaar, C. H. (2001). Die proses van heling en versoening: 'n Pastoraal-

Hermeneutiese ondersoek van die dinamika tussen slagoffer en oortreder binne 'n post-WVK periode. DTh tesis. Stellenbosch: US.

Truth and Reconciliation Commission of South Africa Report (1998). Cape Town: TRC Vol. 5.

THURNEYSEN, E. (1963). A Theology of Pastoral Care. Richmond: John Knox.

VILLA-VICENCIO, C. Telling one another stories: Towards a Theology of Reconciliation. In: VILLA-VICENCIO, Charles/NIEHAUS, Carl ed.: Many cultures, one nation. 1995.

Andreas Hasenclever/Jan Sändig

"I can't live with or without you"

Peace-Building and Reconciliation

Introduction

Peace is a perfect institution: In peace societies settle their conflicts without recourse to force and according to commonly accepted standards of justice. War is the opposite of peace: In war shared principles, norms, rules and procedures failed to coordinate conflicting interests and military force is used to press the opponent into concessions. Whether they occur between or within societies, wars always go along with death and destruction on a large scale. The challenging process of moving a society from war to peace is commonly referred to as Peace-building[1]. It entails confidence-building measures for the prevention of war and the institutionalization of appropriate conflict-settlement mechanisms. Former adversaries are integrated into newly built structures organizing legitimate political decision-making, which then are believed to generate a corresponding sense of community. Trust replaces worse-case scenarios. Peace is a human aspiration. Peace-building, however, is a practical task open to scrutiny and blame in case of failure.

Since the late 1980s Peace-building has been undertaken by a large number of international organizations, most importantly the United Nations (UN), the European Union (EU), the international donor community, and national as well as international non-governmental organizations (NGOs). In countries as varied as Cambodia, Bosnia, Somalia, El Salvador, East Timor and Mozambique international Peace-builders implemented a more or less one-size-fits-all model in which they demobilized and reintegrated former fighters, returned refugees, reformed the security apparatus and justice system, organized elections, encouraged grassroots NGO activities, lifted trade barriers, put up war crime tribunals and occasionally ran truth and reconciliation commissions. Although Namibia and Mozambique are often hailed as success stories proving that "Peace-building works", the overall balance sheet is disappointing: Peace-building has produced many "no war, no peace"-situations (e.g. Bosnia, El Salvador and Cambodia) and in some cases even resulted in the recurrence of warfare (e.g. Angola, Somalia and Rwanda; Mac Ginty 2006).

1 According to former UN Secretary General Boutros Boutros-Ghali Peace-building can be understood as "action to identify and support structures which will tend to strengthen and solidify peace in order to avoid a relapse into conflict" (Secretary-General of the United Nations 1992).

This mixed balance sheet calls for extensive academic research on how peace can be effectively consolidated in fragile post-war settings.

Our contribution reviews the state of the art on Peace-building and discusses two research questions: Firstly, are internationally supported Peace-building missions more effective in consolidating peace than the forces of war, which might also build peace on their own terms? And secondly, what strategies should international actors adopt in Peace-building? The question here is in particular whether reconciliation is necessary to sustain peace. Reconciliation, in our understanding, is the process through which a society moves from a divided past to a shared future (Bloomfield et al. 2003: 12). Justice, truth, healing and reparation contribute to the transformation of conflictive and destructive relationships between adversaries into non-prejudiced and constructive interaction based on mutual trust.

Reconciliation allows us to distinguish two major approaches to Peace-building: The Liberal approach and Communitarian models. The Liberal approach downplays the importance of reconciliation or even treats it as dangerous to the wider efforts of producing stability. Instead, it is occupied with crafting political institutions and spurring the economy in the belief that the newly built institutions serve as arena in which conflicting interests are mediated and commonly agreed policies are decided. This would transform the unregulated exercise of force into coordinated politics, whereby violence becomes dispensable. After years or decades of "normalized" politics, trust would have grown between opposed societal factions resulting in genuine reconciliation – and (to paraphrase Kant) eternal peace. In contrast, Communitarian approaches address the communities in conflict and argue that peace cannot be built unless the groups in conflict are either territorially separated or reconciled. While separation theorists suggest that after long-standing ethnic civil wars trust is only possible within the own community and therefore groups need to be separated into ethnically homogenous states, proponents of reconciliation initiatives challenge this claim by proposing instruments and strategies that seek to reconcile opposed societal factions by promoting justice, truth, healing and reparation.

Our argument is that the liberal approach to Peace-building needs to be complemented by efforts of reconciliation to achieve sustainable peace in the aftermath of civil war. In its current design, liberal Peace-building is overly concerned with establishing political institutions and thereby disregards divisive societal conflicts that disrupt the newly built institutions or even re-ignite civil war. In spite of these grave failings of liberal Peace-building, we do not call for its abandonment as the available alternatives appear worse: Letting war sort out things ("Give war a chance") would be ethically problematic and victor's peace more often than not entails the exclusion of large segments of society from the access to decision-making and public goods, which sows further conflict. Indigenous Peace-building is unlikely to achieve peace as local peace capacities are marginal after long-standing intense violence.

Rather than abandoning liberal Peace-building, we suggest that it needs to be reformed. Separating divided societies would be no realistic reform proposal as forced re-settlements of communities violate international human rights norms. In our opinion, the key to building sustainable peace therefore is complementing the liberal Peace-building agenda by the pro-active promotion of reconciliation through justice, truth, healing and reparation. The underlying assumption of this argument is that, contradicting the view of many separation theorists, reconciliation remains possible even after fierce ethnic wars.

However, we also recognize that there is the potential dilemma of reconciliation opening up of the Pandora box of societal conflicts and triggering a new round of fighting. The solution to the dilemma of how communities that can neither live with or without the opposed communities in post-war settings might achieve reconciliation is largely beyond the current state of academic knowledge. Besides calling for further research, we conclude that a locally grounded, reconciling and ultimately sustainable version of Peace-building requires a hybrid Peace-building framework, in which liberal institutions incorporate local social realities including local power brokers, grassroots organizations and reconciliation initiatives.

The Rise of Peace-Building

Peace-building is an invention of the post-Cold War world in which liberal values have become dominant on a global scale, the principle of national sovereignty is loosened and security is increasingly attributed to human beings rather than to states. During the Cold War UN activities on armed conflict and war were restricted to Peace-keeping, i. e. military and civilian efforts to keep ceasefires and prepare for peace negotiations. The 15 Peace-keeping missions from 1948–1989 (of which five are still ongoing) were followed by 21 major Peace-building operations from 1989–2007 (United Nations 2010b; Paris & Sisk 2009: 2). Today, the UN maintains 16 peace operations (this includes both Peace-keeping and Peace-building) with a total of 124.000 personnel (United Nations 2010a). Compared to 1999 this amounts to a nine-fold increase in personnel strength.

It appears that the strong demand for Peace-building, which we currently witness, is not a temporal spike, but a sustaining trend. This argument rests on the still high number of armed conflicts in the world today, the increase in negotiated war-endings over military victories, the high risk of civil war recurrence (even after internationally supported Peace-building), and the high probability of future rebellions and armed conflict in view of the prevalence of the structural causes of violence in most of the world's developing countries.

The world has become a more peaceful place in recent years, but many armed conflicts[2] are still being fought: In 2008 the number of armed conflicts in the world stood at 36, fought in 26 countries (Harbom & Wallensteen 2009: 578). Five of these armed conflicts were of the scale of wars. In comparison to the recent high of 52 armed conflicts including 18 wars in 1991, the decline in armed conflict is a major improvement. Compared to the recent low of 29 armed conflicts including five wars in 2003, it is, however, an increase by one-fourth. Another indicator of the world becoming more peaceful is the decline in intensity of armed conflict: While in 1950 around 10.000 battle-related deaths were counted per armed conflict/year, this number stands at around 1.000 in 2007 (Human Security Report Project 2010: 24). But this is only part of the picture: Today's armed conflicts, often termed "New Wars", cause more civilian deaths than past wars. Kaldor (2006: 107) finds that while around a century ago 85–90 % of the casualties in war were military, today approximately 80 % of the victims are civilian. Although these numbers are notoriously difficult to estimate, it seems that battle-related deaths account for only a fraction of the "real" (still enormous) human losses and misery caused by armed conflict and war. For instance, the war-induced humanitarian crises in the Democratic Republic of Congo is estimated to have cost, estimations vary, between 860.000 and 2.8 Mio. lives from 2001–2007 (Human Security Report Project 2010: 43).

The nature of conflict termination has also changed importantly indicating a growing demand for international peace consolidation efforts: While during the Cold War 58 % of the armed conflicts ended in military victory, since 1990 this number has been as low as 14 %. Concomitantly, negotiated war endings (comprising both peace agreements and ceasefires) have become more frequent rising from 10 % during the Cold War to 38 % in the post-Cold War world (Kreutz 2010: 246). Research indicates that peace agreements fail at a high rate: Collier et al. (2008) find a 23 % risk of civil war recurrence within the first 4 years and 17 % within the subsequent six years after the end of warfare. Similarly, Walter (2004) indicates that 36 % of the civil wars, which ended between 1945 and 1996, renewed after a failed peace process.

Future rebellions and armed conflicts are most likely to emerge given that vast regions of the world, especially the developing countries in Sub-Saharan Africa, Southern Asia and Central Asia, feature many or even all of the risk factors of civil war. Widespread poverty, social injustices, low state capacities, bad governance and large amounts of unemployed youths substantially increase the risk of civil war outbreak (Collier & Hoeffler 2004; Fearon & Laitin 2003). The all too common discrimination of ethnic and religious

2 Armed conflict is commonly defined as "contested incompatibility that concerns government and/or territory where the use of armed force between two parties, of which at least one is the government of a state, results in at least 25 battle-related deaths". At a death toll exceeding 1000 battle-related casualties per year, the armed conflict is considered as war (UCDP/PRIO 2010: 1).

identities in these regions provides both cause and legitimization to fight (Wimmer et al. 2009). Fortunately, none of the mentioned variables by itself leads to the outbreak of civil war, but they all increase the risk of future rebellion, which might ultimately need Peace-building to consolidate peace.

Non-Intervention is No Alternative

"Give War a Chance", Luttwak (1999) claimed, seemingly in frustration, over the many peace agreements breaking down shortly after their signature. In his opinion, international actors should refrain from mediation, peace-keeping and the wider efforts of Peace-building as this is best done by the victor of war. War should thus be allowed to run until one side has won or all sides are so exhausted that they are truly committed to peace negotiations. The central assumption of the "Give War a Chance"-claim is that peace by military victory is more stable than peace by negotiations. This argument is, however, increasingly challenged by studies showing that externally supported peace agreements do not fare worse in terms of civil war recurrence than military victories (Hartzell & Hoddie 2007: 9; Doyle & Sambanis 2006: 74). But even if war was given free course, would this lead to peace at acceptable costs? Probably not. Many of today's armed conflicts are fought rather for the economic benefit of the belligerents than for political causes. Militias in Uganda, Sudan, Chad, the Democratic Republic of Congo, the Central African Republic, Columbia, Somalia and Afghanistan are often more interested in sustaining control over resource-rich areas than in overthrowing the national government. Their military means are insufficient to strife for becoming the next government. Toft (2010), therefore, suggests that the international community could support rebels for them to achieve military victory. However, in light of the considerable suffering and losses of human life that this strategy entails, Toft's proposition remains unrealistic. Moreover, the proponents of "Give War a Chance" seem to over-estimate the willingness of rebel movements, often based on particular ethnic or regional groups, to become nationalistic governments once in power. Rebel victories after civil war in countries like Uganda, Rwanda, Eritrea and Ethiopia indicate that the ensuing political regimes, based on military repression and ethnic dominance, exclude large parts of society from political participation. This causes further conflict, which could ultimately escalate into civil war.

Non-intervention is also promoted by advocates of indigenous Peace-building stressing that local actors are more capable of building political orders that suit their customs, norms and traditions than the international community (Englebert & Tull 2008; Weinstein 2005). From the historical perspective these scholars claim that it is futile to build states where states have never achieved their function of providing security, distributing public goods and mediating conflicts. In large parts of Western, Central and Eastern Africa and some areas of Central Asia society is more structured and regulated by traditional norms, habits and informal orders than by the state. These local informal mechanisms could, the proponents of indigenous Peace-building argue, produce stable political orders if international Peace-builders refrained from intervention. The much discussed case of Somaliland, the North-western region of Somalia, proves that indigenous Peace-building can produce sustaining peace with participatory institutions and high levels of legitimacy: While Somalia has never developed statehood apart from the temporary colonial state as well as the Siad Barré military dictatorship (1969 – 1991) and remains ridden with armed conflict today, since the early 1990s in Somaliland peace and solid governance structures including a regional government have materialized (Menkhaus 2008; Heyer 1997). Somaliland has developed a "functioning, effective and legitimate political order" that "combines customary institutions – in particular councils of elders (guurti) – and modern state institutions based on free and fair elections, such as a parliament and a president" (Boege et al. 2008: 13). International Peace-builders could hardly have done any better, but did more than once much worse, than the local societal forces in Somaliland. Therefore, Englebert & Tull (2008: 135) "call for recognizing the potential for indigenous recovery in Africa (and elsewhere) and question whether extensive and intrusive external approaches might be as much part of the problem as of the solution".

The success story of indigenous Peace-building in Somaliland, however, is not easily replicable and hence does not suggest that international Peace-building efforts should be abandoned. In terms of the Peace-building triangle developed by Doyle & Sambanis (2006), Somaliland had high local capacities for Peace-building and comparably low levels of hostility: Somaliland is ethnically homogenous, most of the Somali civil war was waged outside of Somaliland and its traditional societal institutions endured colonialism and the military dictatorship. In contrast, recent Peace-building missions in Liberia, Sierra Leone, the Democratic Republic of Congo, Darfur and Southern Sudan are deployed in deeply divided societies after (or even during) substantive and long-term bloodshed. Years or decades of civil war have disrupted indigenous institutions in these countries. Non-intervention in this context would not unfold societal Peace-building forces, but most likely trigger security dilemma between war factions and opposed societal groups, which could lead to the breakdown of the peace process (Walter 1997). We certainly do not want to suggest here that local Peace-building capacities should never be given the chance to build peace, but it seems that after severe violence they require the security and "space" provided by international Peace-building to unfold their peace-contributing effects (Mac Ginty 2008).

Finally, non-intervention is often implicitly demanded by those arguing that international Peace-building cannot succeed where politics is organized along patron-client-relationships. In most of the world's developing countries politics is handled in informal networks, in which loyalties are traded between patrons and clients in exchange for resources (money and other goods; Chabal & Daloz 1999). Formal state bodies facilitate this exchange by generating and transferring resources. De Waal (2009) argues that in clientelistic settings Peace-building interventions become an economic resource in the marketplace of loyalties. Peace-builders (though unconsciously) buy the loyalty of i.a. politicians, officials, administrators, religious authorities and heads of civil society organizations through providing for the means necessary to staff state bodies and create employment for public administrators, former fighters, civil society members and others. Peace-building would thus stabilize peace through investing sufficient resources in informal networks and orders. Tragically, in strict marketplace thinking, these political orders and thereby also peace would break down once the Peace-building missions end and the resources are withdrawn. This inspiring and intuitive economic model of Peace-building requires further clarification on the extent to which Peace-building in practice becomes an economic resource at the hands of local power holders and how intervention strategies should deal with this. Several Peace-building missions of the 1990s that took place in clientelistic settings and were not followed by the recurrence of civil war, however, indicate that peace can be maintained even after the withdrawal from the political marketplace. It would therefore be exaggerated to call for the abandonment of Peace-building on these grounds.

This section highlights that there is no viable alternative to international Peace-building engagement. Peace-building should be undertaken as it produces as stable peace as military victories and at lower human suffering. Indigenous Peace-building succeeds only after short warfare, in undivided societies and where traditional institutions have remained largely intact. In the aftermath of intense fighting local Peace-building capacities can become an important complement to international Peace-building, but no substitute. While clientelistic networks remain a key obstacle to the reform of existing political institutions or the building of state bodies from scratch, they do not make international efforts futile. In the next two sections, we assess the main Peace-building strategies, that is the liberal model and Communitarian approaches, in search for the most promising approach to consolidate peace.

The Liberal Approach to Peace-Building

The liberal approach to Peace-building is the dominant perspective both in practice and in academia. Peace-building efforts by the UN, other international organizations and the donor community attempt to establish democratic political institutions and free markets in countries emerging from civil war. These institutions are believed to stabilize peace according to the magic triangle of political stability consisting of the corners: Coercion (security), legitimacy (participation and local ownership), and self-interest (welfare). Liberal scholars among whom Roland Paris, Michael Doyle, Caroline Hartzell, Nicholas Sambanis and Timothy Sisk research Peace-building largely from a Western, state-centric perspective. For them the key to peace is the replacement of bad political institutions producing authoritarian rule, corruption and inter-group animosity with a set of good institutions including free and fair elections, social justice and the rule of law. Peace results from "the provision of temporary security, the building of new institutions capable of resolving future conflicts peaceably, and an economy capable of offering civilian employment to former soldiers and material progress to future citizens" (Doyle & Sambanis 2006: 5). The solution to the problem of how to consolidate peace, these scholars argue, can be found within liberalism and not without.

Liberal Peace-building reflects European philosophy and the post-Cold War triumph of democracy and market economy. The liberal philosophy behind this approach encompasses Hobbes' idea of the state as security provider in a malign environment, Locke's separation of powers and Rousseau's rule by the people. Kant's argument that peace prevails between democratic states is even extended to the domestic realm. Democracies are thus believed to be externally *and* internally peaceful, or at least more peaceful than authoritarian regimes. In the post-Cold War world democracy appears as ultimate form of human government, whereas non-democratic governance is widely considered as obsolete (Fukuyama 1992). In the economic sphere, the recent demise of the centrally planned economy leaves market economy as the sole remaining economic system. The "economic miracle" of the highly liberalized Southeast-Asian economies including South Korea, Taiwan, Hong Kong, China, Thailand and Vietnam is, albeit in gross simplification, understood as proof that liberal markets create wealthy populations.

The Peace-building missions undertaken by the UN and its partner organizations in the late 1980s and early 1990s were soaked in liberal economic and political thinking. Pejoratively referred to as "quick-and-dirty" interventions, the UN missions in Namibia, Mozambique, Cambodia, El Salvador, Nicaragua, Somalia, Angola, Liberia and Rwanda were of short duration (around 2–4 years). Their task was to facilitate the transition from war to peace through the holding of elections, justice and security sector reform, the disarmament and reintegration of former fighters into civilian life, the lifting of trade barriers, and, in few cases, the establishment of truth and reconciliation commissions. Shortly after the often little democratic elections were held, the UN and most partner organizations left the ground for the assumed peace-enabling effects of democratization and market liberalization to unfold. However, only in Namibia and Mozambique, which were comparably easy cases of Peace-building, this strategy paved the way for lasting peace, economic growth and participatory politics. Following severe and long-standing civil wars, Peace-building did not live up to the expectations: In Cambodia, El Salvador, Nicaragua and Guatemala the "old elites" gradually restored authoritarian regimes that produce widespread insecurity. In Liberia and Angola civil war recurred shortly after the holding of elections and, most disastrously, in Rwanda an internationally brokered peace agreement raised fear and discontentment among Hutu extremists. The ensuing campaign of Hutu extremist propaganda against the minority Tutsi group culminated in the 1994 genocide with an estimated 800.000 victims (Prunier 1995). It was not only the naïve belief in the healing power of political liberalization that discredited "quick-and-dirty" Peace-building, but also the lack of funding and political mandates restricting peacekeepers to peaceful means, when coercive action was utterly needed.

Since the mid-1990s, UN Peace-building has become better funded, more frequently mandated to use coercive means and more extensively engaged in State-building[3] than earlier missions[4]. The conceptual move from "quick-and-dirty" missions to "robust" peace interventions is enshrined in the Brahimi Report (United Nations 2000) rejecting overly optimistic mission planning and urging the UN to be "prepared to confront the lingering forces of war and violence, with the ability and determination to defeat them". Although some of the current Peace-building missions, most strikingly in Darfur and the Democratic Republic of Congo, fall far short of the means necessary to make, keep and build peace in a hostile environment (Eriksen 2005; Tull 2009; De Waal 2007), the recent missions in Bosnia, Kosovo, East Timor and Liberia resemble robust liberal Peace-building. For example, in Bosnia the EU and the UN in the person of the international High Representative exercise full control over the legislature and executive. Mandated to "ensure that Bosnia and Herzegovina evolves into a peaceful and viable democracy on course for integration into Euro-Atlantic institutions", the High Representative may veto or impose laws, dismiss elected and un-elected office holders, create new institutions and even extend its own prerogatives (OHR 2007; Knaus & Martin 2003). In Liberia, where the UN deployed a strong Peace-keeping force, the World Bank exercises full oversight over the financial administration in order to fight corruption and to promote good governance (Andersen 2010). Hence, in recent years Peace-building has become more intrusive, more long-term, and more costly – but also less liberal.

3 State-building can be defined as "[a]ctions undertaken by international or national actors to establish, reform, or strengthen the institutions of the state which may or may not contribute to peacebuilding" (Call/Cousens 2008: 4).

4 Some of the earlier missions were also comparably robust, in particular the (unsuccessful) peace-enforcement mission in the Democratic Republic of Congo (ONUC, from 1960 – 1964), or engaged in State-building, e.g. the UN Transitional Authority in Cambodia (UNTAC, from 1992 – 1993).

Academic Debate on the Liberal Approach

Liberal scholars in the field of Peace-building assess the effects of liberalism, evaluate the design of political institutions and identify patters of sequencing. Studying the failures of "quick-and-dirty" Peace-building in the early 1990s, the enthusiasm on liberalism has been called into question. Most scholars now recognize that liberalization can be conflictive and in contradiction with the goal of building peace in fragile post-war settings (Paris 2004). In many ways liberalization can cause conflicts and reinforce existing societal cleavages: Elections might create situations of insecurity and heightened inter-group tension in post-war settings with little democratic experience, shattered infrastructure and no impartial governing authority. Political entrepreneurs might exploit this situation by rallying followers around ethnic and religious identities to wage war or to maximize votes, influencing election bodies, or impeding the electoral campaign of opposition parties. While democracy is supposed to build peace, paradoxically it might also undermine peace. The "security first"-paradigm, which is increasingly becoming the mainstream liberal Peace-building strategy, attempts to solve the dilemma: "What is needed in the immediate postconflict period is not democratic ferment and economic upheaval, but political stability and the establishment of effective administration over the territory. Only when a working governmental authority has been reestablished should peacebuilders initiate a series of gradual democratic and market-oriented reforms" (Paris 2004: 187–188). Providing for security is "the sine qua non of the beginning of peace" and needs to precede "new courts, human rights, property laws, democracy, and so forth" (Doyle & Sambanis 2006: 338). Paris' "Institutionalization-before-Liberalization"-strategy therefore calls for postponing liberalization until a minimum of security, order and public administration has been established capable of curbing the potentially de-stabilizing effects of political and market liberalization (Paris 2004). Some authors even go one step further – too far into illiberalism, we believe – by suggesting that international actors should take over domestic politics temporarily or even permanently in neo-trusteeships if local power holders are unwilling or incapable of guaranteeing security and well-being of their population (Helman & Ratner 1992; Krasner 2004; Fearon & Laitin 2004).

Power-sharing institutions, which are frequently implemented in international efforts of making and building peace, have also become subject of considerable academic debate. Power-sharing describes the sharing of control over the political realm (fixed quotas of executive and legislative representation), the armed forces (integration of war factions into the armed forces), the economy (public enterprises, exploitation of natural resources) and territory (e.g. regional autonomy, federal structures) between the adversaries. Fixed representation of the war factions and their constituencies in the post-war government, armed forces and economy reduces insecurity and thereby contributes to the consolidation of peace (Walter 1997; Jarstad 2008). After intense inter-ethnic warfare, when security is utterly needed, power-sharing might be the only viable strategy to secure peace (Lijphardt 2004; critically: Horowitz 2002). While earlier research indicated that peace agreements, which contain power-sharing, are more sustainable than peace agreements without power-sharing (Hartzell & Hoddie 2003), more recent studies confirm this effect only for military and territorial power-sharing, whereas political power-sharing seems to have no effect on peace (Hartzell & Hoddie 2005; Jarstad & Nilsson 2008). Power-sharing, however, also contradicts Peace-building in at least three dimensions: Firstly, power-sharing rewards violence as it "creates an incentive structure would-be leaders can seize upon by embarking on the insurgent path as well" (Tull & Mehler 2005: 375). Secondly, there is a trade-off between the short-term goal of ending violence and longer-term democratization (Jarstad 2008). For the sake of ending violence power-sharing agreements often include greedy war factions with dubious human rights records, who are little interested in democratizing the post-war polity in the long-run. Finally, power-sharing arrangements freeze existing societal cleavages (at least at the elite-level) without setting incentives for reconciliation (Horowitz 2002).

Criticism to the Liberal Approach

Many observers criticize liberal Peace-building for at best producing "no war, no peace"-situations (Mac Ginty 2006; Richmond & Franks 2009): With the exception of Namibia and to a lesser extent Mozambique, none of the countries that hosted Peace-building missions today enjoys positive peace, i.e. participatory politics, social justice and economic well-being. Instead, insecurity, social injustices, vast corruption, dire economic conditions and only partially participatory politics prevail. Despite of international Peace-building efforts, many of these countries that just emerged from civil war are at a high risk of renewed warfare. "In practice, what has been achieved in post-conflict environments are the shells of liberal states, reproducing international order, but achieving a virtual peace in a domestic context" (Richmond 2009: 564).

Critical scholars trace the dismal balance sheet of Peace-building not to persistent shortcomings of the missions' equipment and personnel, but to the obsessive focus on State-building along the Western model and the technical character of the interventions. Liberal Peace-building fails to build sustainable peace, these scholars convincingly argue, as it undertakes to solve the social problems of peace and conflict by the technical exercise of replicating state institutions, often in places where states have remained alien throughout history. Implementing a pre-fabricated set of political institutions, essentially the Western democratic model, liberal Peace-building is "acultural, unconcerned with social welfare, and unfeeling and insensitive towards its subjects" (Richmond 2009: 558). While on the positive side liberal Peace-building brought many civil wars to an end, on the negative side the recurrence of civil war remains highly probable as the root causes of violence persist (Mac Ginty 2006: 176 – 177). Not tackling the root causes of violence, in particular societal divisions that undermine the newly built political institutions, liberal Peace-building fails in one of its key assertions: Liberal scholars assume that local actors would integrate their conflicts into the institutions, which would then, as in established Western democracies, mediate these conflicts and reconcile opposed factions of society (Hartzell & Hoddie 2007: 11). In divided societies, however, liberal political institutions do not transform hostile groups and their conflicts in day-to-day politics into stable and peaceful relationships. Therefore, Communitarian scholars, as discussed in the following section, argue that liberal Peace-building needs to take trust seriously and build stable communities while building political institutions.

Communitarian Approaches to Peace-Building

Communitarian approaches encompass a broad strand of literature from the fields of psychology, sociology and critical political sciences. Scholars of this approach, i.a. Chaim Kaufmann, Carter Johnson, Stuart Kaufman, Ervin Staub, Jean Paul Lederach, Daniel Bar-Tal and David Bloomfield, share the assumption that peace cannot prosper unless robust political communities are built. In post-war settings "where neighbor fears neighbor and sometimes family member fears family member, and where each sheds blood", Peace-building needs to make "the emotive, perceptual, socio-psychological, and spiritual dimensions core, not peripheral, concerns" (Lederach 1997: 29). Liberal Peace-building with its emphasis on technical solutions, in particular the replication of democratic states, fails to deliver such robust communities as it leaves the virulent conflicts, suffering and mutual fear of divided societies largely unaddressed. Therefore, Communitarian scholars call for the enlargement of the magic triangle of political stability, on which liberal Peace-building rests, into a magic square consisting not only of coercion (security), legitimacy (participation and local ownership) and self-interest (welfare), but also of trust (community). Trust can be achieved either within the own community, which requires conflicting groups to be separated, or through the reconciliation of divided communities.

Separating Communities

The separation approach to Peace-building argues that the territorial separation of the groups in conflict is the only viable solution to building peace after ethnic war. Two reasons for separating belligerents are often brought forward (Kaufmann 1996: 137): First, "in ethnic wars both hyper-nationalist mobilization rhetoric and real atrocities harden ethnic identities to the point that cross-ethnic political appeals are unlikely to be made and even less likely to be heard". And secondly, "intermingled population settlement patterns create real security dilemmas that intensify violence, motivate ethnic 'cleansing', and prevent de-escalation unless the groups are separated". Kaufmann and other proponents of this approach, therefore, suggest that the international community should give up the futile enterprise of (re-)building multi-ethnic states in deeply divided societies. Rather, with or without the consent of the communities in question, international agents should resettle them into ethnically homogenous states. These mono-ethnic states could then become democratic not facing the risk of elections reinforcing inter-group competition.

The claim made by secession theorists that ethnic identities hardened from decades of animosities, warfare and possibly even genocide cannot be undone seems overly deterministic (Paris 2004: 184). From a constructivist perspective, assuming that identities and inter-group relationships are always socially constructed and can be reconstructed, we assume that even group identities deeply entrenched by ethnic warfare can be made flexible. This would, however, take a long time. The security dilemma-argument for separation seems more convincing: In absence of governing authorities guaranteeing public security, identity groups might engage in collective defensive action (e.g. armament, group-unifying rhetoric and action) to increase their security. Other groups might (mis-)perceive this defensive action as offensive and in turn engage in defensive action, which can spiral into ever more tension. Evidence from Iraq, Bosnia and other cases indicates that such ethnic security dilemma can indeed contribute to the escalation of inter-ethnic violence (Barak 2007; Melander 1999; Melander 2009). For separation to become a *modus operandi* of the international community to solve ethnic security dilemma, it would, however, have to prove both effective and normatively acceptable.

Research on whether the partition of divided societies leads to more stable peace than the building of multi-ethnic states shows mixed results: While Sambanis (2000) and Sambanis & Schulhofer-Wohl (2009) reject the claim that partition reduces post-war violence, Kaufmann (1998) finds partition to have reduced the level of violence in Ireland, India, Palestine and Cyprus. The fact that violence persists in at least some areas of India and Palestine is, according to the author, not due to the strategy of partition, but to its incomplete implementation. Johnson (2008: 143), too, finds that partition prevents the recurrence of war and even of low-level violence. However, this effect can be witnessed only if partition is completed, i.e. mono-ethnic states are established, whereas incomplete partition does not significantly stabilize peace. Partition is thus effective in building sustainable peace "only where populations are already largely separated at the time of intervention [and] where interveners are prepared to separate groups using mass population transfers" (Johnson 2008: 165). Where ethnic groups live highly intermingled as, for instance in Rwanda and Burundi, ethnic un-mixing would require countless re-settlements and become excessively expensive in terms of blood and treasure. The research findings on partition are, overall, rather exploratory as there are only 19 cases of separation to be examined since 1945. It seems that partition can be effective, but only under very specific circumstances.

Assuming that in a given case only few re-settlements would be needed to achieve ethnic homogeneity, who in the international community would become the "ethnic cleanser" carrying out partition? No international agency doing the "dirty work" is in sight because the forced re-settlement of ethnic communities breaches international human rights standards. "Given that the international community is not going to carry out population transfers in the face of violent resistance, effective partition is unlikely to occur except through ethnic cleansing during war" (Horowitz et al. 2009: 203). Once the war factions have completely re-settled opposed ethnic groups, the international community might endow the newly created mono-ethnic states with international recognition as in the case of Kosovo. But even in this scenario, a tangible risk remains that partition merely re-locates internal conflicts into the international arena as in the case of the Eritrean-Ethiopian war (1998–2000).

Separating communities is thus neither necessary to build peace after ethnic war, nor necessarily an effective tool to build peace. The break-up of the former Yugoslavia exemplifies that separation may build stable peace, but at intolerable costs in terms of human suffering. For humanitarian concerns the international community cannot enforce partition and must even prevent belligerents from ethnic cleansing.

Reconciling Communities

Reconciling conflicting ethnic and religious communities is, according to the proponents of this strategy, possible and even necessary to build sustainable peace. Although "reconciliation is extremely difficult to achieve", peace can only be stabilized if the "emotional foundations of hostile political attitudes, and their symbolic expression" is addressed (Kaufman 2006: 202; 215).

Otherwise, the emotion-laden symbolic politics of defining, pursuing and discussing issues of conflict remain constant obstacles to long-term peace. "Reconciliation is not a luxury, or an add-on to democracy. Reconciliation is an absolute necessity" (Bloomfield et al. 2003: 12). Disregarding the peace stabilizing potential of reconciliation might come at the high price of renewed violence: "Without healing, when groups continue to live together, anger and the desire for revenge can lead to violence by former victims" (Staub & Bar-Tal 2003: 735).

Much confusion persists in the literature on reconciliation, in particular about the definition and operationalization of the concept. Most scholars distinguish reconciliation into a process and an end-state. Regarding the process dimension, we understand reconciliation as "a societal process that involves mutual acknowledgement of past suffering and the changing of destructive attitudes and behaviour into constructive relationships" (Brounéus 2003: 3). Essentially, reconciliation describes "socio-psychological processes consisting of changes of motivations, goals, beliefs, attitudes and emotions by the majority of society members" (Bar-Tal 2009: 365). Through cognitive and affective changes, an "ethos of conflict" is gradually replaced with an "ethos of peace" (Bar-Tal 2009: 368 f.). This involves the re-definition of the own goals (moving away from indivisible group-specific goals to societal goals that can be subject to compromise), the humanization, legitimization and personalization of the opponent (attributing action to individuals rather than to groups), and the revision of opposing narratives and interpretations of past events. Reconciliation consists of four elements (Bloomfield et al. 2003):

- justice (punishment of past violence, deterrence of future repetition, restoration of societal norms, establishment of rule of law and respect of human rights),
- truth (addressing various interpretations of history and uncovering unknown events),
- healing (improvement of the psychological, physical and social health of individuals),
- and reparation (real or symbolic compensation for loss).

Although reconciliation is rarely a linear process, it can be fruitfully conceptualized as consisting of three stages (Bloomfield et al. 2003: 19–21): In the first stage, fear, hatred and hostility is gradually replaced by forms of non-violent coexistence guaranteeing physical security and peaceful dispute management. In the second stage, when a minimum of functioning political institutions guaranteeing rule of law and public safety are in place, confidence and trust slowly grows so that the opposing community's members are no longer treated as inhuman, detestable and a threat to the own security. Finally, as all sides come to acknowledge the mutual suffering of the past and the collective responsibility, empathy between the opposed communities grows and former group divisions become increasingly crossed by more flexible and loose identities.

Reconciliation as end-state is, in our understanding, not a perfectly harmonious society, but a society of loose, multiple and malleable identities. Full societal harmony, i. e. the total absence of conflict, is neither realistic, nor desirable. If peacefully mediated into constructive and commonly acceptable outcomes, conflicts keep society alive and intact. Questioning the societal function and inevitability of conflicts by an idealized vision of a totally harmonious society would rather lead us to tyranny than to peace. In the end-state of reconciliation, a "culture of peace" characterized by "justice, respect of human rights, sensitivity, acceptance and respect for cultural differences, values and practices conducive to nonviolent conflict resolution, and above all recognition of the superiority and importance of peace as a value and practice" is achieved (Bar-Tal 2009: 370).

Reconciliation does not require victims to forgive and forget past atrocities. While public opinion and even some scholars hold the view that reconciliation without forgiveness remains shallow (Lederach 1997; Staub 2000), considering forgiveness as indispensable would overload the concept of reconciliation and make it ethically doubtful. There is no doubt that forgiveness contributes to reconciliation, but especially in the first years and even decades after intense ethnic war, the focus of reconciliation should be on justice, truth, healing and reparation, rather than forgiveness. Forgiveness, i. e. the act in which the victim of a crime accepts the pardon of the offender and cancels the offender's moral debt, remains a personal decision. "Many who go through this process experience it as liberating in the sense of discarding burdens of anger, resentment or fantasies of revenge" (Santa-Barbara 2007: 178). Yet, it may take decades until victims are ready to forgive. They simply want the perpetrator to suffer for the crimes committed as they suffer too. Only the victims can decide when and whom to forgive and they may as well decide never to forgive. Public calls for forgiveness, e. g. by Desmond Tutu after the end of Apartheid in South Africa, contradict the victims' right to sorrow and can even be counter-productive. "Engaging in a process of forgiveness is a personal choice and must remain in that realm, whether we are talking about forgiving someone for violating one's dignity or forgiving oneself for robbing others of their dignity. The best one could hope for is to create the conditions that would give rise to forgiveness" (Hicks 2002: 145). Although the concepts of reconciliation and forgiveness are highly interrelated and forgiveness nurtures reconciliation, it needs to be detached from reconciliation for many years following intense violence.

International Peace-building missions have spent little time, money and effort on the promotion of reconciliation. In several Peace-building missions war crime courts and truth and reconciliation commissions were established, but their reach is limited to few actors and events on the national level. Their reconciling effect thus remains marginal. Truth and reconciliation commissions investigate the causes of war, document crimes committed during war and recognize the suffering shared by all societal groups. At maximum, a few thousand individual victims and perpetrators are reconciled in the commissions' meetings, whereas the number of broken relationships remaining unaddressed is much larger. War crime tribunals by the international community are complex, long-term and restricted to high-level cases. For instance, the International Criminal Tribunal for the former Yugoslavia (ICTY), which took up its work already in 1993 when the war in Bosnia was still ongoing, is expected to have completed its task not before February 2014 (Schabas 2006). In total, 161 military leaders and high-level politicians including Slobodan Milošević, Radovan Karadžić, Ratko Mladić, Ante Gotovina and Milan Babić were charged of having violated international humanitarian law (ICTY 2010). While 36 of the trials are still ongoing, 15 years after the end of warfare in Bosnia only 64 of the accused have been sentenced. In the case of Rwanda, only 80 key actors among whom Theonéste Bagosora, Augustin Bizumungu, Jean Kambanda, Hassan Ngeze and Jean-Paul Akayesu face trial at the International Criminal Tribunal for Rwanda (ICTR) out of an estimated total number of 125.000 *génocidaires.* So far, 36 of them have been sentenced (ICTR 2010). International post-war justice is thus of limited reach addressing only the planners, organizers, instigators and leaders of warfare and genocide. This leaves the vast majority of cases to the war-disrupted and often little effective national justice system.

The scant efforts of international actors to promote reconciliation in the aftermath of civil war fall far short of what most Communitarian scholars conceive of as reconciliation strategy. Lederach (1997: xvi) calls for a comprehensive and long-term approach to reconciliation based on "an infrastructure across the levels of a society, an infrastructure that empowers the resources for reconciliation from within that society and maximizes the contribution from outside". Reconciliation efforts should thus address all levels of society ranging from the highly-visible top leadership via the middle-range leadership (e.g. ethnic and religious regional leaders, academics, NGOs) to the grassroots leadership (including leaders of indigenous NGOs, local officials and community developers). Within such an all-encompassing model, Brounéus (2003: 4) argues that the middle-range level, in particular truth commissions and the media, is the most important as it links influential top-level officials with grassroots peace initiatives.

Communitarian scholars suggest numerous instruments that are supposed to reconcile divided societies (Lederach 1997; Brounéus 2003; Bar-Tal 2009; Kaufman 2006): Problem-solving workshops on conflict issues can convene opponents for them to clarify clashing goals and search for solutions to deadlocks. NGOs, peace commissions and grassroots peace activists may promote unbiased and cooperative relationships, provide economic assistance to those worst affected by warfare, and counsel war-induced trauma. The media can transmit information on emerging peaceful inter-group relations into the wider public, make reconciliatory political and religious leaders heard, and produce documentaries and movies humanizing the enemy. The official account of the past that has been produced by public trials and truth and reconciliation commissions can replace incendiary content from public education. These are only some of the many avenues for reconciliation mentioned in the literature. Peace-building and the wider efforts of development cooperation can support reconciliatory actors and their instruments both with technical and financial assistance. This pre-supposes, however, that these actors are truly committed to reconciliation. Donor-driven and externally conceptualized reconciliation efforts contradicting the local elites' agenda could further heat up societal tensions, e.g. by increasing inter-group economic and social inequality. Home-grown reconciliation initiatives are, contrary to international approaches, also more likely to correctly interpret and incorporate local norms, culture and conflicts (Brounéus 2003: 6).

Justice is believed to further reconciliation through breaking with past injustices and ending the prevailing impunity of a culture of conflict. It serves the psychological healing of victims by acknowledging their suffering and restoring their relationships with society, especially with the opposed communities. Breaking with the abusive past through restoring justice makes dispensable the individual desire for revenge, which otherwise could initiate a cascade of recurring violence. Justice can be retributive or restorative (Santa-Barbara 2007: 179–181): Retributive justice refers to the prosecution and punishment of socially inacceptable behavior, for instance by detaining the offender. Thereby, revenge is avoided, guilt is individualized, future perpetrators are deterred and impunity is ended. While retributive justice is more oriented on perpetrators than on victims, restorative justice places the victim in the center of justice. Mediating between the perpetrator, the victim and the wider community, restorative justice returns dignity to victims and heals relationships broken by the transgression of rules. "Restorative justice works with the full participation of the victim and of the relevant communities in discussing the facts, identifying the causes of misconduct and defining the sanctions" (Bloomfield et al. 2003: 111).

Retributive justice in the aftermath of civil war, mostly undertaken by national courts and international war crime tribunals, was in some cases of Peace-building complemented by local approaches to restorative justice, for instance in Rwanda and East Timor. In 2002 the Rwandan government established the *Gacaca* (lit. "justice on the grass") courts tasked to deal with crimes committed during the 1994 genocide ranging from mere damage to property to (assistance in) intentional or unintentional homicide. Based on a traditional conflict resolution mechanism, today *Gacaca* retains, however, only few elements of restorative justice (Rettig 2008). If perpetrators confess and show regret for their deeds, *Gacaca* sentences of up to 25 years of imprisonment or life sentence for murder can be substantially reduced. Restorative justice complemented retributive justice also, albeit after initial reluctance of the UN, in the case of the East Timorese *Nahe Biti* (lit. "laying out the mat"). This is a traditional reconciliation mechanism at the local level, in which local chiefs mediate between perpetrators of minor crimes and victims (Mac Ginty 2008: 154). The *Nahe Biti* is conceived of as "a process that commences with a cause (conflict or mistakes), strives for consensus (reconciliation) and ends up in a state of peace and tranquility (stable social order)" (Babo-Soares 2004: 27 – 28). As both retributive and restorative justice have their assets and drawbacks, it seems that a "combination of domestic trials (where possible), of international punitive reactions *and* of justice mechanisms outside the formal criminal system may well provide the richest possibilities" (Bloomfield et al. 2003: 114; original emphasis).

Truth, which refers to efforts of learning about "causes and conduct of a past war and accounting for crimes and abuses committed during wartime", promotes reconciliation in manifold ways (Mendeloff 2004: 357 – 361): Truth-telling is assumed to be therapeutic to victims as it restores their dignity and allows individuals and groups to make the important shift from blaming entire opposed groups to individual perpetrators. Seeking and concluding an official historical record agreed upon by the adversaries unveils myths, removes contested interpretations of the past and decreases information asymmetries that often are at the core of extremist claims and security dilemmas. Truth-telling thus strengthens moderates in society over extremists by consolidating the respect for human rights and acknowledging "never again". Knowing and telling the truth provides for nothing less than the indispensable groundwork for a new social contract leading to a shared future. While these mechanisms are intuitive, truth-telling has remained without rigorous academic evaluation. Mendeloff (2004: 376) estimates its impact on reconciliation to be limited, "to take a very long time to affect change" and to require a minimum of statehood, democratic freedoms and the willingness of victims to discuss the past. The importance of context in truth-telling, particularly the guarantee of the physical security of the victim, is also highlighted by Brounéus (2008). Her interviews with female survivors of the Rwandan genocide show that telling the truth in *Gacaca*, while being confronted with the perpetrators and insecurity including threats, harassment and direct violence, caused the re-traumatization of several of the interviewed. Hence, truth-telling conceived of as therapeutic and reconciling may as well traumatize victims and impede reconciliation.

Healing encompasses the improvement of physical, psychological and social health of individuals and groups hurt by large-scale violence. War disrupts "normal life": In war people become witness or victim of murder, rape, looting and abduction. They might be forced to flee from their homes, live in poor conditions, deal with constant insecurity and suffer from illnesses and powerlessness. Besides physical injuries, war causes long-term mental traumatization to many individuals, families and entire communities (De Jong et al. 2003). The symptoms of what has become known as "post-traumatic stress disorder" (PTSD) comprise "self-blame, vivid re-experiencing of the event, fear, nightmares, feelings of helplessness, hypervigilance, depression, relationship difficulties, feelings of social disconnectedness, anxiety and even substance abuse-related difficulties" (Bloomfield et al. 2003: 79). The prevalence of PTSD is high after horrific events such as civil war and it might persist for decades: In their survey of Liberia, Johnson et al. (2008) report an estimated national (!) PTSD prevalence rate of 44 %. In the Liberian region Nimba County – almost twenty years after the end of the principal fighting – Galea et al. (2010) still find a 48 % prevalence rate of PTSD. Studying Holocaust survivors, Trappler et al. (2007) show that even 60 years after the end of World War II, traumatization persists among Holocaust survivors. Interestingly, women seem to "have approximately twice the risk of developing PTSD symptoms and their symptoms are more likely to persist than symptoms among men" (Nemeroff et al. 2006: 2; Klarić et al. 2007). An examination of children exposed to severe violence including the killing of their parents finds lower rates of PTSD in younger (age 3–7) than in older children (age 8–13): "[Y]ounger children may be protected from posttraumatic stress by their less developed cognitive abilities" (Schaal & Elbert 2006: 102). Nonetheless, after war PTSD-rates among children are also high (Thabet & Vostanis 1999). Healing PTSD and other traumas can be achieved through individualized psychological counseling (psychotherapy) and psycho-social programs (Bloomfield et al. 2003: 80–86). These programs attempt to heal families and communities, e.g. through self-help groups, grieving and reburial rituals, and re-integration and re-union of dislocated members of the family and community. Healing requires a context of security, justice, the acknowledgement of truth, and, crucially, a culturally-sensitive approach. Whether the Western-based trauma concept of PTSD and related methods of healing are adequate to other cultural contexts or need to be refined is open to debate.

Reparation describes the restitution of what has been lost (if possible) or material and financial compensation for the losses. Losing family members, property and assets not only causes severe psychological harm, but might also entail living life under precarious financial and social circumstances perpetuating the embitterment of past violence on a daily basis. In such a context, individuals and families are often unwilling to engage in reconciliation. Reparation including public services such as schooling, medical services and employment opportunities to individuals (including orphans), families and communities worst affected by warfare can help restore "normal life". "Generally, it seems advisable to have a balanced package of individual and collective, pecuniary and non-pecuniary, and commemorative and reformative reparation measures" (Bloomfield et al. 2003: 158).

Promoting reconciliation after civil war is not without its risks and might, contrary to the supposed effects, even undermine peace by disorienting individuals and further fuel conflict between groups. The phrase "I can't live with or without you" indicates this dilemma of societal groups at the end of inter-group violence: Adversaries might well recognize that re-building relationships is necessary to build sustainable peace, yet the mutual suspicion, fear and hatred prevailing between groups prevents them from embracing reconciliation. Reconciliation is so difficult to achieve because it requires an "act of self-destruction, as recognizing the experiences of the other fundamentally brings into question one's own interpretation of history, the conflict, and the responsibility one holds for the past, present, and future shared realities" (Hicks 2002: 129). In the aftermath of intense inter-group violence, when dire living conditions prevail and trauma, sorrow and mistrust are widespread, it is the own ethnic and religious community that provides safety, meaning and survival in an anarchical environment. There are thus strong incentives not to reach out for reconciliation with other communities. Speeding up reconciliation through Peace-building and development cooperation might be resisted by local actors or cause disorientation: "Too much change too fast can create tremendous upheaval, the felt experience of which is extremely uncomfortable setting off what appears to be a reflexive reaction to protect the threatened views of the self and the world" (Hicks 2002: 133). This is not to argue against external support for reconciliation, but to call Peace-builders to carefully craft their activities and not to over-burden local reconciliation initiatives. Foremost, reconciliation takes time (Brounéus 2003: 49; Bloomfield et al. 2003: 23). Until empathy has grown between former belligerents, years, decades or even generations might have passed.

Academic knowledge on the peace-contributing effect of reconciliation and especially on the dilemma between reconciliation and peace is still very limited. Reconciliation is certainly no panacea, but a long-term and multi-dimensional enterprise consisting of truth-telling commissions, war crime tribunals, psychological healing of traumas, public education reform, grass-roots peace initiatives and many more activities that undertake to transform conflicting inter-group settings into unbiased, constructive relationships.

Conclusion

Liberal Peace-building in the aftermath of severe inter-group violence fails to build sustainable peace characterized by participatory politics, social justice, rule of law and economic prosperity. Instead, Peace-building outcomes are fragile "no war, no peace"-situations with widespread insecurity, injustices and poverty, and a high risk of renewed warfare. Searching for strategies to make peace sustainable, we reviewed – and rejected – most of the widely discussed alternatives to Peace-building such as non-intervention, indigenous

Peace-building, colonial-like neo-trusteeships and the separation approach[5]. We suggest that liberal Peace-building needs to become more social, in particular more reconciliatory. Our analysis of liberal Peace-building reveals that it, due to its overly technical character, fails to solve the many social problems of sustaining peace. Liberal Peace-building transfers Western-based state institutions and conflict resolution mechanisms such as elections, public administration, rule of law, and civil society engagement into divided and war-traumatized societies. However, the fear, mis-trust or even mutual hatred prevailing in the aftermath of most long-standing civil wars makes communities evade political institutions, transform them according to their particularistic needs or even monopolize them. To build sustainable peace, Peace-building would have to seriously engage in reconciling the opposed communities of divided societies through reconciliation initiatives, the promotion of justice and truth-telling, trust-building measures, the building of locally apt institutions and socio-psychological healing. This strategy should rely on traditions, habits and social norms of divided societies and tackle root causes of violence. Over time, such a reconciliatory and locally grounded version of liberal Peace-building would be more likely to produce sustainable peace than the currently employed technical approach of liberal Peace-building.

Our conclusion rests very much on critical Peace-building research arguing that liberal Peace-building needs to incorporate people's social realities including customs, inter-group relations and modes of meaning production. What we define here as hybrid Peace-building has been, with some variation and using many confusing terms (e.g. emancipatory, post-liberal, post-hegemonic, inclusive, participatory and social Peace-building) developed by critical scholars including Oliver Richmond, Roger Mac Ginty, Michael Pugh and Kristoffer Lidén. Hybrid Peace-building, in our understanding, denotes the vast processes and outcomes of the interaction between liberal Peace-building and the local arena including its traditions, conflicts and norms. In a way, Peace-building is always hybridized by local agency (Mac Ginty 2010): "[C]areful analysis reveals the complex negotiations that go on between exporters and importers of liberal peacebuilding, how importers instrumentalize the interventions of external actors, and the ways in which they are 'translated' as they go through these multiple brokering arrangements. Therefore liberal peacebuilding may look very different from how it was originally framed, once it 'hits the ground'" (Goodhand & Walton 2009: 307).

5 We did not elaborate on the possible strategy of establishing authoritarian regimes in post-war settings given that their exclusive and repressive character is incompatible with sustainable peace. Authoritarian regimes "rely on the permanent, forcible suppression of political contestation, rather than on the development of mechanisms that might ultimately be capable of resolving conflicts of interest through conciliation and negotiation" (Paris 2004: 180). Lacking the capacity to mitigate societal conflicts and carrying out repression, authoritarian regimes would even reinforce cleavages and increase the risk of violence.

Given that "many customary approaches to conflict are concentrated on truth-telling, reconciliation and the re-establishment of sustainable relationships", it is surprising how little attention critical studies devote to the reconciliation potential of hybrid Peace-building (Mac Ginty 2008: 158).

Although critical studies have become an important strand of Peace-building research, no coherent and convincing hybrid approach has been developed so far. The debate is mostly on a conceptual level, where the advantages and avenues of hybrid Peace-building are vividly depicted, but not rigorously tested or critically assessed. For instance, Richmond (2009: 578–579) calls for Peace-building to understand local culture, traditions, and ontology and to become "an empathetic, emancipatory process, focused on everyday care, human security and a social contract between society and the polity, which acts as a provider of care rather than merely security". Liberal Peace-builders should, he argues, act as "interface between the liberal and the local" and "mediate the global norm or institution with the local norm". Lidén (2009: 621) urges liberal Peace-building to engage in the "culturally adapted provision of material resources, security, political influence and education without political conditions except for inclusion and non-violence".

Couched in a bloomy and appealing language, these scholars obscure drawbacks and possible trade offs of hybrid Peace-building. The practice of identifying whether local power holders, local "everyday"-structures and traditional norms are still considered as (sufficiently) effective and legitimate by the local population and whether they promote reconciliation is challenging. Research would have to prove that indigenous institutions, which often are oral and informal, can be supported by the highly bureaucratized international Peace-building agencies without disrupting the functioning of the local institutions. Finally, the dilemma that might arise between the promotion of liberal values and the inclusion of often only partially liberal local actors needs to be better understood. Such a trade off between not-so-liberal local "everyday"-structures and liberal efforts of State-building was observed by Chopra (2009) with regard to local peace initiatives in the arid lands of Northern Kenya.

Making hybrid Peace-building work and integrating the concept of reconciliation thus remains a major challenge. It requires the international Peace-building community to "engage historians, anthropologists or other observers who speak local languages and are deeply knowledgeable about local culture and context" in the planning and implementation of Peace-building (Call & Cousens 2008: 14). External actors would have to "take into account the varieties of sociopolitical order that enable or restrict actors in fulfilling their governance functions under conditions of 'state fragility'" (Debiel et al. 2009: 43). These efforts of mapping culture, context and conflicts are indispensable to build locally grounded and reconciliatory Peace-building strategies. Failing to promote reconciliation in Peace-building, peace is unlikely to sustain in the aftermath of intense violence.

References

Andersen, Louise 2010. Outsiders Inside the State: Post-Conflict Liberia between Trusteeship and Partnership. *Journal of Intervention and Statebuilding* 4(3), 129–152.

Babo-Soares, Dionísio 2004. Nahe Biti: The Philosophy and Process of Grassroots Reconciliation (and Justice) in East Timor. *The Asia Pacific Journal of Anthropology* 5(1), 15–33.

Barak, Oren 2007. Dilemmas of Security in Iraq. *Security Dialogue* 38(4), 455–475.

Bar-Tal, Daniel 2009. Reconciliation as a Foundation of Culture of Peace, in De Rivera, Joseph (ed.): *Handbook on Building Cultures of Peace.* New York: Springer, 363–377.

Bloomfield, David/Barnes, Teresa/Huyse, Luc ed. 2003. *Reconciliation after Violent Conflict: A Handbook.* Stockholm: International IDEA (Institute for Democracy and Electoral Assistance).

Boege, Volker, et al. 2008. *On Hybrid Political Orders and Emerging States: State Formation in the Context of 'Fragility'.* Berlin: Berghof Research Center for Constructive Conflict Management. URL: http://www.berghof-handbook.net/documents/publications/boege_etal_handbook.pdf [accessed on 2010-11-11].

Brounéus, Karen 2003. *Reconciliation: Theory and Practice for Development Cooperation.* Stockholm: Swedish International Development Cooperation Agency (SIDA).

Brounéus, Karen 2008. Truth-Telling as Talking Cure? Insecurity and Retraumatization in the Rwandan Gacaca Courts. *Security Dialogue* 39(1), 55–76.

Call, Charles T./Cousens, Elizabeth M. 2008. Ending Wars and Building Peace: International Responses to War-Torn Societies. *International Studies Perspectives* 9(1), 1–21.

Chabal, Patrick/Daloz, Jean-Pascal 1999. *Africa Works: Disorder as Political Instrument.* London: Villiers Publications. (African Issues).

Chopra, Tanja 2009. When Peacebuilding Contradicts Statebuilding: Notes from the Arid Lands of Kenya. *International Peacekeeping* 16(4), 531–545.

Collier, Paul/Hoeffler, Anke 2004. Greed and Grievance in Civil War. *Oxford Economic Papers* (56), 563–595.

Collier, Paul/Hoeffler, Anke/Söderbom, Måns 2008. Post-Conflict Risks. *Journal of Peace Research* 45(4), 461–478.

De Jong, Joop T./Komproe, Ivan H./Van Ommeren, Mark 2003. Common Mental Disorders in Postconflict Settings. *The Lancet* 361(June, 21), 2128–2130.

De Waal, Alex 2007. Darfur and the Failure of the Responsibility to Protect. *International Affairs* 83(6), 1039–1054.

De Waal, Alex 2009. Mission without End? Peacekeeping in the African Political Marketplace. *International Affairs* 85(1), 99–113.

Debiel, Tobias, et al. 2009. Local State-Building in Afghanistan and Somaliland. *Peace Review* 21(1), 38–44.

Doyle, Michael W./Sambanis, Nicholas 2006. *Making War and Building Peace: United Nations Peace Operations.* Princeton: Princeton University Press.

Englebert, Pierre/Tull, Denis M. 2008. Postconflict Resolution in Africa. Flawed Ideas about Failed States. *International Security* 32(4), 106 – 139.

Eriksen, Stein S. 2005. The Liberal Peace Is Neither: Peacebuilding, State Building and the Reproduction of Conflict in the Democratic Republic of Congo. *International Peacekeeping* 16(5), 652 – 666.

Fanthorpe, Richard 2005. On the Limits of Liberal Peace: Chiefs and Democratic Decentralization in Post-War Sierra Leone. *African Affairs* 105(418), 27 – 49.

Fearon, James D./Laitin, David D. 2003. Ethnicity, Insurgency, and Civil War. *American Political Science Review* 97(1), 75 – 90.

Fearon, James D./Laitin, David D. 2004. Neotrusteeship and the Problem of Weak States. *International Security* 28(4), 5 – 43.

Fetherston, A. B. 2000. Peacekeeping, Conflict Resolution and Peacebuilding: A Reconsideration of Theoretical Frameworks. *International Peacekeeping* 7(1), 190 – 218.

Fukuyama, Francis 1992. *The End of History and the Last Man.* London: Hamish Hamilton.

Galea, Sandro, et al. 2010. Persistent Psychopathology in the Wake of Civil War: Long-Term Posttraumatic Stress Disorder in Nimba County, Liberia. *American Journal of Public Health* 100(9), 1745 – 1751.

Goodhand, Jonathan/Walton, Oliver 2009. The Limits of Liberal Peacebuilding? International Engagement in the Sri Lankan Peace Process. *Journal of Intervention and Statebuilding* 3(3), 303 – 323.

Harbom, Lotta/Wallensteen, Peter 2009. Armed Conflicts, 1946 – 2008. *Journal of Peace Research* 46(4), 577 – 587.

Hartzell, Caroline/Hoddie, Matthew 2003. Institutionalizing Peace: Power Sharing and Post-Civil War Conflict Management. *American Journal of Political Science* 47 (2), 318 – 332.

Hartzell, Caroline/Hoddie, Matthew 2005. Power Sharing in Peace Settlements: Initiating the Transition from Civil War, in Roeder, Philip G./Rothchild, Donald ed.: *Sustainable Peace: Power and Democracy after Civil War.* Ithaca: Cornell University Press, 83 – 106.

Hartzell, Caroline/Hoddie, Matthew 2007. *Crafting Peace: Power-sharing Institutions and the Negotiated Settlement of Civil Wars.* University Park: Pennsylvania State University Press.

Helman, Gerald B./Ratner, Steven R. 1992. Saving Failed States. *Foreign Policy* (89), 3 – 20.

Heyer, Sonja 1997. Bedingungen von Staatsbildung und Staatszerfall in Somalia: Überlegungen zu einer Theorie des temporären Staates. *WeltTrends* (14), 81 – 96.

Hicks, Donna 2002. The Role of Identity Reconstruction in Promoting Reconciliation, in Helmick, Raymond G./Petersen, Rodney L. ed.: *Forgiveness and Reconciliation: Religion, Public Policy, and Conflict Transformation.* Radnor: Templeton Foundation Press, 129 – 149.

Horowitz, Donald 2002. Constitutional Design: Proposals Versus Processes, in Reynolds, Andrew (ed.): *The Architecture of Democracy: Constitutional Design, Conflict Management, and Democracy.* Oxford: Oxford University Press, 15 – 36.

Horowitz, Michael C./Weisiger, Alex/Johnson, Carter 2009. Correspondence: The Limits to Partition. *International Security* 33(4), 203 – 210.

Human Security Report Project 2010. *Human Security Report 2009: The Shrinking Costs of War.* URL: http://www.hsrgroup.org/docs/Publications/HSR2009/2009HumanSecurityReport_Complete.pdf [accessed on 2010-11-11].

ICTR 2010. *International Criminal Tribunal for Rwanda: Status of Cases.* International Criminal Tribunal for Rwanda. URL: http://www.unictr.org/Cases/tabid/204/Default.aspx [accessed on 2010-11-11].

ICTY 2010. *Key Figures of ICTY Cases, updated 30 June 2010.* International Criminal Tribunal for the former Yugoslavia. URL: http://www.icty.org/sections/TheCases/KeyFigures [accessed on 2010-11-11].

Jarstad, Anna K. 2008. Power Sharing: Former Enemies in Joint Government, in Jarstad, Anna K./Sisk, Timothy D. ed.: *From War to Democracy: Dilemmas of Peacebuilding.* Cambridge et al.: Cambridge University Press, 105 – 133.

Jarstad, Anna K./Nilsson, Desirée 2008. From Words to Deeds: The Implementation of Power-Sharing Pacts in Peace Accords. *Conflict Management and Peace Science* 25(3), 206 – 223.

Johnson, Carter 2008. Partitioning to Peace: Sovereignty, Demography, and Ethnic Civil Wars. *International Security* 32(4), 140 – 170.

Johnson, Kirsten, et al. 2008. Association of Combatant Status and Sexual Violence With Health and Mental Health Outcomes in Postconflict Liberia. *The Journal of the American Medical Association* 300(6), 676 – 690.

Kaldor, Mary 2006. *New and Old Wars: Organized Violence in a Global Era.* Cambridge: Polity Press.

Kaufman, Stuart J. 2006. Escaping the Symbolic Politics Trap: Reconciliation Initiatives and Conflict Resolution in Ethnic Wars. *Journal of Peace Research* 43(2), 201 – 218.

Kaufmann, Chaim D. 1996. Possible and Impossible Solutions to Ethnic Civil Wars. *International Security* 20(4), 136 – 175.

Kaufmann, Chaim D. 1998. When All Else Fails: Ethnic Population Transfers and Partitions in the Twentieth Century. *International Security* 23(2), 120 – 156.

Klarić, Miro, et al. 2007. Psychological Consequences of War Trauma and Postwar Social Stressors in Women in Bosnia and Herzegovina. *Croatian Medical Journal* 48, 167 – 176.

Knaus, Gerald/Martin, Felix 2003. Lessons from Bosnia and Herzegovina: Travails of the European Raj. *Journal of Democracy* 14(3), 60 – 74.

Krasner, Stephen D. 2004. Sharing Sovereignty: New Institutions for Collapsed and Failing States. *International Security* 29(2), 85 – 120.

Kreutz, Joakim 2010. How and When Armed Conflicts End: Introducing the UCDP Conflict Termination Dataset. *Journal of Peace Research* 47(2), 243 – 250.

Kurz, Christof P. 2010. What You See is What You Get: Analytical Lenses and the

Limitations of Post-Conflict Statebuilding in Sierra Leone. *Journal of Intervention and Statebuilding* 4(2), 205–236.

Lederach, Jean P. 1997. *Building Peace: Sustainable Reconciliation in Divided Societies.* Washington DC: United States Institute of Peace.

Lidén, Kristoffer 2009. Building Peace Between Global and Local Politics: The Cosmopolitical Ethics of Liberal Peacebuilding. *International Peacekeeping* 16(5), 616–634.

Lijphardt, Arend 2004. Constitutional Design for Divided Societies. *Journal of Democracy* 15(2), 96–109.

Luttwak, Edward N. 1999. Give War a Chance. *Foreign Affairs* 78(4), 36–44.

Mac Ginty, Roger 2006. *No War, No Peace: The Rejuvenation of Stalled Peace Processes and Peace Accords.* Basingstoke: Palgrave Macmillan.

Mac Ginty, Roger 2008. Indigenous Peace-Making Versus the Liberal Peace. *Cooperation and Conflict* 43(2), 139–163.

Mac Ginty, Roger 2010. Hybrid Peace: The Interaction Between Top-Down and Bottom-Up Peace. *Security Dialogue* 41(4), 391–412.

Mehler, Andreas 2009. Peace and Power Sharing in Africa: A not so obvious relationship. *African Affairs* 108(432), 453–473.

Melander, Erik 1999. *Anarchy Within: The Security Dilemma between Ethnic Groups in Emerging Anarchy.* Uppsala: Department of Peace and Conflict Research. (Research Report).

Melander, Erik 2009. The Geography of Fear: Regional Ethnic Diversity, the Security Dilemma and Ethnic War. *European Journal of International Relations* 15(1), 95–124.

Mendeloff, David 2004. Truth-Seeking, Truth-Telling, and Postconflict Peacebuilding: Curb the Enthusiasm. *International Studies Review* 6(3), 355–380.

Menkhaus, Kenneth 2008. Somalia: Governance vs. Statebuilding, in: Call, Charles T./ Wyeth, Vanessa ed.: *Building States to Build Peace.* London et al.: Lynne Rienner Publishers, Inc., 187–216.

Nemeroff, Charles B., et al. 2006. Posttraumatic Stress Disorder: A State-of-the-science Review. *Journal of Psychiatric Research* 40, 1–21.

OHR 2007. *Introduction.* Office of the High Representative in Bosnia and Herzegovina. URL: http://www.ohr.int/ohr-info/gen-info/default.asp?content_id=38519 [accessed on 2010-11-11].

Paris, Roland 2004. *At War's End: Building Peace After Civil Conflict.* Cambridge: Cambridge University Press.

Paris, Roland 2010. Saving Liberal Peacebuilding. *Review of International Studies* 36 (2), 337–365.

Paris, Roland/Sisk, Timothy D. 2009. Introduction: Understanding the Contradictions of Postwar Statebuilding, in: Paris, Roland/Sisk, Timothy D. ed.: *The Dilemmas of Statebuilding: Confronting the Contradictions of Postwar Peace Operations.* London et al.: Routledge, 1–20.

Prunier, Gérard 1995. *The Rwanda Crisis: 1959–1994 History of a Genocide.* London: Hurst.

Prunier, Gérard 2010. Rwanda and Darfur: A Comparative Approach to Two Peacekeeping Failures. *Journal of International Peacekeeping* 14(1–2), 117–133.

Pugh, Michael 2005. The Political Economy of Peacebuilding: A Critical Theory Perspective. *International Journal of Peace Studies* 10(2), 23–42.

Rettig, Max 2008. Gacaca: Truth, Justice, and Reconciliation in Postconflict Rwanda? *African Studies Review* 51(3), 25–50.

Richmond, Oliver P. 2009. A Post-Liberal Peace: Eirenism and the Everyday. *Review of International Studies* 35(3), 557–580.

Richmond, Oliver P. 2010. Resistance and the Post-Liberal Peace. *Millennium – Journal of International Studies* 38(3), 1–28.

Richmond, Oliver P./Franks, Jason 2009. *Liberal Peace Transitions: Between State-building and Peacebuilding*. Edinburgh: Edinburgh University Press.

Sambanis, Nicholas 2000. Partition as a Solution to Ethnic War: An Empirical Critique of the Theoretical Literature. *World Politics* 52(4), 437–483.

Sambanis, Nicholas/Schulhofer-Wohl, Jonah 2009. What's in a Line? Is Partition a Solution to Civil War? *International Security* 34(2), 82–118.

Santa-Barbara, Joanna 2007. Reconciliation, in Webel, Charles/Galtung, Johan ed.: *Handbook of Peace and Conflict Studies.* New York: Routledge, 173–186.

Schaal, Susanne/Elbert, Thomas 2006. Ten Years After the Genocide: Trauma Confrontation and Posttraumatic Stress in Rwandan Adolescents. *Journal of Traumatic Stress* 19(1), 95–105.

Schabas, William A. 2006. *The UN International Criminal Tribunals: The former Yugoslavia, Rwanda and Sierra Leone.* Cambridge et al.: Cambridge University Press.

Secretary-General of the United Nations 1992. *An Agenda for Peace: Report of the Secretary-General pursuant to the statement adopted by the Summit Meeting of the Security Council on 31 January 1992, A/47/277.* URL: http://www.un-documents.-net/a47-277.htm [accessed on 2010-11-11].

Staub, Ervin 2000. Genocide and Mass Killing: Origins, Prevention, Healing and Reconciliation. *Political Psychology* 21(2), 367–382.

Staub, Ervin/Bar-Tal, Daniel 2003. Genocide, Mass Killing, and Intractable Conflict: Roots, Evolution, Prevention, and Reconciliation, in Sears, David O., Huddy, Leonie/Jervis, Robert ed.: *Oxford Handbook of Political Psychology.* Oxford: Oxford University Press, 710–751.

Thabet, Abdele A./Vostanis, Panos 1999. Post-traumatic Stress Reactions in Children of War. *The Journal of Child Psychology and Psychiatry* 40(3), 385–391.

Toft, Monica D. 2010. Ending Civil Wars: A Case for Rebel Victory? *International Security* 34(4), 7–36.

Trappler, Brian/Cohen, Carl l./Tulloo, Rajeshree 2007. Impact of Early Lifetime Trauma in Later Life: Depression among Holocaust Survivors 60 Years after the Liberation of Auschwitz. *American Journal of Geriatric Psychiatry* 15(1), 79–83.

Tull, Denis M. 2009. Peacekeeping in the Democratic Republic of Congo: Waging Peace and Fighting War. *International Peacekeeping* 16(2), 215–230.

Tull, Denis M./Mehler, Andreas 2005. The Hidden Costs of Power-Sharing: Reproducing Insurgent Violence in Africa. *African Affairs* 104(416), 375–398.

UCDP/PRIO 2010. *UCDP/PRIO Armed Conflict Dataset Codebook.* Uppsala Conflict Data Program/Peace Research Institute Oslo. URL: http://www.pcr.uu.se/digitalAssets/19/19230_Codebook_UCDP_PRIO_Armed_Conflict_Dataset_v4_2010.pdf [accessed on 2010-11-11].

United Nations 2000. *Report of the Panel on United Nations Peace Operations (Brahimi Report, UN doc. A/55/305–S/, 21 Aug. 2000, para. 51).* URL: http://www.un.org/peace/reports/peace_operations/docs/a_55_305.pdf [accessed on 2010-11-11].

United Nations 2010a. *Fact Sheet: United Nations Peacekeeping.* URL: http://www.un.org/en/peacekeeping/documents/factsheet.pdf [accessed on 2010-11-11].

United Nations 2010b. *United Nations Peacekeeping: List of Operations.* URL: http://www.un.org/en/peacekeeping/list.shtml [accessed on 2010-11-11].

Walter, Barbara F. 1997. The Critical Barrier to Civil War Settlement. International Organization 51(3), 335–364.

Walter, Barbara F. 2004. Does Conflict Beget Conflict? Explaining Recurring Civil War. Journal of Peace Research 41(3), 371–388.

Weinstein, Jeremy M. 2005. Autonomous Recovery and International Intervention in Comparative Perspective. Center for Global Development (Working Paper).

Wimmer, Andreas/Cederman, Lars-Erik/Min, Brian 2009. Ethnic Politics and Armed Conflict: A Configurational Analysis of a New Global Data Set. American Sociological Review 74 (April), 316–337.

About the authors

Susan Flämig is a PhD researcher in Peace Studies at the University of Bradford. She works on police reforms in El Salvador. Her research interests include post-conflict peacebuilding, cultural and institutional change, critical security studies and reconciliation. Susan holds an M.A. in Political Science, Intercultural Communication and Sociology from the University of Jena. As a research assistant at the Faculty of Theology in Jena, she worked on the Programme 'Religions as Agents of Reconciliation' and organised the Summer School 'Societies in Transition'.

Martin Leiner is Professor of Systematic Theology and Ethics at the Faculty of Theology of the Friedrich-Schiller-University in Jena, Germany. He studied Philosophy and Protestant Theology and completed his doctorate at Heidelberg University with a text published in 1995 under the title: *Psychologie und Exegese. Grundfragen einer textpsychologischen Interpretation des Neuen Testaments* (Gütersloher Verlagshaus). His second thesis (habilitation), at Mainz University, was a study on Martin Buber. It was published in 2000 under the title: *Gottes Gegenwart. Die dialogische Philosophie Martin Bubers und der Ansatz ihrer theologischen Rezeption bei Friedrich Gogarten und Emil Brunner* (Gütersloher Verlagshaus). From 1998 – 2002 he was Professor of Systematic Theology and Hermeneutics in Neuchâtel/CH. Since 2002 he is in Jena and since 2003 he works on issues of peace, reconciliation and human rights.

David Tombs is Assistant Professor on the Belfast-based M. Phil. in Conflict Resolution and Reconciliation for the Irish School of Ecumenics, Trinity College Dublin. His publications in political theology include *Latin American Liberation Theology* (Leiden: Brill, 2002) and an edited collection with Joseph Liechty on *Explorations in Reconciliation: New Directions for Theology* (Aldershot: Ashgate, 2006). He is currently conducting research on crucifixion as an instrument of torture.

Matthieu de Nanteuil is a sociologist and professor in the Louvain School of Management at the Université catholique de Louvain (UCL) in Belgium. He is a member of the "Centre de recherches interdisciplinaires Développement, Institutions, Subjectivité" (CriDIS) at UCL and associated member of the

"Grupo de Investigación en Teorías Políticas Contemporáneas" (TEOPOCO) at the Universidad Nacional de Colombia.

Mariana Chacón is a lawyer who graduated from the Faculty of Law of the Pontifical Catholic University of Peru (PUCP). She is the assistant to the coordination of the PUCP's Masters Program, offered by the Institute for Democracy and Human Rights of the Pontifical Catholic University of Peru and her main academic research revolves around transitional justice and international law, specifically the contribution of the Inter American Human Rights Court to the transition processes in the Latin American region.

Witold Mucha, M.A., is a Ph.D. candidate in peace and conflict studies at the Department of International Relations, Peace and Development Research, University Duisburg-Essen. He holds a Heinrich Böll Foundation scholarship and is doing his doctorate in peace and conflict studies. He received a B.A. in social sciences at Heinrich-Heine University Düsseldorf in 2005 and a M.A. in international relations and development studies at University Duisburg-Essen in 2008. Besides lecturing at Heinrich-Heine University of Düsseldorf and University of Wuppertal, he draws on fieldwork in Bolivia, Cameroon and Chile.

Elizabeth Lira is a psychologist. She is the Director of the Center of Ethics of the Alberto Hurtado University, Santiago de Chile. She is member of the Commission for the Recognition of Disappeared, Executed and Tortured victims in Chile (2010–2011). ***Brian Loveman*** is professor emeritus of political science at San Diego State University. He published recently "No Higher Law: American Foreign Policy and the Western Hemisphere" (2010). He is the author of the most well-known history of Chile in English: "Chile, the Legacy of Hispanic Capitalism", (3rd edition, 2001). They have published together more than ten books on Chilean Political Reconciliation since 1999. Their recent research includes Reparations Policies, Justice and Memory in Chile.

Hugo Rojas teaches Sociology of Law and Legal Reaserch at Alberto Hurtado University (Chile). He has worked as advisor for the Presidency of Chile, as volunteer for the National Commission on Torture and Political Imprisonment and at the Council for Transparency in Chile. At the moment he is a graduate student in Law & Anthropology at London School of Economics and Political Science.

Katharina Freudenberg studied Protestant Theology at University of Leipzig (Germany), Martin-Luther-University of Halle-Wittenberg (Germany) ISEDET in Buenos Aires (Argentina), and Friedrich-Schiller-University Jena (Germany). In 2009 the German National Academic Foundation supported her fieldwork project in Contemporary Church History focused on the context of the Argentinean Dictatorship.

Kanan Kitani is a Research Fellow of the Japan Society for the Promotion of Science (JSPS) and a doctoral student of the School of Theology at the Doshisha University, Kyoto, Japan. Her field of research is practical theology, specializing in missiology. Currently, she serves on the program area committee on Faith, Mission and Unity of the Christian Conference of Asia (CCA).

Christo Thesnaar grew up in the former Transkei. Before being appointed at the Stellenbosch University he lectured at the Huguenot College (Unisa) in Wellington as a lecturer in Youth work with a specialisation in pastoral care and counselling. He was appointed in 2009 as Senior Lecturer in Pastoral care and counselling within the Faculty of Theology at the University of Stellenbosch. He also played a role in setting up an NGO called the Institute for the healing of Memories and is currently a board member of this institute. His areas of interests are: reconciliation, forgiveness and justice. He is married to Nelmarie and they have two children.

Andreas Hasenclever is Professor of International Relations at the Eberhard-Karls-University of Tübingen. His chief research interests are in the field of peace and conflict studies with particular reference to the analysis of the democratic peace, regime analysis, and the impact of religious traditions on political conflicts. On these topics he authored numerous articles and books. His book „Macht der Moral in der internationalen Politik" (Campus 2001) was awarded with the Helmuth-James-von-Moltke-Preis 2003 endowed by the German Society for Military Law and the Law of War.

Jan Sändig is research assistant and lecturer at the Cluster of Peace and Conflict Studies at the Institute of Political Science, University of Tübingen. His main fields of research are ethnic conflicts, terrorism, Peace-Building and development cooperation. He undertook field studies as development consultant and intern in Mali, Ethiopia, Nigeria, Liberia and Rwanda. Jan Sändig studied political science in Potsdam and Paris and earned a Diploma degree from the University of Potsdam in 2009.

List of Abbreviations[1]

AAA	Alianza Anticommunista Argentina
ADN	Acción Democrática Nacionalista
ANC	African National Congress
ANC	Asamblea Nacional Constituyente
ARENA	Alianza Republicana Nacionalista
AUC	Autodefensas Unidas de Colombia
CCP	Confederación Campesina del Perú
CDPAZ	Corporación Derechos Para la Paz
CIASI	Corporación de Investigación y Asesoría Sindical
CNI	Central Nacional de Informaciones
CNT	Central Nacional de Trabajadores
CODHES	Consultaría para los Derechos Humanos y el Desplazamiento
CONADEP	Comisión Nacional sobre la Desaparición de Personas
CONAPA	Comisión Nacional de Pueblos Andinos, Amazónicos y Afro peruanos
CriDIS	Centre for Interdisciplinary Research on Development, Institutions, and Subjectivity
CSUTCB	Confederacíon Sindical Unica de Trabajadores Campesinos de
CUT	Central Única de Trabajadores
DANE	Departamento Administrativo Nacional de Estadísticas
DELPS	Deutsche Evangelische La Plata Synode
DIGESTYC	Directorate of Statistics and Census
ELN	Ejercito de Liberación Nacional
ENS	Escuela Nacional Sindical
EPL	Ejercito Popular de Liberación
ERP	Ejército Revolucionario Popular
DINA	Dirección de Inteligencia Nacional
FAC	Freedom of Association Committee
FARC	Fuerzas Armadas Revolucionarias de Colombia
FIDH	Fédération Internationale des Droit de l'Homme
FMLN	Farabundo Martí National Liberation Front

1 List of abreviations by Peggy Stöckner

FSM	Federación Sindical Mundial
GEIH	Gran Encuesta Integrada de Hogares
IBGE	Instituto Brasileiro de Geografia e Estatística
IERP	Iglesia Evangélica del Río de la Plata
ILO	International Labor Organization
IMF	International Monetary Fund
INDEPA	Instituto Nacional de Desarrollo de los Pueblos Andinos Amazónicos y Afroperuanos
ISEDET	Instituto Superior Evangélico de Estudios Teológicos
MAS	Movimiento al Socialismo
MEDH	Movimiento Ecuménico por los Derechos Humanos
MESEP	Misión para el Empalme de las Series de Empleo, Pobreza y Desigualdad
MIR	Movimiento de la Izquierda Revolucionaria
MOVICE	Movimiento Nacional de Victimas de Crimenes de Estado
MNR	Movimiento Nacionalista Revolucionario
MSM	Movimiento sin Miedo
NGO	Non-Governmental Organization
OAS	Organisation of American States
ONUSAL	Misión de Observación de las Naciones Unidas en El Salvador
PCN	Partido de Conciliacion Nacional
PCP-SL	Peruvian Communist Party-Shining Path
PDDH	Ombudswoman for the Defence of Human Rights
PIR	Plan Integral de Reparaciones
PNC	Policia Nacional Civil
PRIF	Peace Research Institute Frankfurt
PRIO	Peace Research Institute in Oslo
RAF	Rote Armee Fraktion ("urban guerrilla" group in the 1970 s)
SAP	Structural Adjustment Program
SIPRI	Stockholm International Peace Research Institute
SSR	Security Sector Reform
TRC	Truth and Reconciliation Commission
UCKG	Universal Church of the Kingdom of God
UN	United Nations
UNESCO	United Nations Educational, Scientific and Cultural Organization
UP	Union Patriotica
USIP	U.S. Institute of Peace

Index